Women in the
Spanish Novel
Today

Women in the Spanish Novel Today

Essays on the Reflection of Self in the Works of Three Generations

Edited by
Kyra A. Kietrys *and*
Montserrat Linares

McFarland & Company, Inc., Publishers
Jefferson, North Carolina, and London

LIBRARY OF CONGRESS CATALOGUING-IN-PUBLICATION DATA

Women in the Spanish novel today : essays on the reflection of
self in the works of three generations / edited by Kyra A.
Kietrys and Montserrat Linares.
        p.   cm.
    Includes bibliographical references and index.

    ISBN 978-0-7864-4354-3
    softcover : 50# alkaline paper ∞

    1. Spanish fiction — 20th century — History and criticism.
    2. Spanish fiction — Women authors — History and criticism.
    3. Women and literature — Spain — History — 20th century.
    4. Women in literature.   I. Kietrys, Kyra A.   II. Linares,
Montserrat.
    PQ6144.W66 2009
    863'.64093522 — dc22   209000151

British Library cataloguing data are available

©2009 Kyra A. Kietrys and Montserrat Linares. All rights reserved

*No part of this book may be reproduced or transmitted in any form
or by any means, electronic or mechanical, including photocopying
or recording, or by any information storage and retrieval system,
without permission in writing from the publisher.*

Cover image ©2009 Shutterstock

Manufactured in the United States of America

*McFarland & Company, Inc., Publishers
    Box 611, Jefferson, North Carolina 28640
        www.mcfarlandpub.com*

To Mark, Nikolai, and Aleksei
and
to Chris

Table of Contents

Introduction: Reflecting the Self
Kyra A. Kietrys and *Montserrat Linares*   1

PART I. POSTWAR WRITERS

Carmen Martín Gaite's *Irse de casa* or the Metafictional Creation of the Self
    Vilma Navarro-Daniels   9

Space and the Construction of the Self in the Narratives of Josefina Aldecoa
    Carmen T. Sotomayor   21

PART II. GENERATION OF THE TRANSITION TO DEMOCRACY

Historia de un abrigo: Women's Search for an Anchor in the Modern World
    Joanne Lucena   39

Naturalism and the Self in Rosa Montero's *La hija del caníbal*
    Ellen Mayock   57

Women, War, and Words in *La voz dormida* by Dulce Chacón
    Kathryn Everly   77

The Wounded Self and Body in Dulce Chacón's *Algún amor que no mate:* A Haunting Discourse
    Esther Raventós-Pons   93

Female Characters in the Novels of Clara Sánchez: Reflection and Mirage
    Mary Ann Dellinger   113

Part III. New Writers of the 1990s

Looking for the Other: Peninsular Women's Fiction after Levinas
    Nina L. Molinaro   133

Revaluing the Mother in Lucía Etxebarria's *Un milagro en equilibrio*
    Sandra J. Schumm   153

Negotiating Girlhood: Mediating Bodies and Identities in Novels by Care Santos
    Parissa Tadrissi   171

The Elusive Self in Eugenia Rico's *La muerte blanca*
    Kyra A. Kietrys   191

Fragmented Identities: The Narrative World of Espido Freire
    Montserrat Linares   205

About the Contributors   219

Index   221

Introduction: Reflecting the Self

Kyra A. Kietrys and *Montserrat Linares*

> I shall speak about women's writing: about *what it will do*. Woman must write her self: must write about women and bring women to writing, from which they have been driven away as violently as from their bodies — for the same reasons, by the same law, with the same fatal goal. Woman must put herself into the text — as into the world and into history — by her own movement.
> — Hélène Cixous, *The Laugh of the Medusa*

At the turn of the millennium, as women in Spain continue to find their voices in a world of shifting, complicated freedoms, where oppression exists but is not always overt, we find that many women writers explicitly or implicitly comment in their novels upon women's search for identity. This collection of essays examines the representation of the female self in narrative works by Spanish women of three successive literary generations, all of whom published new novels between 1990 and 2005.* This fifteen-year span represents a pivotal chapter in Spain's literary history, a chapter which mirrors larger political and social changes. While not all the works studied explicitly address 20th century Spanish history, we are using Spanish history in general — namely, the Franco regime, the transition to democracy in the late 1970s and early 1980s, and the consolidation of democracy in the 1980s and

---

*Our classification follows that which Carmen de Urioste proposes in "Narrative of Spanish Women Writers of the Nineties: An Overview": postwar, boom, and *nueva narrativa* [new narrative]. The authors from the three generations studied in our volume are: (1) Carmen Martín Gaite (b. 1925) and Josefina Aldecoa (b. 1926); (2) Soledad Puértolas (b. 1947), Rosa Montero (b. 1951), Dulce Chacón (b. 1954), and Clara Sánchez (b. 1955); and (3) Belén Gopegui (1963), Marta Sanz (b. 1966), Luisa Castro (b. 1967), Lucía Extebarria (b. 1966), Care Santos (b. 1970), Eugenia Rico (b. 1972), and Espido Freire (b. 1974).

1990s — to define the three generations of writers represented in this collection: women born in the 1920s who experienced firsthand the Spanish Civil War and whose first works were published during the Franco dictatorship (1939–1975); women born in the 1940s and 1950s whose literary careers flourished either during the transition to democracy or shortly afterward; and finally, women born during the 1960s and 1970s who started publishing in the solidly democratic 1990s. Each generation is marked by unique historical and political events that emphatically defined the women's movement — or lack thereof— in Spain.

Women in the Spanish Novel Today incorporates the perspectives of individual women of different ages who have lived distinct personal and historical realities. Our cross-generational study not only bridges the past and present by revealing some recurring common concerns of women writers in Spain, but also debunks the frequent monolithic, reductive perception of "Woman," thereby reversing the negative connotations normally associated with the term "women's writing." As Carmen de Urioste points out in her article "Narrative of Spanish Women Writers of the Nineties," the publishing world in the '90s and the beginning of the 21st century simultaneously promotes and devalues women's writing. This irony "reflects the dual effect of an editorial market that promotes the emergence of a new culture within the framework of an open society, but at the same time hinders its development due to the fleeting character of the texts" (284). Both the media and literary critics constantly emphasize the unprecedented number of women writers successful in both publishing and sales. The reality, however, is quite different as there is a "desproporción entre esa visibilidad y su presencia real, que es mucho más modesta" [disparity between that visibility and their real presence, which is much more modest] (Freixas 35). Hispanist Christine Henseler notes that "the media functions to cover up the absence of women's full-fledged existence in powerful roles by hyping the power of a select number of women; such as the editors Beatriz de Moura and Esther Tusquets, the literary agent Carmen Balcells, and the writers Espido Freire and Lucía Etxebarría" (13). Along with the hype over women's control of the literary world, there appears to be a consensus within Spanish literary criticism that the majority of women's literary production is simply a product of marketing which is incompatible with literary quality. There exists a tendency to classify all works written by women under the category of "commercial literature," that is, of little serious merit. Laura Freixas, author and critic, notes that "mientras que la identidad masculina de un escritor, de sus personajes o de sus lectores nunca es objeto de comentario por parte de los críticos, en cambio la femenina se menciona con cierta frecuencia y prácticamente siempre con carácter peyorativo" [while the male identity of a writer, his characters, or his readers is never the object of critical commentary, the female identity is frequently mentioned, and almost always with a negative connotation] (Freixas 40). Freixas's project demonstrates that this alleged advancement of women's literature is a fallacy, given that the media presence of a select number of women writers is held as an indication of women writers "invading" the literary field. The reality is that, particularly in the academic sphere and as far as serious literary criticism is concerned, still only minimal attention is being paid to the work of women writers. For this reason it is necessary to begin a process of "normalization" through anthologies of women's writing and critical studies it so that women writers gain authentic recognition. We purposefully include authors who are at different stages of their personal and professional lives, ranging from internationally known, canonized novelists to newer, more experimental writers. This multiplicity of voices offers a thorough exploration of the many ways in which Spanish women of different ages and experiences view and define the female self— how women understand their psychology; how they view their bodies; how they see themselves in literature, history, and society; in sum, what it means to be a woman in contemporary Spain and the ways in which this meaning is found.

Our project elucidates some common concerns while emphasizing that each novelist interprets the self in a singular way. The need to recover the voices of women lost to history, for example, is a recurring theme, as well as the need to establish connections between those lost women and Spanish women today. Time and time again the need to reclaim a literal or metaphorical space — whether in the public or private sphere — resurfaces in these novels. Also prevalent is the need to repair broken relationships of the past, particularly mother-daughter relationships. Several essays emphasize other female relationships — women as friends or sisters — and their role in building strong female communities. Still other essays analyze the quest for self-discovery or self-creation. In short, the essayists find in these novels a kaleidoscope of concerns, but central to all is the position of the female self.

While all of the contributors to our volume are Hispanists trained in literary history, they approach the texts from varying critical perspectives such as feminism, psychoanalysis, and phenomenology, among others. Some essays study individual novels, others a group of novels by the same author, while others consider various novels by authors from a specific generation. In the opening essay, Vilma Navarro-Daniels explores the metafictional search and creation of self as experienced by Amparo, the protagonist of *Irse de casa*

(1998) by Carmen Martín Gaite (b. 1925), one of Spain's most widely studied authors. Navarro-Daniels argues that as Amparo reads and rewrites the movie script her son wrote about her life she is creating a metaphor of her own recreation. In the next essay, Carmen T. Sotomayor studies a trilogy by Josefina Aldecoa (b. 1926), who belongs to the same generation as Martín Gaite (*La generación de la posguerra* or Postwar Generation), but whose literary career did not flourish until the 1990s. Sotomayor examines the relationship between public and private spaces and the construction of identity and the female self in *Historia de una maestra* (1990), *Mujeres de negro* (1994), and *La fuerza del destino* (1997).

The third essay marks the shift from the postwar generation to the Generation of '68, of the transition to democracy, or "boom" of Spanish feminine narrative. Joanne Lucena focuses on the need for female self-fulfillment in *Historia de un abrigo* (2005) by Soledad Puértolas (b. 1947). Lucena studies several female characters from different vignettes that thread this novel and who suffer the consequences of adhering to fixed female stereotypes: unhappiness, spousal abuse and anorexia. She claims that although the author does not provide a concrete solution to these contemporary problems, she does advocate the intervention other women. For Puértolas, it is other women, be they mothers, sisters, or friends, that make the modern world navigable.

Ellen Mayock approaches the female protagonist of *La hija del caníbal* (1997) by Rosa Montero (b. 1951) from a naturalist perspective claiming that such a reading permits a vision of the female self as it meets and comes to term with its own history, familial influences, and physical surroundings. Mayock furthermore proposes combining a naturalist reading with more contemporary themes and techniques such as the integration of the public and the private, the literary and the "real," and the destruction and construction of the self.

The next two essays study works of distinct genres written by Dulce Chacón (b. 1954). In a sense, we can say that both texts address the silencing of women but from different perspectives. Kathryn Everly's essay centers on the concepts of visibility and invisibility of the female perspective in the making and remembering of history in *La voz dormida* (2002). She claims that the novel goes beyond recovering the lost feminine voice and creates a new literary approach to history that combines factual and narrative elements with patriarchal and marginalized forms of language. Everly concludes that this approach results in a more complete rendering of historical events. Esther Raventós-Pons examines the effects of aggression and repression on the female body and the female self in her analysis of *Algún amor que no mate* (1996).

For Raventós-Pons, the physical aggression (wounded body) and psychological repression (wounded self) that the protagonist suffers are examples of how society silences women through violence. She postulates that this silencing ends up as an absence full of signification and that women's denied meaning becomes a source of meaning.

Mary Ann Dellinger considers the different models of women's self-perception and self-definition in three novels by Clara Sánchez (b. 1955): *Desde el mirador* (1996), *Últimas noticias del paraíso* (2000) and *Un millón de luces* (2004). Dellinger affirms that a new female self emerges through the author's use of reflection and mirage, and of direct and indirect voice. Separating themselves from traditional patterns, the women leave the restrictive domestic space and enter in multiple roles in a postmodern society.

Nina L. Molinaro's essay marks the shift to the third generation of writers in our collection — those born in the 1960s and '70s. She uses Emmanuel Levinas's theory regarding ethical subjectivity to examine *La fiebre amarilla* (1994) by Luisa Castro (b. 1966), *Tocarnos la cara* (1995) by Belén Gopegui (b. 1963), and *El frío* (1995) by Marta Sanz (b. 1967). Molinaro analyzes the disparate ways in which the three novels foreground the construction of female selves in relation to the other, how women characters see and speak their subjectivity, and how and why they recognize and respond to others.

Sandra J. Schumm employs feminist theory and Carl Jung's perspective of the archetypal mother to study the reincorporation of the mother figure in Spanish literature as exemplified in Lucía Etxebarria's (1966) *Un milagro en equilibrio* (2004). She postulates that the portrayal of the mother-daughter relationship offers a counterbalance to the Virgin Mary model imposed by Franco's government, and thus presents a new paradigm for female communication.

Parissa Tadrissi studies the role of technology in shaping and defining young women's identity through an analysis of Care Santos's (b. 1970) *Laluna.com* (2003) and *Operación Virgo* (2003). Tadrissi argues that through the mediums of literature and Internet communication, Santos offers teenage girls a sense of belonging, allowing them to understand that they fit into a community despite an increasingly globalized world, disintegrating families, and transient friends.

Kyra A. Kietrys analyzes the elusive self in Eugenia Rico's (b. 1972) *La muerte blanca* (2002). She claims that the narrator, through her attempt to recreate her deceased brother, ultimately writes an identity for herself. While sensitive to women's historically subordinate role in society, the narrator is paradoxically unaware of how she is rewriting this role through her own writing.

Our collection closes with Montserrat Linares's study of *Irlanda* (1998) and *Diabulus in Musica* (2002) by the youngest author studied in our collection, Espido Freire (b. 1974). Linares argues that Freire proposes a new type of novel in which the adolescent female characters search for their identity through fantasy as an alternative to contemporary realism.

In closing, we hope that our collection offers a more inclusive view of women's situations in Spanish literature at the turn of the millennium, specifically with a focus on the female self and the gender politics implied therein. We do not wish to imply that the women novelists are transgressing societal norms simply because they are women who are writing. Rather, we aim to offer a legitimate space where their works can be studied. Without a doubt, the essays in this collection foster an awareness of the literary production of Spanish women, but even more important, they demonstrate a recognition — by the novelists and essayists alike — that much remains to be gained socially, politically, and economically, and that women continue to exist within both public and personal systems of power and control.

Works Cited

Freixas, Laura. *Literatura y mujeres. Escritoras, público y crítica en la España actual.* Barcelona: Ediciones Destino, 2001.

Henseler, Christine. *Contemporary Spanish Women's Narrative and the Publishing Industry.* Champaign: University of Illinois Press, 2003.

Urioste, Carmen de. "Narrative of Spanish Women Writers of the Nineties: An Overview." *Tulsa Studies in Women's Literature* 20.2 (2001): 279–295.

PART I. POSTWAR WRITERS

Carmen Martín Gaite's *Irse de casa* or the Metafictional Creation of the Self

Vilma Navarro-Daniels

Irse de casa (1998) by renowned author Carmen Martín Gaite tells us about the world of Amparo Miranda, a successful fashion designer who lives in New York. After forty years in the United States, she decides to go back to Spain to visit the city where she was born and grew up, a city whose name is never revealed to the reader. In her trip, Amparo carries with her a script written by her son, who aspires to make a film about his mother's life. Before giving the funds for such a project, Amparo wants to closely examine the script in order to know if it faithfully depicts her. On the other hand, she wants to recover her own life story, which had been suddenly interrupted when she and her mother left Spain to find more opportunities abroad. As a single mother and a seamstress, Amparo's mother looked for a better economic situation in America. In the novel, Amparo returns to Spain alone because she feels that she must reconstruct the fragments of her life on her own helped only by the script for the biographical film. The reference to this script makes this novel profoundly metafictional. Several times, Amparo thinks of herself as a character in the film. This way, there is a counterpoint between Amparo's memories and the script, which becomes her interlocutor.

Traditionally, metafiction has been considered a mode of writing that distances fiction from life, in the sense that the texts turn inward to reveal how they are constructed. In this study, however, I contend that Carmen Martín Gaite, rather than postulate a disconnection between life and literature, uses metafiction to explore reality and the ways we understand and create it—in this case, Amparo's life and personal story. In other words, Martín Gaite makes us understand that fiction is an integral component both of Amparo's life and of the perceptions of her own reality and self.

In her essay about this novel, Joyce Tolliver posits that this literary work is precisely "about feminine identity" (258), highlighting the aforementioned fictional component of selfhood. In this manner, Tolliver sustains that Amparo creates and represents a personage. Through clothing, plastic surgery, as well as the name that she adopts—Miranda Drake—she produces an image of herself, and she spatially and temporarily re-places herself (258–9). Tolliver also emphasizes the fact that the "mask" assumed by Amparo allows her to return to her native city without being recognized (260). Her clothes and sophisticated appearance, for example, cause people to see her like something she is not: a foreigner (261). Amparo rejects thus everything that could fix her identity, and opts, instead, for defining herself and being defined by others (261). It is in this context that Tolliver understands the cinematographic script of Amparo's son as a way to track all the re-positions of his mother:

> Amparo's son, Jeremy, attempts to track these displacements in the film he plans to make, which would trace the life of a female character who is a thinly-fictionalized representation of his mother. Amparo's constant redefinition of herself through performance is literalized in Jeremy's project; at many points in the narrative, we encounter a shifting of the boundary dividing the experiences of Amparo Miranda, protagonist of the story we are reading, and those of the unnamed woman of Jeremy's film [261].

During her stay in Spain, the fiction contained in the script that Amparo reads, leads her to attentively observe and question the world referred to in the script, a world that comes to be the "reality" at the diegetic level of the narration. Nevertheless, this world sends Amparo back again to the script, in an unending round trip between "life" and fiction. This two-way movement allows us to understand identity as a process rather than a final product. The act of reading allows Amparo to understand the world that surrounds her and also question and lead a new life simultaneously.

Irse de casa is a deeply metafictional novel. It is necessary to understand metafiction as a dynamic concept. In addition to emphasizing the self-referential nature of metafiction, Patricia Waugh also underlines the implications of metafiction in the extra-textual or "real" world:

> *Metafiction* is a term given to fictional writing which self-consciously and systematically draws attention to its status as an artefact in order to pose

questions about the relationship between fiction and reality. In providing a critique of their own methods of construction, such writings not only examine the fundamental structures of narrative fiction, they also explore the possible fictionality of the world outside the literary fictional text [2].

In this manner, "self-reflectiveness" is one of the most important characteristics in a metafictional work. Self-reflectiveness is understood as an exploration of fiction in itself—in other words, a metafictional work can be seen as a theory about fiction — through making fiction (2). In *Irse de casa* we see this self-reflectiveness in the allusions to theater, literary language, and very well known literary works.*

Most importantly, the metafictional nature of *Irse de casa* is emphasized by the inclusion of several characters who are either writers — besides Jeremy — or very well versed readers. I would like to mention three secondary characters who illustrate this tendency which permeates the whole novel. Ricardo, the young receptionist at the Hotel Excelsior, introduces himself as a writer, in spite of not yet having written a book. Towards the end of the novel, Amparo leaves him a letter. By means of this letter, she invites him to join her and Jeremy in the enterprise of filming *La calle del olvido*, arguing that "necesitamos una persona de buen oído y olfato literario como tú para que colabore con los diálogos" [we need someone who has good literary senses of both hearing and smell, someone like you to collaborate in writing the dialogues] (344). Susana, the keeper of Amparo's hotel room, is described as someone who has an "enfermiza afición por las novelas policiacas y de espionaje" [insane inclination toward detective and spy novels] (334), which leads her to invent her own version of the elegant and sophisticated woman who she waits on for one week. The narrator says that Susana plots her story "siguiendo pautas novelescas" [following novelistic patterns] (335). Marcelo, the young assistant of the zarzuela troupe, extensively discusses the importance of Aníbal, a secondary personage in *Luisa Fernanda*, the zarzuela that the group of artists is presenting in the city. Marcelo enhances this character, making him gain a relevance that no one had seen up to that time. Even more, during the last performance of *Luisa Fernanda* before departing to another town, Marcelo appropriates his character and makes him say things that are not written in the script. By so doing, Marcelo transforms Aníbal's heroic gesture into a defense of art in a society that has

---

*These literary references include works such as *Macbeth*, *The Odyssey*, *Jane Eyre*, *Rebecca*, and *Hamlet*, and writers such as Lope de Vega, William James, John Keats, Joseph Conrad, and Henrik Ibsen. Martín Gaite also refers to philosophers like Jacques Monod, George Bataille, Henri Bergson, and Simone de Beauvoir.

become more and more consumerist. Although these characters — with the exception of Ricardo — are not directly involved with Amparo, their presence, along with the literary references, creates an atmosphere full of metafictional connotations.

Very often in the novel some characters realize that they follow models learned either in films or in literary works. These characters are so deeply influenced and shaped by the personages they know through reading and movies that they cannot establish a very clear limit between their identities and the identities of those fictional beings. As readers, we witness how these characters build their own discourse resorting to a language full of references to texts in which life is fictionalized. Patricia Waugh has highlighted the importance of fiction in one's own selfhood creation as well as the creation of what we call reality:

> If, as individuals, we now occupy "roles" rather than "selves," then the study of characters in novels may provide a useful model for understanding the construction of subjectivity in the world outside novels. If our knowledge of this world is now seen to be mediated through language, then literary fiction (worlds constructed entirely of language) becomes a useful model for learning about the construction of "reality" itself [3].

Thus, Manuela Roca, the lawyer who dies in a car accident when driving to her family summer house and with whom Amaro has a brief encounter in her hometown, is a good example of a personage that is perfectly aware of the theatricalness of her behavior. After a divorce that has left her sunk in a deep depression that prevents her from going ahead with her life, Manuela keeps up a very personal conversation with Rufina, her maid. The narrator asserts that the scene is a representation that could be labeled as a scene in a theater of absurd play (80). Later, the narrator adds that Manuela, as a reader of Golden Age literature, knows very well that in plays written by Lope de Vega, Tirso, Moreto, and Cervantes the reader can find ladies who confide in their maids and tell them secrets. Notwithstanding, such a confidence and complicity is always based on the lady's wishes to amuse herself. The difference, thus, is the genre: while the Golden Age heroines are characters in a comedy, Manuela is totally conscious of the tragedy of her meaningless life (81).

Irse de casa also is abundant with discussions on literature, film, and the act of artistic creation. Diverse characters, main and secondary, are involved in conversations whose subject is fiction itself. This includes the frivolous gatherings of the ladies nicknamed "the Greek choir" by Ricardo, the receptionist, and the conversations on literature held by the young people who meet at the bar Oriente, as well as the dialogues between Amparo and the people who really seem to be able to have a more intimate connection with her, people who recognize her or notice something deep and hidden behind the "mask" that Amparo adopts in her incursions in her native city.

All these examples point to what Waugh considers to be the main assumption in metafiction: the understanding of the world as if it were a book (3). This implies that extra-textual reality is not exempt of fiction: if human experience of the world is mediated or indirect — which means that it must be narrated or told to be understood — then such experience is, to some degree, built. That is why the concern about fiction is tied to the question about "how human beings reflect, construct and mediate their experience of the world" (2). In *Irse de casa*, the inclusion of a character who is a script writer can be taken as a metaphor for the necessity of a narration that tells one's life in order to make it understandable. In this way, Jeremy — Amparo's son — comes to be a key character in spite of his very few explicit interventions in the story. In the first part of the novel, Jeremy sustains a conversation with an actress, Florita, a young woman in whom he has found the perfect performer for the main role of his motion picture. While he tries to convince her to accept the role in his movie, Jeremy and she talk about the script and film in general, always linking the fiction presented in films with life. When Jeremy gives Florita a printed copy of the script, he asserts: "Leída la entenderás mejor. Te la puedes quedar, está guardada en mi ordenador. No es la versión definitiva, ¿sabes? Llevo dos años trabajando en ello, y no paro de corregir, bueno, es la vida la que lo corrige" [If you read it you'll understand it better. You can keep it, I've saved it in my computer. It's not the definitive version, you know. I've been working on it for two years, and cannot stop making corrections, well, it's life that corrects it] (13). Jeremy's explanation about how life corrects the script underlines an inner tension present at the very heart of metafictional works. That tension involves both the self-referential nature of the work and also the undeniable presence of real life-like elements (Herzberger 419–35). As a metafictional novel, *Irse de casa* makes the reader understand that there is a very deep bond between what we call "real life" and the ways we find to interpret it, making also very clear that such an interpretation must resort to a narrative model to be told. In *Irse the casa*, Martín Gaite appeals to a cinematographic script. In other novels, the author makes her characters write letters, essays, novels, or journals, in other words, they need a narrative model which enables them to tell their own story. We cannot understand our world and life if we do not try to make them comprehensible and meaningful through a narrative model, which implies a fictional frame.

Martín Gaite conceives a character — Jeremy — who in turn creates a character for the film he plans to make. But, the doubling of the act of creation does not stop there. The personage invented by Jeremy is based upon the little information that he knows about his mother's past. However, it is amended and, thus, recreated by Amparo. This triple act of creation — by Martín Gaite, Jeremy, and Amparo — equates all these processes of imagination, making visible the high degree of fictionalization that the creation of one's own identity involves. As has been already said, Amparo creates an identity for herself as Miranda Drake, a very sophisticated woman who is taken to be a foreigner in Spain. Nevertheless, while in her country and by reading her son's script for the biographical film, Amparo questions the path her life has taken during the last four decades. The script itself arises as a voice that forces her to be more active — creative — and, in this way, to find a more genuine life for herself. By means of this literary resource, Martín Gaite emphasizes the importance of and need for invention whenever we try to organize the different events of our personal history. According to Linda Hutcheon, the process of narrating has become a crucial feature of our comprehension of the real, because it is the way we impose an order on the confused flow of happenings: "Narrative is what translates knowing into telling[...]. The conventions of narrative in both historiography and novels, then, are not constraints, but enabling conditions of possibility of sensemaking" (121). However far Jeremy's script may be from what Amparo considers the "truth," it works as the counterpoint of her dusty and dispersed memories. Amparo contrasts what the script says with what she remembers and also with what she finds during her excursions in her hometown. Linda Hutcheon has pointed out the importance of a narrative order to understand and assimilate the past, which indicates the paradoxical admission that the facticity of the past can be approachable only through textualization (114). *Irse de casa* proposes that, although we try to establish a dividing line between the script and Amparo's life, those limits are blurred. In fact, Jeremy maintains that the script "se va cambiando al hilo de las situaciones imprevistas" [changes according to the thread of unexpected situations] (21). This emphasizes the convergence of one's own life and the fiction that narrates it, which undermines the apparent autonomy of each sphere, life and fiction.

Thus, Amparo understands herself, interprets her own history, and projects herself towards the future using fiction as one of her main points of departure. In this way, the act of reading and criticizing her son's script is one of the most important elements that allows her to find a more genuine self. It is in the act of creation where, according to Martín Gaite, one's own selfhood is revealed and shaped. In "El Gato con Botas," Martín Gaite explains her theory about every human being's need of fictionalizing her/his own life. The essay opens sustaining that "todo es narración" [all is narration] (143). Martín Gaite argues that children like to imagine themselves as story tellers, which set them free from the narrative patterns imposed by someone else (144). The author extols the talent of knowing how to tell stories, because "ser narrador capacita para rectificar lo que parecía irremediable y roturar su magma impreciso, otorga el don de la revancha. [...] Contar alivia de ese peso insoportable con que nos abruma lo meramente padecido, nos convierte en protagonistas, nos ayuda a sobrevivir y a rechazar, somete a los demás a la órbita de nuestra influencia" [Being a story teller enables us to rectify what seemed irremediable and to break up its imprecise magma, it grants us the gift of revenge. [...] Telling stories relieves us from the unbearable weight of merely being a passive character, it transforms us into protagonists, it helps us to survive and reject, it subdues the others putting them under the orbit of our influence] (144). This, indeed, is precisely what Amparo does.

After two days in her native city, she starts taking notes about the places she has visited. As time passes and Amparo accumulates more experiences, the narrator tells us that "necesitaba tomar notas de todo aquello, rumiarlo a solas. Ya empezaba a haber argumento" [She needed to take notes about it, meditate about it by herself. A plot had started to sprout] (187). When Amparo decides to have a second look at Jeremy's script, she writes down on the manuscript some details about the different people she meets by chance. On her sixth day in Spain, Amparo concludes the reading. Then, "...supo con certeza no sólo que ese texto había sido el desencadenante del viaje emprendido, sino que se había movido a su dictado desde que llegó" [...she knew without a doubt that the script not only had triggered her trip but also that she had continually acted out the script] (207). It is then when she expresses her wishes to become autonomous: "Me quiero salir del guión de Jeremy — dijo —. Ir de verdad a la calle del Olvido" [I want to move out of Jeremy's script — she said —. To really go to Oblivion Street] (207). This is the precise moment in which Amparo decides to be the author of herself. From then on, she will be more active in relation to the script, becoming its writer as well. She does not simply become *any* writer but one who is able to make the script truly alive. This attitude agrees with Jeremy's self-criticism, because he is aware about the artificiality of his story. Jeremy's script, in Amparo's opinion, is an incomplete story, full of mysteries that remain in darkness. Amparo doubts the quality of the text and also tells us about the decisions she makes in order to complete and overcome her lack of information. It is a story that needs other stories: the stories that Amparo rescues and recreates through her errant walks in her natal city.

Towards the end of the novel, Amparo decides to produce her son's film after reviewing and correcting what he has written. In this way, Amparo plays the double role of reader and writer. As a reader, Jeremy's words help her to understand herself and her life. As a writer, she can start to think of the possibility of accomplishing a project that could bring plenitude to her life. Thus, the script written by Jeremy works as a *writerly text*. Roland Barthes distinguishes between *readerly texts* and *writerly texts*. The former "are products (and not productions)" (*S/Z* 5), and need a passive reader. The purpose of a *writerly text*, on the contrary, "is to make the reader no longer a consumer, but a producer of the text" (*S/Z* 4). Even more, it is possible to sustain that Amparo, by correcting the script, appropriates the authorial function: on the one hand, Jeremy is Amparo's author, at least the author of the unnamed woman who is the main character in the script. She is a fictional being who will shape the extratextual Amparo (at the diegetic level of the novel), as she becomes the only reader of the script. On the other hand, Amparo uses her son's script as her counterpoint, a voice with which she is able to dialogue. In other words, Amparo actively reads the script, transforming it, which also means transforming herself. She perceives the reinvention of herself to be closely tied to the writing and reading of the text in which she has been fictionalized (the script). However, Amparo resists the idea of being a character created by someone else and becomes instead a character that creates her own self, deconstructing the script from a *readerly text* in order to reconstruct it into a *writerly text*. This process agrees with what Carmen Martín Gaite has said about self-definition not only in some of her essays, but also in several of her novels. The author thinks that every human being needs to create and tell his or her own story. It is through the creation and narration of the story of one's own life that someone can gain an identity before other people and, most importantly, before oneself. In this way, living and narrating become deeply imbricated.

In fact, as Joyce Tolliver has noticed, Amparo eventually abandons the role of the character depicted by her son and places herself behind the camera, which denotes a deep change from a passive to an active role in the filmic depiction and also creative representation of her own life:

After seven days in her home town, and on the day of her birthday, Amparo consciously decides to play the protagonist, not of Jeremy's imagined story of her life, but of her own newly-awakened story. She thus steps into her newly chosen role, "performing" in the life she would most like for herself. Ironically, this last performance allows her, finally, to begin to control the spectacle of her life, for it is at this point that she resolves literally to step behind the camera and to become a producer of films, starting with the film of her own life [267–8].

Amparo's attitude coincides with Carmen Martín Gaite's idea about telling stories: "Cuando vivimos, las cosas nos pasan; pero cuando contamos, las hacemos pasar" [When we live, things happen to us; but when we tell stories, we make them happen] ("La búsqueda" 22).

Martín Gaite's novel proposes that Amparo's personal story and the one of the woman protagonist of the script are deeply related, so much so that when Amparo understands her she also illuminates some obscure zones of herself. Amparo travels and rambles through her native city carrying a script that supposedly tells her life. Nevertheless, the first addressee of such a narration is Amparo herself. Jeremy's script impels her to embark on a temporary and geographic trip, according to Tolliver. However, this is a trip towards her own intimacy. Her son's script takes the place of the voice of the Other, a voice that interpellates and questions her; a voice that forces her to undertake a task she has avoided for decades: the task of being able to know who she really is. In order to succeed in attaining this goal, the presence of another's voice is essential because it helps the individual to understand her or himself, which also means to understand one's own life. This process necessarily implies the action of telling one's own story to someone else, which makes evident the need of an interlocutor.

In *Irse de casa,* the role of the interlocutor is to help create the identity of the individual with whom it is interacting. It is Olimpia, Amparo's sole friend during her youth, who taught her about the need of having an interlocutor: "Olimpia decía que era muy divertido hablar una sola, y hasta inventar a alguien que te contesta" [Olimpia used to say that it was very amusing to talk to oneself, and even to invent someone who answers you] (55). Later in the novel, we learn that Olimpia has a very lonely life, suffers insomnia, and begs for the company of someone who could rescue her from such isolation. In this context, Olimpia creates her own interlocutor. Inside her spacious and empty house, Olimpia declaims with her strong voice Macbeth's invocation to the witches (218); on another occasion, she recites a poem that reveals her unbearable solitude (313–4). As in Olimpia's case, Amparo also has a very lonely life. Behind a façade of a very successful life, Amparo has found herself in the need of inventing someone to address and share her intimate wanderings. This need of communication is framed within the theory about the search of the dreamed interlocutor elaborated by Martín Gaite.

In her essay "Los malos espejos," Martín Gaite explains the human need of being observed and appreciated the way one is, a need the author understands as "sed de ser reflejados de una manera inédita" [longing to be reflected in a totally new way] (16). According to Martín Gaite, the solitary effort to reach one's own inner part is not enough, because what one pursues "solamente una mirada ajena podría hacer creíble y reivindicar" [only someone else's eyes could make believable and vindicate] (18). In "La búsqueda de interlocutor," the writer postulates that one who has experienced radical solitude also desires an encounter with a utopian interlocutor, in order to break such loneliness (28, 32). In "El interlocutor soñado," Martín Gaite sustains that we imagine our encounter with someone with whom we will be able to establish an authentic communication, endowing our addressee with exemplary and magnificent features (139). In other words, we invent our dreamed interlocutor while we wait and hope that person finally appears. Jeremy, through his script, plays the role of the dreamed interlocutor to Amparo. He is the one who has the special talent to "enterarse de lo más oculto" [to perceive the most hidden things] (55), which, in Amparo's opinion, immediately labels him as a good writer. As she says to Ricardo: "Los buenos escritores tienen que amar lo secreto" [Good writers must love secrecy] (205), and her own son certainly fits into that description.

We can conclude that in *Irse de casa* Carmen Martín Gaite shapes a narrative where she opens the possibility for exploring selfhood. This selfhood is based on the creative quest for an identity on Amparo's part which is deeply related to the redefinition of herself. Thus, Martín Gaite brings out the fictional nature of the creation of our own identities. Reading, writing, acting, discussing literature and film not only link human beings to the world of literature and art but also permit us to gain reality. Although it is true this novel reveals its own fictionality, it is no less true that it relates to "life" as long as Amparo is now connected to a life that seems to be more real to her. Carmen Martín Gaite stresses the ability of Amparo to act upon her own history in order to change it. The novel refers to different literary genres as well as to diverse types of discourse in which the characters—mainly Amparo—interpret themselves, either rejecting those genres or embracing, questioning, or changing them. Zarzuela, philosophy, Golden

Age theater, popular music, film, detective novel, poetry, among others, are investigated as possible channels of understanding personal reality.

Amparo, as the main personage, as well as some of the secondary characters show their nonconformity to their own life styles, and consequently search for a genuine identity through a longing for finding and creating an authentic self. By resorting to fictional works, Martín Gaite points out the interests and motives of different characters, revealing facets of them that usually remain hidden. In this way, the metafictional nature of *Irse de casa* becomes a powerful instrument for analyzing identity through the abandonment of the daily roles and the exploration of alternative ones. Martín Gaite examines the relationship between life and fiction highlighting how the latter can promote the transformation of the first one, encouraging the characters — and, by extension, the readers — to acquire an identity, dismantling the masks that have kept them far from their own fulfillment.

Works Cited

Barthes, Roland. *S / Z*. Trans. Richard Miller. New York: Hill and Wang, 1974.

Herzberger, David K. "Split Referentiality and the Making of Character in Recent Spanish Metafiction." *MLN* 103.2 (1988): 419–35.

Hutcheon, Linda. *A Poetics of Postmodernism. History, Theory, Fiction*. New York and London: Routledge, 1999.

Martín Gaite, Carmen. "La búsqueda de interlocutor." *La búsqueda de interlocutor y otras búsquedas*. Barcelona: Destino, 1982. 21–34.

———. "El gato con botas." *El cuento de nunca acabar (apuntes sobre la narración, el amor y la mentira)*. Barcelona: Destino, 1997. 141–9.

———. "El interlocutor soñado." *El cuento de nunca acabar (apuntes sobre la narración, el amor y la mentira)*. Barcelona: Destino, 1997. 133–40.

———. *Irse de casa*. Barcelona: Anagrama, 1998.

———. "Los malos espejos." *La búsqueda de interlocutor y otras búsquedas*. Barcelona: Destino, 1982. 11–20.

Tolliver, Joyce. "The Geography of Time: Martín Gaite's *Irse de casa*." *Disciplines on the Line: Feminist Research on Spanish, Latin American, and U.S. Latina Women*. Eds. Anne J. Cruz, Rosilie Hernández-Pecoraro and Joyce Tolliver. Newark, Delaware: Juan de la Cuesta, 2003. 257–68.

Waugh, Patricia. "What Is Metafiction and Why Are They Saying Such Awful Things About It?" *Metafiction. The Theory and Practice of Self-Conscious Fiction*. London and New York: Routledge, 1990. 1–19.

Space and the Construction of the Self in the Narratives of Josefina Aldecoa

Carmen T. Sotomayor

The study of the influence of our spatial surroundings on the social and historical conditions of human beings has become one of the most significant intellectual developments of our era. Wesley A. Kort in *Place and Space in Modern Fiction* (2004) affirms that in the present time "we are beginning to read places as our cultural 'scriptures' and to identify and evaluate ourselves and other people spatially" (5). Kort's theory about spatial relations and narrative constructions provides a relevant theoretical frame for the study of contemporary narratives by women, for "space and place are important in the construction of gender relations and in struggles to change them" (Massey 179). This essay focuses on the study of the relationship between space and the construction of identity in the trilogy by Spanish writer Josefina R. Aldecoa: *Historia de una maestra* (1990), *Mujeres de negro* (1994), and *La fuerza del destino* (1997). While weaving complicated spatial relations, Aldecoa seduces the reader with characters of great psychological depth that relay many socio-cultural issues, including the elaborate interplay between power and control, the public and the personal spheres and women's private and public struggles to find their place in a changing society.

Kort advocates the need to recognize the diversity of languages in narrative discourse. These languages can be designated as the languages of character, of action and events, of the teller's interests or attitudes, and of place or environment. They are not only present but also related to and interactive with one another within a narrative discourse. In the works of Aldecoa, who devotes part of the narrative discourse in her fiction to the description and construction of specific locations, the language of place and space acquires real prominence. Aldecoa highlights the relationship of her protagonists with their surroundings, as it is while immersed in them that they construct their own sense of self, in consonance with Kort's assertion that "personal place-relations are crucial to the actualization of human potential and integrity" (165). He distinguishes between three types of place or space relations: cosmic or comprehensive relations, social-political relations, and personal-intimate relations. Cosmic or comprehensive space focuses not only on the language of natural space, but also on the gaps and margins created by human constructions, by the transitions between social spaces. On the other hand, social space tends to "conceal, swamp, or determine both comprehensive and personal or intimate spaces" (157). In Aldecoa's narratives, space is not just a passive "setting," the décor where the action takes place.* Rather, her writings elaborate on the function of space, which becomes an important carrier of meaning in her works.

The narrative voice in the first volume of the trilogy, *Historia de una maestra*, is that of a female protagonist, Gabriela López Pardo, who is talking to her daughter Juana — who is listening to her life story — and, by extension, to us, the readers. The account of the memories of her early years as a public school teacher will be marked by the figure of Franco, from the recounting of his wedding to Carmen Polo in October 1923 (the same day Gabriela received her diploma as a public school teacher) to the events of July 1936. *Historia de una maestra* closes down with the beginning of the Civil War and General Franco assuming a leadership role in the governance of Spain for the next thirty some years.† Although Gabriela will continue to teach children after the war, she will never again, like many Republican teachers, be allowed to do so in a Spanish public school.

Gabriela's account of her life until 1936 is divided into three sections: *El comienzo del sueño, El sueño, El final del sueño*. The metaphor of the dream is the leitmotiv of this first narrative, as Gabriela tells the interlocutor/reader about her desire to achieve certain goals and the problems she faces as she

---

*In contrast with other narrative components such as character and action the term "setting" does not imply content and therefore is an inappropriate way of referring to space, as it erases the referential possibilities of the language of space.

†In *La fuerza del destino*, Gabriela mentions the fact that she was able to keep her promise never to return to Spain as long as Franco was alive. This decision had a significant impact in her life, as she remained voluntarily exiled in Mexico and displaced from her home country, as well as from her daughter Juana and her grandchild, Miguel, who returned to Spain before 1975.

tries to realize them. Gabriela's first years as a teacher are spent in remote villages where, young and inexperienced, she has to struggle to develop her potential as an educator. The surrounding social and personal spaces are negative and restricted, as she lives in rental rooms in very isolated villages, without running water or electricity. She, like her father, projects her understanding of the sacred to everything around her: "El mar y el monte y el hombre son Dios" [the sea and the mountain and man are God] (29). She strives to create around her pleasant environments, as when she decides to clean and paint one of her first schools because "no podemos trabajar en un lugar tan feo" [we cannot work in such an ugly place] (23). She makes every effort within her power to teach the children in these secluded villages, using geography as a way to help them to place themselves in the world and to combat their ignorance.* As she reflects upon the scarcity around her, she compares herself and her students to Robinson Crusoe, as they all live in a land isolated from civilization and progress. Aldecoa's portrait of these villages' precarious conditions in the 1920s and 1930s is profoundly moving. Through the point of view of her protagonist, she is able to communicate the sense of social and economical segregation and the difficulties of life in those inaccessible and forgotten places far from the urban centers: "nosotros vivíamos encerrados en el circo de montañas, prisioneros de la geografía y la miseria" [we lived enclosed by a ring of mountains, prisoners of geography and misery] (49).

When Gabriela finally has a chance to choose her own school, she exchanges the cold winters of northern Spain for the unbearable tropical heat of Equatorial Guinea. Aldecoa attempts to show the relational character of identity, as her protagonist encounters new people and new places that contribute to the evolution of her personality. In her struggle to reach some level of autonomy, Gabriela will grow as an individual but will also submit herself to a social environment that defeats her desire to develop as a human being: "Si fuera hombre ... pensaba. Un hombre es libre. Pero yo era mujer y estaba atada por mi juventud, por mis padres, por la falta de dinero, por la época" [If I were a man ... I would think. A man is free. But I was a woman and I was tied down by my youth, by my parents, by the lack of money, by the times] (53). Gabriela tries to balance her challenge regarding her gen-

---

*"Nunca han oído estos niños una explicación sobre el lugar que ocupa la Tierra en el Universo, Europa en la Tierra, España en Europa. Creo que ni siquiera están seguros del punto de España en que se encuentran" [These children have never heard an explanation about the place that the planet Earth takes in the Universe, Europe within Earth, Spain within Europe. I believe that they are not even sure about where in Spain they are located] (32-33).

der and her social and financial limitations with a clear understanding of her mission as an educator. However, what brings her to Africa is not just her educational mission, but her thirst for new adventures, as Gabriela is also searching for the possibility of finding a place where she might be able to exercise some personal freedom. Nevertheless, she is not able to establish close relationships with most people. The only profound bond that she develops is with a young black African doctor, Émile. As the companionship grows, so does the alarm of the white European community and soon the social space around her starts raising racial barriers against their friendship.

After her return to Spain — forced by her debilitated physical condition caused by fevers — Gabriela marries a fellow teacher, Ezequiel, who reminds her that there is no need to travel far as there are many Guineas within Spain. When Gabriela settles down with her husband, and shortly after gives birth to a baby girl, Juana, she tries hard to relate in a positive manner to the two spaces that connect her life experience, her school, and her home. The creation of a positive home environment is a major goal for the protagonist who would agree that "our house is the corner of the world. As has often been said, it is our first universe, a real cosmos in every sense of the word. If we look at it intimately, the humblest dwelling has beauty" (Bachelard 4). Gabriela has derived this sense of belonging from her parents' home, anchored in her memory by the affection and sense of security that her parents had conveyed to her through their configuration of their intimate space, their home. The house could be comprehended as a metaphorical space that may signify a place of safety as well as a place of restraint:

> The limitation of women's mobility, in terms both of identity and space, has been in some cultural contexts a crucial means of subordination. Moreover the two things — the limitation on mobility in space, the attempted consignment/confinement to particular places on the one hand, and the limitation on identity on the other — have been crucially related [Massey 179].

The access to a private place relates directly to economic and social factors, as it impacts a person's cultural and personal values. As Virginia Woolf discusses in *A Room of One's Own*, there is a profound connection between the enjoyment of a private space and one's sense of creativity and personal worth. The relationship between self-esteem and a private place can also be expanded to establish a connection between the private and a person's sense of spirituality. Gabriela's struggle to provide for herself and her family a home is a sign of her maturity: "Con nosotros viajaba nuestra casa donde quiera que fuéramos. El hogar está en la cabeza, en el corazón o, como diría

Regina, por todo el cuerpo. Nosotros tres éramos nuestro hogar y conducíamos nuestro destino. Yo veía mi sueño navegando hacia puertos seguros" [Our house traveled with us wherever we went. Home is in the mind, in the heart, or, as Regina would say, all over the body. The three of us were our home and we drove our own destiny. I could see my dream sailing toward safe harbors] (148–49).*

Within the limitations of a humble income, Gabriela surrounds her daughter with a sense of well-being that emanates from the kitchen, the place where the family gathers, the center of the house, which has a magnetic force transforming itself into a major zone of protection (Bachelard 31). However, the characters are faced with their own solitude as they try to struggle with the issues of their daily life. As Ezequiel is drawn into his quest for social justice, he turns away from the home and spends more of his time in the public space, the village square, where he participates in the insecure events taking place before the Civil War. In contrast, Gabriela decides to focus on her work as an educator and on motherhood, dividing her time between the school and the kitchen.

From the moment she began experiencing her pregnancy, Gabriela felt a strong bond between herself and her child, a connection that reflects her intimate relation with the land. This cosmic perception of the self comes from a personal understanding of the inner self and motherhood. On the other hand, Gabriela understands the limitations brought about by her view of maternity, as she realizes that "ser madre es una gloria y una condena al mismo tiempo" [to be a mother is a glory and a condemnation at the same time] (174). Her introspective look at herself brings her to the conclusion that, although she has always been on the side of progress in her career — supporting co-education, for instance —, nevertheless in her private life she has followed the traditional pattern of expected behavior. She thinks of her marriage as a life-long commitment, as she could not conceive of challenging this notion, reinforced by the presence of a child, also a difficult obstacle for divorce.† When Gabriela thinks back about Guinea, she sees it as a lost opportunity, the road to her own freedom, which she failed to pursue further. Instead, she brought herself within the traditional expectations, becoming a good wife, a good mother, and a good citizen. She concludes her reflections by recognizing that "la trampa se cerraba sobre mí" [the trap

---

*This is a variation of the old saying "We bring our lares with us" (Bachelard 5).
†Although she is "happily married" to Ezequiel, she shows signs of wariness in her thoughts about their relationship.

was closing in on her] (176). Gabriela renounces her own desire for adventure, accepting her role as "a stable symbolic center," while accepting to have her identity as a woman to be tied up with the notion of the "home-place" (Massey 180).

Contained by the boundaries of the home there is also a web of interconnections, of relations of power. In the recounting of her life, Gabriela acknowledges the important role of other women in her existence. The memory of several of those women (her mother, her underprivileged neighbors, Regina and Marcelina, and the adolescent Mila while she lived in Spain; Remedios, in the Mexican *hacienda*) make her reflect that "Si voy mirando hacia atrás siempre encuentro en el pasado una mujer que me ha ayudado a vivir" [if I look back, I always find in my past a woman that has helped me to live] (173).* As Gabriela struggles with her duties as a teacher and a homemaker, she finds support from lower-class workingwomen. In fact, Gabriela's situation recalls McDowell's reference to the engagement of women in the working place and their need to negotiate a solution between their time requirements to pursue a career and having to seek assistance for housework and the caring of their children (184). Gabriela requests these women's help without any regrets. However, she treats them with respect and care, and reciprocates their help by other venues. Gabriela's struggle to live a life "not defined by family and husband" (Massey 198) is put into question by Marcelina, who comments: "Ustedes, las que han estudiado, mucho predicar pero a la hora de dar trigo, ¿qué? Ni trigo ni ejemplo ni nada. ¡Pobres mujeres!" [You, those who have studied, you preach a lot but when the time comes to produce, then what? Nothing! Not a very good example. Poor women!] (175).

As Gabriela observes the women around her, she realizes that they are prepared from the cradle to be submissive, and she tries in her own small way to fight the gendered spaces that limit a woman's place in society. She helps the women in the villages by organizing classes for adults, seeking to advance their knowledge of good practices related to personal hygiene and caring for their children. She also supports co-education and takes a chance with it, even though she feels certain social pressure to abandon the initiative. If gender is the social organization of sexual difference (McDowell 15), Gabriela has an acute perception of the profound inequalities that the co-education initiative is helping to correct. By bringing down spatial barriers among her male and female students, Gabriela challenges long-held assumptions about the place of women in Spanish society.

The division of the social space affects Gabriela as a citizen as well as a woman. Her description of the villages where she teaches makes clear the barriers that cut across between social classes, races, genders and professions. Societal and cultural values are well delineated by the division of the social space, especially in these small communities. Even though the size of urban spaces tends "to occlude comprehensive space and swamp personal spaces" (Kort 207), in the small communities described by Aldecoa, migration to the urban centers is seen as an act of liberation. This thought is implied by Ezequiel when he reveals to Gabriela his dreams regarding Juana: "Esta niña no vivirá aquí, saldrá de los pueblos, estudiará en una ciudad lo más grande posible, Gabriela. En Madrid o en Barcelona se pueden hacer revoluciones. Aquí, no" [This little girl will not live here, she will go away far from the village life, she will study in a city, the bigger the better, Gabriela. In Madrid or Barcelona people can bring about revolutions. Not here] (126). As Kort indicates, cities have been places where women "have sought and found greater freedom of movement, economic opportunity, and places to actualize their identities and integrity" (217).

The second narrative of the trilogy, *Mujeres de negro*, is presented from Juana's perspective. It is divided into three sections entitled *Los vencidos, El destierro* y *El regreso*. The underlying metaphor of exile and return is the leitmotiv of this account, as Juana struggles to recuperate her past and to delimit her personal relationship with the spaces that have the most influence in her development as an individual: Spain and Mexico. The storyline encompasses Juana's recollections of her early childhood in northern Spain during the Civil War, her adolescence in Mexico, and her return to Spain as a young university student. From her daughter's perspective, the reader is also invited to reconstruct Gabriela's life, as she takes another chance at marriage and the opportunity to live in a beautiful *hacienda* near the city of Puebla (Mexico), in the company of her second husband, Octavio Guzmán.

As Juana reminisces about those times, the reader learns that the loss of her father and her grandfather at the beginning of the armed conflict, and the disappearance of her grandmother later, have a profound impact on the child, who is also dealing with the difficulties of war. Her mother and grandmother's efforts to shelter the little girl are encapsulated in Juana's assertion: "fuera de nuestra casa había una guerra" [there was a war outside of our home] (10). The social pressure of war times is expressed by external symbols, such as the coercion to decorate the balconies and windows with the Spanish traditional flag. Spaniards were forced to belong to a new order. Those who refused to follow orders became enemies of the new repressive regime and had to either flee or hide. The trip to Mexico is in Juana's words a way to escape, the result of Gabriela's determination to getaway from the difficulties of the repression years after the war. The aftermath of the war is a key factor in the vanishing of her intimate space, as living in Spain becomes a reminder of her personal tragedies, including the death of her husband and parents. Furthermore, she has to face the loss of her social status, as she suffers the labeling of being one of the defeated and is denied the credentials to continue practicing her profession. Gabriela, echoing Mariano José de Larra, admits to Juana: "Tengo miedo de no poder vivir en una cárcel, porque ya todo es una cárcel" [I am afraid of not being able to live in a prison, because everything is already a prison] (58).

As Juana leaves for Mexico in the company of her mother, the latter becomes the only stable point of reference in Juana's life until she develops the normal desires for independence that surge with adolescence. During her years in "la capital" (a reference to León), Gabriela is under an emotional shock that is apparent to her child, who finds her withdrawn, elusive and distant: "My mother hardly ever emerged from a gloomy realm, impenetrable to me" [Mi madre apenas salía de un mundo neblinoso, impenetrable para mí] (19). Luckily, Juana will recuperate her mother as they establish themselves in a new constructive environment.

The solitude of the large colonial house outside of Puebla provides a refuge for the newly formed family, and allows them to configure new relationships among themselves and with those around them. Remedios, the old cook who supervises the household needs, provides through the intimacy of her warm soul and her kitchen, a place of comfort for the young and insecure Juana. As she grows up, Juana finds other persons to share her intimacy with, such as Soledad, Gabriela's school assistant, who invades the household with her radiant personality. At the same time that Juana feels more rooted in her new surroundings, she also develops a certain level of anxiety as she does not want to lose her connection to the land of her birth and the memories of loved ones that she has left behind. In her dreams, she revisits her grandmother's house in the countryside, a symbol of all the positive memories of her childhood. As was the case with Gabriela, this house becomes the referent of secure and happy remembrances. As Juana faces her anxieties over "losing her past," Gabriela provides her emotional support and attempts to pass on to her child a feeling of belonging not through identification with Spain but rather through a solid foundation in one's chosen destiny in life. She asks Juana to think of the world as her motherland and to let go of emotional attachments to "las patrias pequeñas" [small homelands] (80).

The positive environment of the *hacienda* expands as Gabriela is given a second chance at rebuilding her life, including the opportunity to teach again. Rather than displacing Remedios as the housekeeper, Gabriela welcomes the opportunity to help her husband in his business and to organize a small private school to teach the children of the Indian families that live in Octavio's farmlands. Gabriela attains empowerment as she locates and prepares the space for her little school. However, she faces once more the constraints of an established social space that limits the access to education for these children. As was the case in the villages in Spain, she finds herself going against the social forces that benefit from the ignorance of these illiterate people that are chained to the land from generation to generation and exploited by the landowners. While the chance to teach again invigorates Gabriela's intimate space, renewing her interest in life through her enthusiasm to work with these disadvantaged children, the story repeats itself, as "we live in societies that are structured by relations of power" (McDowell 247). The established patriarchal society (represented by such figures as the priest and the Public Education Bureau Inspector) acts repressively in fear that the structures of power may crumble under the influence of the educational goals of progressive teachers such as Gabriela. The parallelism between the small schools in northern Spain and the little school in the *hacienda*, reminds the reader of the penury of those social spaces.

While Gabriela settles down in the *hacienda* and finds ways to feel useful, Juana approaches adolescence and with it, the desire to become more independent. As Juana receives her mother's support to study in Mexico City first and then in Madrid, Merceditas, Octavio's daughter, accepts the fact that she will be denied the opportunity to leave the familiar spaces, since societal pressures restrain the mobility of young upper-class women: "A mí no me dejarán salir de aquí" [They will not let me to get out of here] (109). Merceditas will remain within the close oversight of her father and aunt. She will marry young, with the responsibility for her own life choices shifting from her father to her husband. However, Merceditas accepts the limitations of her social space, as she confesses to Juana in a letter: "Ya tengo dieciséis años pero yo no soy como tú. Yo no quiero irme a estudiar lejos, no quiero vivir sola" [I am sixteen years old but I am not like you, I do not want to go far away to study, I do not want to live alone] (142). On the other hand, young Juana's experience in Mexico City and later in Madrid echoes her father's wishes for her to have more opportunities in life. Although Juana resents her mother's stern and resigned outlook in life (which Juana connects to the Castilian "mujeres de negro"), she is given the freedom to leave the family's realm. Furthermore, Gabriela respects Juana's choices while she lives in Spain and encourages her to travel and live in other European cities.

Juana is given the opportunity to establish her identity as she seeks answers to her personal dilemmas. When she is invited to enter the social spaces of the Spanish exiles in Mexico City, she finally comes to terms with her own notion of exile and loss. She recuperates her memories, through the collective remembrances of the exiled Spaniards with whom she interacts and through language, as she will listen again to her native Castilian. Juana's words resonate Pablo Neruda's view of the Spanish language as "the common space," the point of contact of all of the cultures that use the Spanish language to bridge their differences: "El idioma, mi única, mi verdadera patria" [the language, my only, my true homeland] (117). In her recollections, Juana refers to her mother's views regarding the exiled, which included a reconciling notion of not blaming either those who left or those who remained in Spain. For Gabriela, "hace falta tanto valor para irse como para quedarse. [...] Hace falta mucho coraje para seguir viviendo allí sin rendirse por dentro" [It is as hard to go as to remain. [...] One must have a lot of courage to continue living there without giving up inside] (97).

Juana's youthful dilemma about her sense of belonging to Spain and/or Mexico is central to the notion of a cosmic space and to her ideological development. Her stay in Madrid during those formative years leaves a lasting impression on her at a personal, social, and philosophical level. Within the freedom of renting a room in Madrid and being without a direct supervisor, she enters the "confusing labyrinth of passions" (128) as a forming adult. Through the discovery of intimacy and sex in her relation with Sergio, Juana shapes her personal space, as she learns about herself and establishes a positive connection with her body and her intimate relationships.

She is also an observer of social spaces in the capital, as she is exposed to many public intersections of the city. Those include the high-class neighborhoods (with the influential power of the well-to-do families), the suffocating intellectual life in the university's classrooms and the political repression (she gets involved in the students' political resistance against the dictatorship), the poverty and misery of the slums, and the middle-class fight to survive the hardships of life in the post-war period. Madrid becomes for Juana a place of discovery and a familiar realm, as she refers to the public place where she gathers with her new friends as "nuestra taberna" and she learns from her friends how to find shelter from the lack of civil liberties under the Franco regime. Her political involvement is limited and although she feels the call to engage in underground political activities, she remains neutral, as her family's past places her in a vulnerable situation. Juana will question the sincerity of her political/social engagement, as she remains an "active observer" during her university years in Madrid from 1949 to 1954. Her trip to León to visit a childhood friend, Amelia, is a turning point in the story, as Juana recognizes the rural Spain of her youth, aggravated by the still visible marks of the Civil War. Her story is circular in its conception, as it begins with her departure into exile in Mexico and ends with her return to her adopted land, signaling the closing of an epoch for Juana, as she comes back to Mexico more mature and with the desire to find her own way in life, as indicated by Vásquez: "In electing to make her life in Mexico, Juana rejects the shadows — 'mujeres de negro'— to move and stake her space within what she sees as a greater light. Hers is not, however, a capricious election. It is a choice, fully as much of generation as of place, for a way of being female and against another female mode." (269)

Juana acknowledges the difficulty of reaching a decision at that turning point in her life, as she finds herself one more time the victim of a split, caught in the middle of the bridge that united her two homelands. Her divided sense of attachment reclaims her to Mexico and those she loves. It will only be later, as she regains a solid emotional/personal space with Sergio and finds a worthy mission for her social conscience, that she will finally return to Spain.

The third and last novel of the trilogy fast-forwards the narration to the events after November 20, 1975. That day Juana informs her mother of Franco's death and asks her to join her in Madrid. Gabriela narrates the last of the novels in the trilogy, *La fuerza del destino*, mainly from the perspective of her uncertain present in an unknown city and in a country that she no longer recognizes.* The novel is likewise divided into three sections: *El plazo, La esperanza y El silencio*. As in the previous novels, there is profound connection among its three parts, while it also weaves into a dialog with the preceding narratives. This time, as Gabriela finds herself without an interlocutor, she narrates her story to herself. Her account includes remembrances from the past and events from the present, mixed progressively with dreams and an internal debate, as she realizes that her brain is deteriorating. Her monologue becomes a reflection of the character's loneliness, solitude being her main disease, as she confesses in one of several references to her personal

---

*Pascual Solé analyses the trilogy from the perspective of exile in her article mentioned in the bibliography.

discontent after her return.* The reader learns that she is living alone in a fancy upper-class suburb in the outskirts of Madrid, as she declines to join her daughter and husband in the city. Her refusal to move into Madrid is tied up with a feeling of personal emptiness, to which Gabriela makes multiple references: "He pasado a convertirme en un ser inútil" [I have become a worthless being] (21).

Aldecoa's critique of life in the suburbs is also prominent in her novel *El enigma* (2002). In both narratives, the writer criticizes these "colonies" of "casitas aisladas" [isolated little houses] as contributors to seclusion and loneliness, since people come and go into the city for their daily work. There is a lack of shared social spaces in the planning of the suburbs, of places where people may meet one another and have a chance of creating a supportive community. Furthermore, many women who do not work outside of the home may feel isolated in the suburbs. The division between public and private, and the confinement of women to the private sphere of the home are clearly identifiable in Gabriela's case but not in her daughter's. While Gabriela wrestles all her life, without much success, to break away from this confinement, Juana will establish her life style on the basic premise of her capacity to negotiate her own space in her personal as well as in her professional life, including politics, which was and still is highly dominated by males. While Juana and her husband craved the isolation of life in the suburbs as they were establishing themselves socially as a couple (Sergio had to go through the process of a nasty divorce), eventually they moved back into the city and participated actively in the social and political spaces of the capital. As Gabriela comments on Juana's ability to create a comfortable home and social space around her, including her love and appreciation of beautiful objects since childhood, she recognizes the importance of their different educational foundation.†

Gabriela, who was brought up conditioned by her parents' austerity, was able to put together her need to belong in a place — school — with her need to have a mission in life, inculcated by her father. This explains why Gabriela longs for her pupils even as she enjoys a life without any financial worries: "La noche es larga cuando no tienes a nadie a quien cuidar. Un niño, por pequeño que sea, te hace olvidar el miedo. Pero cuando nadie te necesita, empieza la soledad. Y el miedo a la soledad" [Night seems long when you do not have anyone to take care of. A child, no matter how small it is,

---

*"Lo único que me duele es la soledad" [The only thing that hurts is this loneliness] (202).
†See Vásquez's essay for a study of Juana's character formation and contrast with Gabriela's.

makes you forget fear. However, when no one needs you, solitude begins. And with it, the fear of solitude] (15–16). Gabriela's strategy as a young woman to leave the realm of the home is to devote her life to teaching, a professional venue with a higher proportion of women than most and established as a reputable career for them. In Gabriela's case, it provided her with objectives that would greatly contribute to shape her mission as a human being.* As the protagonist relives the most important events in her life and scrutinizes her actions, she refers to character as destiny† and concludes by saying that "Por eso, nadie escapa a su destino, porque nadie escapa a su carácter" [no one escapes their destiny, because no one can escape their character] (102). It is in her temperament to accept cultural restrictions, while at the same time she craves to be adventurous. There is nostalgia in Gabriela's reflections about her past life that connects her desire to serve others with her yearning to travel, to see the world. Her grandchild, Miguel, a young man who wishes to be a photographer and to report about social issues in different places in the world, embodies Gabriela's ultimate desire to bring together a curiosity for the outside world with a mission to serve others.‡

Through Gabriela's monologues in *La fuerza del destino*, the reader witnesses her attempt to unearth her most intimate spaces. We witness a daily ritual that commences with remembrances of the past linked to the predictable life events in the suburbs and to the historical events of the country (such as the referendum on the 1978 Spanish Constitution and the 1981 failed coup d'état) and ends with the view of the sunset from the top of a nearby hill. This symbolic ceremony is part of the protagonist's ritual to prepare herself for her final refusal to nourish her body, as well as to face death: "Morirse es despedirse de uno mismo" (215). As Gabriela equates this stage of her life to getting ready for the final departure, she recalls those most important spaces in her life: "De toda mi vida volvería a tres momentos. Uno, Guinea, con mis niños negros, la escuela de la playa, el calor. Y Èmile todas las tardes. [...] Otro, el día que nació Juana [...] Y luego México, con Juana niña y el amor de Octavio que transformó mi vida" (From all my life, I would return to three moments. First, Guinea, with my black children, the

---

*Gabriela refers to her mission to "educate those abandoned in cultural deserts": "educar a los abandonados en sus desiertos culturales" (54). She has devoted her life to help others, a knowledge that makes her strong in her convictions: "He dedicado lo mejor de mi vida a ayudar a los demás. Y en eso no me he equivocado." [I have devoted the best part of my life to help others. And I have not been wrong in doing so] (80).

†"el destino es el carácter" [destiny is character] (65).

‡Miguel is described by his grandmother as a "ciudadano del mundo" [citizen of the world] (102).

school at the beach, the heat. And Èmile every afternoon.... Second, the day that Juana was born. [...] And then Mexico, with little Juana and Octavio's love, which transformed my life)" (216).

Gabriela reflects upon her life in terms of her exile in Mexico and her return to Spain, where she lives "una vida aislada en un país que me da poco y al que yo no doy nada" [isolated life in a country that gives me little and to which I do not give anything] (113). She is anticipating her death as she wonders about the impact of her life on either country. She feels attached to both lands through her connections with the people in each place. She followed Octavio to Mexico, driven by her passion for him and pushed her remembrances of her childhood to the background, an indicator of her desire to live in the present, of her personal drive during those years. Now Mexico, the cycle of ardent passions, has closed and she has returned to Spain to be near her daughter and grandchild. Gabriela experiences a strong connection between her notion of a cosmic space and her personal space as, for her, both are related. This conviction she inherited from her parents' creed about their relations with their personal spaces, which would include a sense of rectitude and cleanliness applied to their bodies, home, social relations and code of ethics. As Gabriela begins closing her life cycle, she dreams frequently about the spaces of her childhood and her parents' home. Antonio Machado's words reverberate in Gabriela's personal philosophy and approach to material possessions throughout her life: "Lo que hay aquí no es mío. Si yo tuviera que abandonar este cobijo, emprendería el viaje, una vez más, sólo con mi maleta, hacia el nuevo destino" [None of these things here are mine. If I had to abandon this shelter, I would commence my journey, once more, with just my luggage, on towards the new destination/destiny] (148). The last novel of the trilogy is truly a journey for Gabriela. The reader witnesses her act of dispossession, as she begins losing consciousness and submerges herself in total solitude and refusal. Gabriela equates death to total alienation, "la desaparición total" (216): "Cuando se abandona un lugar en el que se ha vivido durante cierto tiempo, comienza enseguida el desprendimiento de la pequeñas o grandes rutinas. Hay un afán de distanciamiento inconsciente que trata de hacer menos dolorosa la partida" [When one leaves a place where one has lived for a while, soon one begins a process of distancing oneself from the trivial or even perhaps the significant daily routines. There is an unconscious need to make the departure the less painful] (190). As Gabriela is getting ready to depart from this world, she mentions that "he entrado en un mundo lleno de agujeros por los que se escapan las ideas, los recuerdos, los proyectos" [I have entered a world full of holes, through which ideas, remembrances and projects escape] (217).

Aldecoa, joining the effort to not forget Spain's recent history, refers to these novels as her "trilogy of memory" (*En la distancia* 216). She provides the reader, especially the younger reader, an account of the historical memory of this tragic era. Her trilogy is a generational saga in this regard and the third novel in particular, a piercing account from the perspective of someone who suffered greatly the consequences of the Civil War and the postwar period.* In the three narratives, Gabriela is presented as an itinerant character, portrayed as someone who wants to shake off old values and notions about womanhood and citizenship. Within the constrictions of her time, she travels and lives in a number of places; however, her life is centered on her passion for teaching. As she tells Juana in *Mujeres de negro*: "elige algo que pueda ser para ti el cimiento de tu existencia. Algo a lo que te puedas agarrar en los momentos malos, algo que nadie pueda quitarte. Las personas, los afectos pasan, pero tu profesión está ahí. Es como tu esqueleto que soporta tu cuerpo y te permite andar y moverte de un lado a otro, un delicado mecanismo que regula el equilibrio de tu vida" [Choose something that can be for you the foundation of your existence. Something to hold on to when things are not going well, something that no one can take from you. People, affections move on, but your profession will always remain. It is like your bone structure that provides your body support and allows you to walk and to move from here to there, a delicate mechanism that regulates the balance in your life] (73).

According to Massey, space needs to be conceptualized as "constructed out of interrelations, as the simultaneous coexistence of social interrelations and interactions at all spatial scales, from the most local level to the most global" (264). Josefina Aldecoa's female characters reassert their value as human beings as they cross the boundaries of the private into that of the public sphere by virtue of their narratives. Leggott remind us of the fact that "the majority of women deploy the more private forms of the diary or the journal to record the stories of their lives" (21). Women feel caught in a dilemma, as they are not used to moving freely across the boundaries of the public and the private spheres. Gabriela reclaims her place in society by way of recounting her personal struggle. Juana, who recalls her memories of childhood in Spain and exile in Mexico, finally returns to Spain and finds her place in Spanish society. Furthermore, through her political involvement during the Transition years to democracy, she actually contributes to the groundwork "writing" of a democratic Spain, the 1978 Constitution. As María Elena Soliño sustains, their testimonies are "extremely personal texts

---

*See in this regard the article by Cinta Ramblado-Minero mentioned in the bibliography.

that allow us to glimpse the lives and struggles of the mothers and grandmothers who must not be forgotten in the democratic Spain for which they, too, laid the foundation" (37).*

Aldecoa's account confirms the claim that "the spatial is integral to the production of history, and thus the possibility of politics" (Massey 269). Although their relative importance varies within each narrative, Josefina Aldecoa's close attention to the construction of space and to the interaction of her characters with their surroundings is indicative of her perception of the significance of space and spatial relations in society. Her trilogy corroborates Kort's assertion that "narrative discourses are sites of our experiences of and search for positive place-relations" (223). At the end of her narration, Gabriela, who had struggled throughout her life to find "her place," in a holistic sense, expresses the culmination of her journey through the music that reverberates in her head and compels her to travel through memory, bringing her forth to the ultimate placeless and timeless experience.

Works Cited

Aldecoa, Josefina. *Historia de una maestra*. Barcelona: Anagrama, 2005.
_____. *Mujeres de negro*. Barcelona: Anagrama, 2004.
_____. *La fuerza del destino*. Barcelona: Anagrama, 2002.
_____. *En la distancia*. Madrid: Punto de lectura, 2005.
Bachelard, Gaston. *The Poetics of Space*. Boston: Beacon Press, 1994.
Kort, Wesley A. *Place and Space in Modern Fiction*. Gainesville: The University of Florida Press, 2004.
Leggott, Sarah. *History and Autobiography in Contemporary Spanish Women's Testimonial Writings*. New York: The Edwin Mellen Press, 2001.
Massey, Doreen. *Space, Place, and Gender*. Minneapolis: University of Minnesota Press, 1994.
McDowell, Linda. *Gender, Identity and Place*. Minneapolis: University of Minnesota Press, 2003.
Pascual Solé, Yolanda. "*Historia de una maestra, Mujeres de negro* y *La fuerza del destino* de Josefina Aldecoa. Una trayectoria vital: del exilio al no destierro." *Exilios femeninos* (2000): 397–407.
Ramblado-Minero, Cinta. "Novelas para la recuperación de la memoria histórica: Josefina Aldecoa. Ángeles Caso y Dulce Chacón." *Letras Peninsulares* 17.2 Fall/Winter 2004–2005: 361–379.
Soliño, María Elena. "Tales of Peaceful Warriors: Dolores Medio's *Diario de una maestra* and Josefina Aldecoa's *Historia de una maestra*." *Letras Peninsulares* 8.1 (1995): 27–38.
Vásquez, Mary S. "Space, Voice and Identity in Josefina Aldecoa's *Mujeres de negro*." *Monographic Review / Revista Monográfica* 13 (1997): 261–272.

*Gabriela's life span covers many significant events of 20th-century Spain, from 1904 to 1982.

PART II. GENERATION OF THE TRANSITION TO DEMOCRACY

Historia de un abrigo: Women's Search for an Anchor in the Modern World

Joanne Lucena

As a middle aged woman, Mar, drives home from the supermarket she dreads unpacking the groceries that await her in the trunk of her car. She starts to daydream about her deceased mother's black astrakhan coat. She would much rather be wandering the streets enveloped in its soft maternal warmth alone without a care in the world than leading her mundane life. The search for the coat that represents female protection from the cruel world is the first vignette that opens Soledad Puértolas's latest novel, *Historia de un abrigo* (2005). The novel itself is composed of many such vignettes; each introduces a new character tenuously linked to the prior chapter. The rapid changing pace of each chapter reflects the different narrators (Puértolas alternates between first and third person) and their attempt to establish their identity as women in the modern world. Once again, Puértolas employs the themes of nostalgia and memory to achieve this end. In each carefully crafted vignette Puértolas examines contemporary Spain and analyzes the traditional roles assigned to women that hinder their personal development. Using Abraham Maslow's humanistic psychological theories on self-esteem and fulfillment to analyze each character, I propose to demonstrate how societal pressures and norms influence women's self.

Historia de un abrigo is the Zaragozan writer's tenth novel and shares many of the same characteristics, such as the search for identity and the presence of loneliness, of her first works. She is a prolific writer and has penned numerous articles, essays, short stories, and novels.* All of Puértolas's works are concerned with the psychology of the characters and not the action in itself. Catherine Bellver affirms that "Soledad Puértolas avoids dramatic conflict in the structure of her plot, preferring instead to expose the evolving human relationships of her characters (6). Bárbara Mujica also underlines the propensity of Puértolas to limit the narrative action in her introductory paragraph of *Queda la noche*: "Este tipo de narrativa en la que un principio parece que *no pasa nada*, consiste, sin embargo, en una gran tela de araña en la que vamos localizando una galería de tipos cotidianos y una serie de escenarios" [This type of narration where at first it seems as though nothing is happening, however, really consists of a large spider web where we start to situate a gallery of everyday people and a series of scenes] (417). Mujica establishes that each character is highly delineated with all of their psychological nuances, "los tipos, dentro de su aparente normalidad, nos mostrarán cómo cada persona, por muy común y normal que nos parezca, tiene dentro de sí una serie de inclinaciones que la mueven a actuar de manera determinada" [The characters, within their apparent normality, will show us how each person, as normal and common as they might appear to be, has within him or her a series of inclinations that impel them to act in a specific way] (417). Mujica determines that this particular novel, written during Spain's formative *movida* years, reflects the country's slowly changing customs: "Los escenarios son descripciones perfectas del mundo cotidiano y reflejos de una España en lento cambio, un perfecto retrato de una sociedad en la que las costumbres se alteran poco a poco" [The scenes are perfect descriptions of a daily world and reflect Spain's slow change, a perfect portrait of a society where customs are altered little by little] (417). Puértolas continues this reflection of modern society in *Historia de un abrigo* but this time she is principally concerned with problems affecting women.

Although the author narrates the histories of a few male characters, it is done so in relation to the women in the text. All of the women analyzed in *Historia de un abrigo* discover that they do not need men in order to feel fulfilled. Friendship with other women is much more rewarding and satisfying and doesn't require the establishment of set stereotypical roles. One man, Borja, can't believe that his wife, Mabel, isn't having an affair in her

---

*Her first novel, *El bandido doblemente armado*, was published in 1980 and received much accolades. Her other acclaimed novels are *Burdeos* (1986), *Todos mienten* (1988), *Queda la noche* (1989) (which was awarded the Premio Planeta literary prize), *Días de Arenal* (1992), *Si al atardecer llegara el mensajero* (1995), *Una vida inesperada* (1997), La señora Berg (1999), *La rosa de plata* (1999) and *Con mi madre* (2001).

free time but rather prefers to spend it in the company of a female friend. Blanca, Mar's sister, travels to Italy in the company of women. She and two other Spanish women, Elena and Amalia, form an inseparable trio that spends their days pondering men, love, routines and the prosaic things that form this life. Here, women are travelers, in part because the author herself is not. Men no longer interest Blanca. She is expected by a traditional society to tend to her ailing father as she is the only unmarried female child. The trip to Italy allows her to escape from this stereotypical role.

In this novel, Puértolas addresses the consequences of adhering to fixed female stereotypes: unhappiness, spousal abuse and anorexia. Women can not reach self-fulfillment if their basic needs are not met. According to Abraham Maslow, a renowned humanistic psychologist of the 1950s,* if people do not satisfy the essential needs of physical comfort, safety, love, and esteem (an important issue especially for women), self-actualization can not be reached. These needs are divided into a pyramid and if each level is not fulfilled a person cannot move up to the next level. The bottom of the pyramid is characterized by biological and physiological needs: air, drink, food, shelter, warmth, sex, sleep. These basic needs are all vital to human survival. The next level consists of safety needs: protection, security, law, order, stability etc. This is followed by love and belongingness which is concerned with family, peers, professional groups, relationships, and forming part of a community. The category of esteem is the fourth level and consists of achievement, need, status, and responsibility where the participant wants to gain approval and recognition. The last classification is self-actualization. If these five basic needs of physiological, safety, love, esteem, and self-actualization are not gratified, a dysfunction or imbalance results, i.e.— lack of vitamins causes malnutrition or lack of love causes depression. However, the restoration of this gratification consequently restores the dysfunction.† Self-

---

*Although Maslow's theories were widely applied during the 1950 and1960s, they are still highly cited and employed today in academic journals such as *The Journal of Humanistic Psychology*. Many experts in the field of business management and organizational behavior also examine Maslow's texts to provide optimal output and happiness for the participants. Furthermore, many psychologists have incorporated his humanistic theories into educational practices. Huitt affirms that Maslow's theories continue to be relevant today to the study of human behavior and motivation (2).

†In a free choice situation, gratification of lower needs will normally take precedence over gratification of higher needs (Feshbach 164). According to Maslow, "higher need satisfaction produces better health, longer life, and a generally enhanced biological efficiency." Furthermore, higher need satisfaction is productive and beneficial not only biologically but psychologically as well because it produces deeper happiness, peace of mind, and fullness in one's inner life" (164).

actualization, the ultimate achievement, is defined by a person doing what he is fitted for: "a musician must make music, an artist must paint, a poet must write, if he is to be ultimately happy" (Maslow 383). These higher needs are defined by one's social context and environment.*

The search for one's identity and the goal of self-actualization is best exemplified by one of the principal characters, Mar. Mar is one of nine children though Puértolas concentrates on her relationship with her three sisters, Blanca, Estrella, and Malica. Her five brothers are barely mentioned except in reference to their respective wives, Mar's sister in laws, whom Mar questions as to the whereabouts of the astrakhan coat. Mar's mother is deceased, and her sister Blanca is responsible (as the single daughter) for tending to Mar's father, Florencio Campos. Although married with children, Mar is unable to feel fulfilled as a person because she is still seeking to complete the basic need of love. She keenly feels the loss of her mother and tries to return to the feelings of warmth and protection provided by her by obsessively searching for the tattered astrakhan coat that her mother often donned: "me gustaría estar envuelta en ese abrigo tan pesado en lugar de tener en el maletero del coche tantas bolsas llenas de comida que hay que guardar en cuanto llegue a casa. Me gustaría estar andando por la calle con el abrigo de mi madre, paseando, mirando los escaparates de las tiendas, sin nada que hacer" [I would like to be enveloped in that very heavy coat instead of having the trunk of the car filled with so many bags full of food that must be put away as soon as I arrive home. I would like to be walking on the street with my mother's coat, strolling along, window shopping, and not have to do anything] (9–10). Mar's sister, Blanca, in a conversation with a close friend, recognizes that Mar has not been able to recover from her mother's death: "No supera la muerte de su madre. No soporta ir a la casa donde fue feliz, donde siempre estaba su madre esperándola. No soporta que su padre apenas habla de su madre, como si esa larga etapa hubiera sido borrada" [She can't get over the death of her mother. She can't bear going to the house where she was happy, where her mother was always waiting for her. She can't tolerate that her father hardly speaks of her mother, as if that long period had been erased] (88). The quest for the lost coat also represents Mar's pursuit

---

*Maslow also examines a series of conditions of deficiency that occur when these needs aren't satisfied. The first four categories are defined as deficient needs because they encourage the individual to action if something is lacking in their life. Maslow affirms that the thwarting of the needs in the love category is very common in cases of maladjustment and even severe psychopathology. Lack of self-esteem which allow one to feel worthy, satisfied, strong, and capable can produce feelings of inferiority, weakness and helplessness which may consequently trigger basic discouragement or compensatory or neurotic trends (Maslow 382).

of her identity in the modern world. She is not satisfied with her status as a house wife and mother where her husband and children barely notice her existence. Mar needs the coat as a confidante, to establish a rapport with another being (although only on a symbolic level): "Por eso quiero el abrigo. Quiero contárselo todo, al fin. Quiero tener el abrigo sobre los hombros y sentirme protegida del mundo y decidir lo que quiero contar y lo que no" [That's why I need the coat. After all, I want to tell it everything. I want to have the coat on my shoulders to feel protected from the world and to decide what I want to tell and what I don't] (15). Ironically, although Mar technically belongs to a group, that of her family, she does not feel protected and therefore can not move up to the next level of Maslow's need hierarchy which is self esteem, much less attempt to attain self-realization which would allow her to develop a sense of worth in the modern world.

Marguerite Intemann in her critical text, *El tema de la soledad en la narrativa de Soledad Puértolas* (1994) defines this inability to form part of a group as *la soledad personal* [personal loneliness] and each character of Puértolas's appears to suffer from this existential angst:

> Los personajes de las obras de Puértolas experimentan y expresan muchos aspectos diferentes de este tema existencial. Representan todas las etapas de la vida humana-son jóvenes, adultos y viejos. La mayoría de ellos parecen sufrir dentro de la condición solitaria que eligen. Su angustia se refleja en la pasividad y la cualidad estática de sus vidas. Se centran en sus memorias, pero no pueden ponerse de acuerdo con ellas. Sus adaptaciones al presente resultan infructuosas.
>
> [The characters in Puertolas's works experience and express many different aspects of this existential theme. They represent all of the stages of life-they are youth, adults and old people. The majority appear to suffer within the confines of the solitude that they choose.Their anguish is reflected in the passivity and the static quality of their lives. They focus on their memories, but they can't reconcile them. Their adaptations to the present are fruitless.] [8].

An integral part of this feeling of solitude is the lack of interpersonal communication (23) which is amply demonstrated in *Historia de un abrigo* by Mar and her immediate family.

Eva, another female character trying to establish herself, demonstrates the theme of solitude in the works of Puértolas. Eva is recently divorced with three children and is an English teacher at an elementary school. Her husband abandoned her and she was forced to survive with no job and the sole responsibility of the children. She is the most appropriate, as she speaks English and has time off for the Christmas holidays, to rescue her sister,

Amalia, in New York. Amalia, an ex-model, was a close friend of Blanca's when Blanca traveled to Italy, and is married to an abusive American, Billy. Although Eva's esteem has been constructed through her ability to survive adverse circumstances such as the divorce, in Maslow's need hierarchy she is finally able to gain resolution and self-actualization through her travel to New York to support her sister. She receives strength from an anonymous letter hidden in a bible that she discovers in her hotel room in New York. The reader knows that Eva will continue to survive and thrive as she has been able to overcome such difficult conditions and even concentrate on another's well-being.

In New York, Eva randomly meets a former student of hers from Spain, Japi (Ramón Campos, the nephew of Mar and Blanca), who is accompanying his uncle. They spend New Year's together embraced in each other's arms. She is able to feel an immense tenderness towards Japi because she recognizes him in a similar ability to survive in difficult circumstances: "Pero Japi ha sobrevivido. Sobrevivimos los dos en este año nuevo tan lejos de casa" [But Japi has survived. We both survived this New Year's so far from home] (177). Japi needs to separate himself from his mother in order to receive her love. He is a rebel because he knows that if he shows her that he needs her, she will reject him. Although Japi is able to comfort his former teacher, he is a cause of strife for his own mother, Gracia (one of Mar's sister in laws who aids her in the search for the astrakhan coat) who feels marginalized by her own flesh and blood: "No habla con nosotros, nos mira siempre con el ceño fruncido, pero sus amigos le llaman Japi. No entiendo nada. Ya nunca voy a entender nada. Me he quedado al margen" [He doesn't speak to us, he always frowns at us, but his friends call him Happy. I don't understand. I am never going to understand anything. I have been excluded] (32). When he is at home, Japi locks himself in his room and listens to music all day. Both characters, although cohabitating the same house, are separated by their sensations of loneliness. They are unable to communicate. Nevertheless, both Japi and his mother thrive when they aren't following the stereotypical roles assigned to them by society. Puértolas underlines the fact that personal happiness must come from within and should not be based on traditional relationships. Gracia feels ignored in her own house and finds outside affirmation from a complete stranger in a park who tells her a strange dream that he has had. They share a cigarette and imagine things together. Gracia returns to her unfulfilled marriage but for one brief moment she has felt realized as a person. Japi also excels when he is independent and able to move around the world with ease.

The search for identity is a salient theme in the works of Soledad Puértolas and can be related to travel and the pursuit of self-realization. The author declared in a recent interview that all of her characters suffer from this quest: "La lucha por la identidad es un asunto muy arduo y yo he tratado de acercarme a ese misterio" [The struggle for identity is an arduous matter and I have tried to close in on that mystery] (Puértolas). This pursuit of auto discovery ties in with Maslow's need hierarchy within the categories of love and belonging: one cannot feel part of a group until they know who they are as a person. Many of the characters in *Historia de un abrigo* travel abroad in the hope that they might discover something about themselves. According to Daniel Kilbride, a critic who has studied European travel, "Travel, moreover, had the potential to reshape individual and group identity" (549). He affirms the introspective nature of the journey that accentuates self discovery when mixing among strangers (549). Eric J. Leed, another travel critic, underlines the liberating and transforming role of travel which is seen as "the paradigmatic experience, the model of a direct and genuine experience which transforms the person having it" (145). In Puértolas's novel, Dani, a young athlete in a long term relationship, and Augusto Riofrío (an ex-lover of Mabel, Mar and Blanca's sister) meet on a plane to Manchester, England. Dani wants to take his girlfriend, Irene (who at these moments is plagued with doubts about her relationship with the young marathon runner) to Manchester so that she too can experience something different. The journey and its absurdities are liberating as they free him from the banality of everyday life: "La sensación de que este rato no existe en realidad sino que se ha quedado al margen de todo, deshilvanando, le proporciona un profundo sentimiento de liberación. Repentinamente, se siente cómodo. Incluso, alegre" [The sensation that this moment doesn't exist in reality, rather, it is outside of everything, detaching itself, gives him a profound sense of liberation. Suddenly he feels comfortable. Even happy] (112). The journey of self-discovery and its subsequent liberation of its participant play an integral role in the development of Blanca Campos. Blanca is another principal protagonist as she is the sister of Mar and is mentioned in various chapters. She is emancipated from the family yolk when she travels to Italy and discovers the fulfillment of female friendship. Blanca is single and lives with her dog, Tasia, on whom she bestows all of her affection. She hopes to escape the drudgery of her job and the continuous demanding phone calls of her father who expects her to wait on him hand and foot even though she does not live at home with him anymore: "Olvidarse, sobre todo, de su padre, de sus continuas llamadas telefónicas pidiéndole que le vaya a ver, del continuo reproche que le hace, unas veces veladamente y otras no, por tener una vida independiente de la suya" [To forget about everything, above all, her father, his continuous phone calls asking her to come see him, his continuous reproaches to her, sometimes veiled, other times not, to be able to have a life independent of his] (139). She doesn't tell her father that she is traveling to Venice, as he would blame her for abandoning him and consigning him to a period of loneliness. Mar, in Chapter One, underlines their father's absolute dependence on Blanca. He can't conceive that she would have anything else to do with her time: "Sé que mi padre depende de Blanca, no concibe que ella tenga otras cosas que hacer aparte de venir a verle, no le cabe en la cabeza que Blanca trabaje. Ya que vive sola, debería dedicarse enteramente a él" [I know my father depends on on Blanca; he can't conceive that she might have other things to do aside from coming to see him. It doesn't enter into his mind that Blanca works. Since she lives alone she should dedicate all of her time entirely to him] (16). Blanca is unable to feel self-actualized, according to Maslow's hierarchy because she isn't able to do what she is fitted for as society expects her to attend to her father's needs. Puértolas is openly criticizing Spanish society, that although has adapted to modern standards where women work, the female gender is still culturally expected to tend to their male counterparts, either as a wife or as a daughter. Blanca is able to subvert this societal pressure by telling her father that she has a business trip in Paris, when she in fact has an organized tour to Venice. She is able to recognize her own parental oppression by traveling abroad and leaving her normal environment. Mary Procida, an expert on women's travel narrative, notes that feminist scholars of travel texts "have discerned a proto-feminist stance in many women's writings" (186). She asserts that: "women's recognition of their oppression may be inferred from their empathetic response to the plight of the colonized natives as fellow victims of European male dominance" (186). Although Blanca doesn't reflect on the troubles of the colonized natives; she is able to recognize her own patriarchal imprisonment while in the company of other women. Procida adds that "conversely, women authors may be seen as boldly proclaiming women's public role and social value by demanding the attention of the reading public through the publication of their works" (186). Here, Puértolas underlines the liberating role of travel and the value of an independent woman who does not need to depend on a man to establish her own identity.

Blanca is no longer interested in men. Although she bears no bitterness towards them, they do not attract her anymore. Her three sisters have not been able to find happiness through their relationships with men. In her depiction of Blanca, Puértolas underlines the importance of female friendships. Blanca ruminates on the fates of her two sisters, who are also unlucky in love. Estrella, a character only mentioned in passing, still searches for her prince charming who she is convinced will resolve all of her problems. Mar, is forever complaining and is forever sick. Blanca's criticism of her sisters indicates that Puértolas advocates a stronger community of women to be used as social support, something that she has confirmed in an interview: "Es muy interesante la idea de la amistad femenina, para mí es algo esencial en la vida" [The idea of female friendship is very interesting; for me, it's something essential in life] (Urbanc). It is in Venice that Blanca is able to form strong bonds of friendship with two other travelers: Elena, a receptionist in a small hotel, and Amalia, a model who has a very close relationship with her sister, Eva. Eva has always supported her and defended her even to their parents: "y la confianza que tiene con ella no tiene límites. Se lo puede contar todo — sea lo que fuere ese todo — nunca la juzga, siempre se pone de su parte" [and the trust she has in her has no boundaries. She can tell her everything — no matter what, she never judges her, she always takes her side] (144). This tight fraternal union is of utmost importance later in the novel when Eva travels to New York to rescue Amalia from the abusive hands of her boyfriend, a theme I will expand later. Blanca, Amalia, and Eva, much like the modern day characters of Candice Bushnell's *Sex in the City*, to which Puértolas would be have been amply exposed as it aired on primetime Spanish television, philosophize over love, sex, relationships and affairs with married men: "ha habido muy buenos ratos alrededor de una mesa, bebiendo cerveza o vino, o licores, hablando de hombres, del amor, de la rutina, de las pequeñas cosas de la vida. A veces, un poco de las grandes. Sí, también han hablado de cosas grandes, de filosofías, de ambiciones, de sueños" [There have been really good times at the table, drinking beer or wine, or liquors, speaking of men, of love, routines, the small things in life. Sometimes, a little bit of the big things. Yes, they have also spoken of big issues, of philosophies, ambitions, and dreams] (152). This friendship between women is of immense satisfaction to all of its participants. All of the women feel self-fulfilled and realized and Blanca's trip to Venice aids her in navigating her otherwise banal existence to which she must return.

Malica is another Campos sister whose story is told in various chapters and her narration also represents the theme of travel and self-discovery. Puértolas uses the narrative voice of the third person to relate Malica's adventures and confesses that the narration of first and third person is determined by the distance to the narrator: "está narrada en primera y en tercera persona, en función de si los personajes están más cercanos o alejados del narrador" [it is narrated in first and third person depending on whether the characters are close to or distant from the narrator] (Puértolas). The reader never reads a personal account of Malica but is able to discover through the other characters that she travels around the world to exotic places like India trying to direct movies. She is not fulfilled in her romantic relationships and thus treats disdainfully her current love interest. She is still stuck in the level of love in Maslow's hierarchy. Her dissatisfaction in her romantic relationships can be attributed to the fact that she had to escape a controlling relationship where her ex-husband convinced a movie star like herself to live in an isolated small town and work in a bakery. Celia, a young adolescent in this same small town, narrates part of Malica's history. She vows to leave the village so that the same thing will not occur to her: "Cuando me casara, sería con alguien que tuviera un poco de mundo, pero que no me llevara a un pueblo desconocido y me hiciera poner una panadería" [When I get married, it will be with someone who is worldly and who won't take me to a strange town and who won't make me work in a bakery] (53). Celia, at the novel's end, manages to escape to Madrid and flees the provincial life of a small town. Puértolas once again underlines the fact that the younger generations of women have hope for the future and are willing to implement changes even though Spain might not have adapted to modernity and contemporary gender mores in much of its small towns.

Puértolas also emphasizes the importance of female friendship in her description of Mabel, another principal character that finds happiness with her female friend, Blanca. Mabel, who has recently turned fifty, decides that it is time to do things that she had never dared to tackle before. Her children no longer live at home and she is frustrated with her husband who, after work, opens a beer and throws himself on the sofa with no desire for conversation or communication. Thus, Mabel establishes an agreement with her husband, Borja, to have one day and one night a week free for herself, liberated from his incessant demands. According to Maslow, she too would be limited by her necessity to fulfill the requirement of love. Puértolas is criticizing traditional gender roles assigned by the institution of marriage where women are just expected to serve their husband without any concern for their own well being. Nevertheless, Mabel discovers that this lack can be fulfilled with a female friend: "Es cuando se siente mejor. Recién llegada a casa después de haber pasado la tarde con una amiga. Es una sensación que hacía mucho tiempo no tenía, algo que roza la felicidad" [It is when she feels the best: arriving home after having spent the afternoon with a friend. It is a sensation that she hasn't felt for a long time, something that borders on happiness] (78). The one time Mabel does decide to meet an old lover, Augusto Riofrío (the aforementioned traveler on the plane to Manchester), she realizes how pretentious and self absorbed he really is. He doesn't stop talking about himself and asks Mabel nothing about her own life. This is a positive moment for Mabel as she realizes she does not need affirmation from a man in order to survive. Her friendship with other women is far more fulfilling and once this need is satisfied she can continue on the path to self-realization. Borja spies on her one day and can't believe that his wife is so relaxed in the company of other women. He observes that as she nears their house, her shoulders become hunched, her head drops and she appears defeated, a significant statement by Puértolas that once again emphasizes the loneliness of each character and the danger of adhering to fixed gender roles. Borja uses the same opportunity of freedom to meet another woman, Elena, and embark on an affair that lasts ninth months. He recognizes that she too spoke much but he didn't listen as her stories about her family didn't interest him. He is unable to reach a level of fulfillment as he looked for a quick solution in something that provided no emotional stability. Nor was he willing to provide the communication necessary for establishing a viable relationship.

The chapter concerning an abused woman, Amalia, underlines an important theme in women's literature. Self-esteem is of utmost importance in self-realization and fulfillment. Furthermore, lack of self-esteem can produce feelings of inferiority, weakness and helplessness which may consequently trigger compensatory or neurotic trends (Maslow 382). Without self-esteem and confidence women may be oppressed by others. Psychological studies have demonstrated that women continue in abusive relationships because of low self esteem, a sense of self-blame and feeling that they deserve the punishment meted out by a loved one [Violencia]. Both the victim and the abuser suffer from this low self-esteem: "En la violencia familiar las víctimas poseen muy baja autoestima, ya que por un lado, la víctima es alguien al que maltratran sin que ésta pueda poner límites y no se da cuenta de que está siendo abusada" [With domestic violence, the victims have very low self-esteem since, on the one hand, the victim is someone who can be abused who won't establish limits and won't realize that she is being abused] [Portal]. This chapter, narrated in first person singular, describes how a young promising model, Amalia, gives up everything to marry a man who turns out to be drunk and abusive. Billy, her American husband, is sullen and rude when he visits Amalia's family in Spain and does nothing but drink and escape to a world of his own. Amalia, who was once the rebel child and contradicted her parents in everything, has turned into a meek shadow of herself, overly affectionate in her desire for any kind of demonstrative approbation: "Había venido a Madrid con ese fin: a darles calor a mis padres, el calor que nadie le daba a ella" [She had come to Madrid for that reason: to show affection to her parents, the affection that no one gave to her] (160). Her parents feel sorry for their daughter and often exclaim, "Amalia no ha tenido suerte" [Amalia has not had any luck] (158) but then again, neither has her sister, Eva. As mentioned before, she was abandoned by her husband with no savings and was forced to care for her children by herself. However, she manages to resolve her life, get divorced, find a steady job and maintain a daily routine which allows her to continue forward. Puértolas underlines the notion that women are capable of survival and self-realization without a man on which to depend. Amalia and Eva choose not to inform their parents the true reason for Amalia's hospitalization choosing instead to let them believe that it was a viral infection. Amalia is not forthcoming with any information regarding the abuse when Eva inquires if it was the first time: "Prefiero no hablar de esto, Eva, dice Amalia-. Ya se ha terminado. El lo sabe también" [I prefer not to talk about it, Eva, Amalia says, I know it's over. He knows it too] (167).

This theme of spousal abuse and physical violence against women is a reflection of contemporary Spain and the problems that have only recently been brought out into the open. Amalia is not capable of addressing the issue in a direct manner although she is lying in a hospital bed with bruises all over her face and her head in bandages. Although the abuser is an American man, the abused woman is Spanish and was raised in a society that did not acknowledge the widespread incidence of such atrocious acts until 1998 when the *I Plan de Acción contra la Violencia Doméstica* was initiated after the brutal assassination of Ana Orantes by her husband in 1997. Juan Avilés contends that spousal abuse was an issue that was handled in the private sphere but in recent years, has become a salient social issue "que tradicionalmente quedaba al margen de la preocupación pública, por entenderse que lo que ocurría en el seno de la familia era una cuestión privada, pero que se ha convertido en España durante los últimos años en un problema que genera auténtica alarma social" [that traditionally, in public, people were not concerned because it was understood that what happened within the family was a private issue but it has become in Spain within the last few years, a problem that generates authentic social alarm] (1).* The last few years have shown an increase in reported cases of domestic violence against women presented to the National Police and the Civil Guard but Juan Avilés attributes this more to the fact that women are finally breaking the wall of silence imposed on them for years. Puértolas, by openly addressing this issue in her novel, underlines the need for developed societies to continue in the struggle to obtain equality for all of its members. The community and family atmosphere affect female self-esteem:

> La autoestima es el sentimiento valorativo de nuestro ser, de nuestra manera de ser, de quienes somos nosotros, del conjunto de rasgos corporales, mentales y espirituales que configuran nuestra personalidad, además es aprender a querernos y respetarnos, es algo que se construye o reconstruye por dentro. Esto depende, también del ambiente familiar, social y educativo en el que estemos y los estímulos que éste nos brinda.
>
> [Self-esteem is how we value ourselves, the way we are, who we are, the combination of physical, spiritual and mental traits that make up our personality. It is also about learning to love ourselves, to respect ourselves; it is something constructed or recreated from within. This also depends on our domestic, social and educational environment and the stimuli which they provide.] [Portal].

Women need to find their voices (much as Amalia needs to regarding the issue of her own abuse in order to confront it) to protest years of subjugation and oppression. Puértolas provides the reader with a glimmer of hope for the future of Amalia. She recognizes that she is an abused woman and knows that she will not return to Billy. Furthermore, she is not willing to return to the familial home to resolve her problems; rather she opts to stay in New York: "De momento, me quedaré aquí—dice. Tengo que resolver mi vida y tengo que hacerlo aquí" [For the moment I will stay here, she says. I have to resolve my life and I have to do it here] (167). When Eva says goodbye to her sister, the nurse reassures her with a complicit look that Amalia will survive and thrive: "Los ojos de Amalia se llenan de lágrimas al

---

*The institution of Plan I consequently produced services specifically dedicated to the protection of women such as SAM (associated with the National Police), ENUME (associated with the Guardia Civil), women's shelters in each autonomous community, information centers and aid within the legal system, legal changes designating psychological violence as a crime, and the establishment of restraining orders (2). In 2001, Plan II was initiated which furthered Spain's dedication to preventing violence against women. Coordination between the various agencies, public and private, an improvement of current legislation, and educational programs based on dialogue, respect and tolerance were some of the furthered Spain's dedication to preventing violence against women. Coordination between the various agencies, public and private, an improvement of current legislation, and educational programs based on dialogue, respect and tolerance were some of the objectives established.

abrazarme, la enfermera jefa de la planta me estrecha la mano con fuerza y me mira fijamente, como si quisiera transmitirme una gran firmeza, una gran confianza. Todo irá bien" [Ana's eyes fill with tears as she hugs me. The floor nurse forcefully shakes my hand and looks at me firmly as if to transmit a feeling of strength and confidence. Everything will be fine] (179). Eva informs the reader (via information that she receives from her mother) that Amalia does in fact recover after separating from Billy. She lives with two roommates and works selling perfume at Bloomingdales but has other plans and aspirations. She does not intend to return to Spain. She is able to overcome adverse circumstances and move forward with her life neither without having to depend nor on a man nor her family to find happiness.

Another prominent contemporary theme concerning modern Spanish women that Puértolas addresses is that of the high incidence of anorexia. Teresa, Celia's (the young girl from the small town mentioned before) twin is diagnosed with anorexia and has stopped eating. Celia escapes to Madrid from her village to avoid the family drama. Celia attributes her sister's eating disorder to a bad relationship and can't understand why her sister would let herself be controlled by a man in such a way. Teresa is able to receive run the clock care with a live-in nurse who invigilates her every move. There is hope that she will recover.

Anorexia nervosa is considered a serious disease in developed societies and its incidence is rising each year. Ten years ago, Spain had the least amount of diagnosed cases of Anorexia and Bulimia in Europe; however, in the last two years it has lead the European Union. Eighty thousand cases were diagnosed last year with 500 of them requiring hospitalization and one hundred that resulted in death. The representative of Adaner (Association for the Defense of Anorexia Nervosa) proclaims that 500 is in fact a conservative estimate and that mostly likely the actual numbers were much higher: "esa cifra es muy superior, alrededor de medio millón" [That number is much higher, around half a million] (Quintana 1). The majority of experts attribute the cause of the disease to young girls trying to obtain an impossible standard of beauty established by models and clothing manufacturers. Carmen Quintana argues that the primary source of the disease is that young people have personal problems that they don't know how to resolve and instead of confronting them, they elect to lose weight as a coping mechanism: "deciden adelgazar como mecanismo para ser aceptados, queridos y admirados por los demás creyendo que lo conseguirán pareciéndose a esos modelos que — creen ellos — lo tienen todo" [They decide to lose weight as a mechanism to be feel accepted, loved and admired by others, thinking they will achieve this by looking like those models, that they think, have everything] (2). Quintana proclaims that those suffering must address the internal conflict and try to boost their self-esteem. She adds that unfortunately people try to tackle the problem from a physiological standpoint instead of a psychological one and it is not helped by the fact that manufacturers have just altered the clothing sizes and have not concentrated on the actual causes of the disease.

The latest psychology emphasizes finding the direct origin of the conflict and resolving it. This entails family therapy where other members of the family are encouraged to build the patient's self-esteem, many times destroyed by these same family members. Unfortunately in Spain, many doctors are not trained to combat Anorexia and Bulimia and are witness to the deaths of one hundred people every year. The patients are sent to endocrinologists who address the problem as an alimentary one and not psychological and they are sent home to once they have gained enough weight to be stabilized. Others are sent directly to centers where they are surrounded by paranoid schizophrenics, psychotics and rapists and consequently fall into an abject depression. Rosa Calvo Sargadoy, a clinical psychologist at La Paz hospital in Madrid, contends that many of the cases in people younger than eighteen are due to a problematic relationship with their parents, specifically a controlling and authoritative mother. In order to succeed, the parents need to be reeducated and the family dynamic must be altered (Quintana 4).*

Much like Maslow's need hierarchy, if sufferers of Anorexia or Bulimia do not have self esteem and feel part of a group, they will never recover from the disease nor will they ever able to feel fulfilled as a person or self-actualized. Puértolas is criticizing a developed society that pressures young adults to aim for impossible standards especially in the case of Teresa, when it was imposed by a case of a bad relationship. Women need to discover within themselves coping mechanisms such as friendship to be able to overcome these adverse circumstances and regain control of their own lives.

The last chapter in *Historia de un abrigo*, closes the story of Mar, this

---

*The Spanish government has tried to help prevent the disease by establishing a website complete with a contest, "Saludactiva.com," which attempts to address the problems of Anorexia and Bulimia by fomenting the mental health of the participants: "El propósito (del cibersitio) es emitir mensajes positivos entre ellos, incidiendo en los aspectos básicos del problema: la alimentación, el consumo, la autoestima, los valores y los modelos de la sociedad actual" [The purpose of the site is to send positive messages that focus on the basic aspects of the problem: food, consumption, self-esteem, values, and models in today's society] (España). The goal is to create a fictional character that is able to confront difficult situations that must be overcome. The idea is that the participants will then apply these same skills to their daily lives.

time narrated in third person. She receives a phone call from an ex-lover of hers, Vicente, and realizes that he is only calling to make himself feel better. Mar is able to recognize that she entered into that relationship as a way to escape the emptiness of her own life when her mother was dying. Although she still feels empty and lonely she realizes that embarking on a bad relationship will not solve her problems. Mar's doctor recommends a long walk each day and while this is not a panacea, it does allow her to collect her thoughts. On one of these long walks she encounters Roberto Enciso, her ex-brother-in-law, ex-husband of her sister Malica who spews bitter vitriol against Mar's father, Florencio Campos, who viewed every male as a rival that would detract the women's attention from him. Mar suddenly realizes that her father treated her mother very badly, blaming her for his own failure as a photographer as he had to find a job to support the family. Here, Puértolas is overtly criticizing traditional gender roles that keep women oppressed within the confines of their own home.

Roberto informs Mar that Palmira, the doorman's wife in their old house and recipient of her mother's astrakhan coat, has now opened a small clothing repair shop on Manises street, exactly where Mar is at this moment in time. Palmira, in fact, still has the coat and has used the material to create a jacket from it. Mar is relieved to find that it hasn't been sold to a stranger and in some way the presence of her mother continues to live on through the jacket and through her mother's friendship with Palmira. She is conscious of all of the friendships that her mother established of which she was not aware. She only knew a small part of her mother's life: "porque eso es lo que conocemos de las vidas de los demás, partes, trozos, fragmentos, incluso de las personas a quienes creemos conocer mejor" [because this is what we know about other peoples' lives; parts, pieces, fragments even of those people who we think we know the best] (236). This theme underlines the fragmented style of the novel and justifies Puértola's use of a series of vignettes to narrate the different histories of each character. The vignettes reflect women's search to discover their niche in an alienating world. Mar is able to continue with her life and feels less estranged knowing that a part of her mother continues to live on in Palmira's astrakhan jacket. Symbolically, another woman has transformed a mother's maternal warmth and affection (Palmira was also a recipient of Mar's mother's approbation) into a useful object. A jacket, which does not envelop one in its comfort, still provides protection from the cold (loneliness of the outside world). The coat/jacket represents a haven for women in a world filled with solitude and demonstrates the need for women to form a support system amongst themselves.

Although Puértolas does not provide concrete solutions to contemporary problems such as unhappiness, spousal abuse and anorexia, she does advocate other women intervening. It is other women — mothers, sisters, or friends — that make the modern world navigable and allow women to discover their own voices.

Works Cited

Avilés, Juan. "La violencia contra la mujer en la España de hoy: el ámbito familiar." *Análisis* 47 (2002). Gees. 9 pp. 1 May 2006. <http://www.gees.org/articulo/325/>.
Bellver, Catherine G. "Two New Women Writers from Spain." *Letras femeninas* 8.2 (1982): 3–7.
"España: con juego en Internet combatirán la anorexia y bulimia." *Mujereshoy* (2003). 3 May 2006. <http://www.mujereshoy.com/secciones/1295.shtml
Feshbach, Seymour, and Bernard Weiner. *Personality*. Boston: Houghton Mifflin, 1986.
Huitt, W. "Maslow's Hierarchy of Needs." *Educational Psychology Interactive* (2004). 25 April 2006. <http://chiron.valdosta.edu/whuitt/col/regsys/maslow.html>.
Intemann, Marguerite Dinonno. *El tema de la soledad en la narrativa de Soledad Puértolas*. Lewiston: Mellen University Press, 1994.
Kilbride, Daniel. "Travel, Ritual, and National Identity: Planters on the European Tour, 1820–1860." *The Journal of Southern History* 69.3 (Aug. 2003): 549
Leed, Eric J. *The Mind of the Traveller: From Gilgamesh to Global Tourism*. New York: Basic Books, 1991.
Maslow, Abraham. "A Theory of Human Motivation." *Psychological Review* 50 (1943): 370–396.
Mujica, Bárbara. *Milenio: mil años de literatura española*. New York: John Wiley and Sons, 2002.
"Portal de desarrollo personal." 15pp. 20 Oct 2006. <http://www.sitio-de-exito.com/articulos/201_249/228.htm>.
Procida, Mary A. "A Tale Begun in Other Days: British Travelers in Tibet in the Late Nineteenth Century." *Journal of Social History* 30.1 (Fall 1996): 185–209.
Puértolas, Soledad. *Historia de un abrigo*. Barcelona: Anagrama, 2005.
Quintana, Carmen. "Anorexia: 80.000 casos nuevos y 100 muertes al año." *Discovery DSalud* (2006). 4 pp. 3 May 2006. <http://www.dsalud.com/numero5_1.htm>.
"Soledad Puértolas vuelve a la novela con *Historia de un abrigo*." *Periodistadigital.com*. Agencia EFE. (2005) 5 may 2006. <http://www.periodistadigital.com/libros/object.php?o =60701>.
Urbanc, Katica. "Soledad Puértolas: he vuelto a la realidad de otra manera." *Espéculo* (1998). 6 May 2006. <http://www.ucm.es/OTROS/especulo/numero8/k_urbanc.htm>.
"Violencia doméstica." 9 pp. 20 Oct 2006. <http://www.ispm.org.ar/violencia/images/Hechos/v-domestica.html>.

Naturalism and the Self in Rosa Montero's *La hija del caníbal*

Ellen Mayock

> Pero en realidad yo no soy la que fui ni la que seré; como mucho, no soy más que este instante de conciencia en la negrura, y ni siquiera estoy segura de ser eso, porque a menudo me veo a mí misma desdoblada.
> (Lucía in *La hija del caníbal*, 52)

Rosa Montero bills her 1997 blockbuster novel, *La hija del caníbal*, as a book about "the difficulties of growing up" (Conversation with Rosa Montero, May 1998). Most critics view the work, winner of the 1997 Premio Primavera, as an intriguing detective novel that also brings to light the themes of physical and emotional development.* The female protagonist featured in the novel experiences a mid-life crisis, motivated by her husband's supposed kidnapping, which forces her to examine both her own and Spain's history and the environment that has conditioned her development. In a sense, this novel focuses on the aging self and how it does or does not resemble its younger counterpart, which was influenced by a physical, historic, and familial environment heavily influenced by Francoist mores.

The narrative approach of *La hija del caníbal* reveals a poetics of unfolding — unfolding of the detective intrigue of the kidnapping of the protagonist's husband and of the protagonist into other characters, times, and selves.

---

*See Marisa Postlewate's "The Use of the Detective Story as a [Pre]text for Self-Realization in *La hija del Caníbal*" for a lucid examination of the detective story as an apt structure for the story of Lucía's self-discovery in the novel.

This emphasis on split events and personages reflects the development of the main character Lucía, whose depiction, which vacillates between first- and third-person narration, allows for frequent and smooth movements into characters of different ages and sex. The fluid movement of and among the "selves" in this novel provides ample space for disquisitions on consciousness, identity, aging, and death, the fundamental themes of Montero's works, what Javier Escudero calls Montero's "preocupación metafísica" [metaphysical preoccupation] ("La presencia del no-ser," 24). Davies looks in Montero's works at the "humanist feminism," which she describes as: "una problemática feminista a través de la cual se critican, entre otros aspectos, el machismo, el discurso falocéntrico, la violencia masculina, la represión erótica, la desigualdad laboral que afecta a la mujer y las dificultades de comunicación entre los sexos" [a feminist framework through which, among other items, *machismo*, phallocentric discourse, masculine violence, erotic repression, labor inequity which affects women, and difficulties of communication between the sexes are criticized] (Escudero, "La presencia," 21).

In Hippolyte Taine's *Histoire de la littérature anglaise*, the author proposes "trois sources différentes [qui] contribuent à produire cet état moral élémentaire: *la race, le milieu* et *le moment*" [three different sources which contribute to the production of this elementary moral state: *race, environment, and moment*] (23). These three "sources" are the pillars of the naturalism adopted and practiced by Emile Zola throughout the end of the 19th century. In this study of *La hija del caníbal*, I use a naturalist perspective to explore how self is reflected through the lens of humankind's environment, historic moment(s), and familial inheritance. In essence, this naturalist lens allows an examination of the individual protagonist's coming to terms with her self (or selves, as Virginia Woolf has said [Kakutani]) and of a collective reckoning with contemporary development of identity. The multiple literary genres, the historical foldings and unfoldings of twentieth-century Spain, and the replete array of literary techniques presented in Montero's 1997 novel allow for a unique view of how the form and foundation of many novels featuring Spanish women mesh with these three salient principles of naturalism — environment, historic moment, and genetic inheritance. Specifically, I examine here the protagonist Lucía's encounters with a contemporary, highly urban Madrid of the post–Transition period and how these very encounters frame her views of life as literature, her own dissatisfactions at middle age, her husband's disappearance, the new friendships she develops over the course of the novel, and the evolving way in which she is able to view her parents and their influences upon her.

In an interview with Escudero and González in 2000, Rosa Montero compares today's world with that of the Middle Ages, and ponders the grander questions of the individual versus the collective, the effects of an increasingly secular society, and humankind's more urgent need to relate with others in an environment that does not necessarily facilitate such communication (215–16). When asked if she considered her work to be pessimistic, Montero replied:

> En mis novelas, incluso muchos críticos señalan esa especie de vitalismo y de voluntarismo. Sin embargo, lo que ocurre es que tengo un sentido de la realidad de finales de siglo XX que es imposible que no sea, por lo menos, melancólico. Y digo finales del siglo XX y digo siempre, porque la vida, como nos enseñaban nuestros padres, es un valle de lágrimas y la existencia es complicada. La existencia es un chispazo entre tinieblas. Si, además, a finales del siglo XX no hay respuestas posibles, encontrarle un sentido a la existencia es difícil intelectualmente. El sentido melancólico de la existencia es imposible no tenerlo y eso, evidentemente, se transluce en las novelas.
>
> [Many critics signal that type of vitality and volunteerism in my novels. Nevertheless, the situation is that I have a sense of the reality of the end of the twentieth century that is impossible not to be, at the very least, melancholic. And I mean the end of the twentieth century, as I always say, because, as our parents taught us, life is a valley of tears and existence is complicated. Existence is a big spark among the shadows. If, besides, at the end of the twentieth century, there are no possible answers, finding some sense of existence is intellectually difficult. It is impossible not to experience that melancholic feeling of existence and that, evidently, shines through my novels.] [216].

Much of what Montero notes about the end of the 20th century in this interview echoes the preoccupations of the naturalist writers of the end of the 19th century. At the end of the 19th century, industrialization and urbanization had wrought a society that was more complex and that brought with it a heightened sense of anonymity and individualism, occurrences that might have spoken to a Darwinist impulse. Increased secularism and the advent of organized labor movements had individuals questioning traditional institutions, such as the Church, government, military, and the family. Scientific developments, the environment, and the impact of positivism allowed for advancements but made humankind question its role in a world that often seemed overpowering. As a result, fatalism and humankind's fear of and struggle against death manifested themselves as recurring themes in much of the literature of the turn of the century. In a sense, the "palpitating question" set forth by Emilia Pardo Bazán at the end of the 19th century — whether or not literary naturalism can succeed in a fundamentally Catholic nation (*La cuestión palpitante* 156–58)— resurfaces at the end of the 20th century. In fact, the phenomenon of the great increase in "non-practicing Catholics" within the Spanish citizenry might support further an examination of naturalist elements in literature produced at the turn of the current century.

Given Montero's background as both journalist and novelist, it may come as no surprise that naturalism's powerfully negative depiction of a specific reality manifests itself to some extent in all of Montero's works. Escudero speaks of this effect with respect to Baba, of *Bella y oscura*, and to Lucía, of *La función Delta*:

> En última instancia, lo que prevalece en la novela es una reflexión muy pesimista sobre la condición humana, en la que los seres están determinados no sólo por una fatalidad existencial inexplicable sino también por su intrínseca maldad, la cual les lleva a destruirse unos a otros.
>
> [In the last instance, what prevails in the novel is a very pessimistic reflection on the human condition, in which human beings are determined not only by an inexplicable existential fatality, but also by an intrinsic evil, which leads them to destroy each other.] ["La presencia del no-ser," 34].

Escudero uses the word "inexplicable" to describe the sense of fatalism experienced by Montero's characters. I argue that a naturalist reading of *La hija del caníbal* brings to light several explanations for the existential angst of the characters and that, in the end, this novel's complex mixture of genres and primary characters offers something of a humanist solution to angst concerning fatalism.* Maite Zubiaurre uses Zimmerman's term "expanded realism" to describe this thrust of Montero's fiction (92).

Montero employs a complex narrative structure through which characters and time periods unfold. Along with the highly existentialist flavor of her novel, Montero creates a very real, very concrete environment that makes the complex unfoldings not only highly believable, but also downright compelling and often humorous. The first of Taine's precepts to be explored here — the *milieu*, or environment, of the novel recalls, in 20th century format, the urbanization and anonymity so prevalent in the 19th century novel. The novel begins in the hustle and bustle of a regular day at Barajas International Airport in Madrid. The airport setting evokes the elements of the

---

*In 1993 Rosa Maria Grillo speaks of an increased optimism in later works by Montero: "L'apertura verso il futuro e l'evidente ottimismo costituiscono una novità rispetto ai precedenti romanzi" [The opening towards the future and evident optimism constitute something new in comparison to previous novels] (33).

contemporary world: hurrying from one place to another, stress, anonymity. In fact, the protagonist Lucía Romero finds herself not only in Barajas Airport, but right outside the men's bathroom in Barajas, as she waits for husband to emerge and catch a flight to Vienna with her. Montero effects the scene by providing contemporary, urban, global, and even scatological details. Lucía must enter the men's bathroom in order to ascertain the whereabouts of her husband. This naturalist detail heightens the urgency of the detective genre and presages the "excremental" question of the deterioration and decomposition of Lucía's relationship with her husband.* As in naturalist novels of the 19th century, the city is depicted as an environment of iniquity. The narrator refers to more visible criminal elements of the city when she mentions the "zona salvaje" [wild zone] of Madrid (45). In addition, Lucía Romero portrays a lonely, uninhabited city that reflects her own disconnectedness (121). In another section of the novel, Félix compares taurine Madrid to Barcelona (171). In short, the reader is provided a look at the contemporary Spanish capital from plural points of view.

Minute details in the descriptions of the environment of Lucía and her octogenarian friend Félix, the two "co-protagonists" (Escudero and González, 217), who continue to work on the mystery of Ramón's kidnapping, include gory details about Ramón's severed finger in which Lucía bluntly describes the finger as "ese pedazo de persona [que] no era más que un fragmento de basura orgánica" [that piece of a persona which wasn't anything more than a bit of organic garbage] (104). In addition, there appears a lengthy enumeration of the potions and lotions used to stave off old age: "Todos esos frascos, frasquitos, botellones, tubos, estuches, cajas, pomos, tarros, ampollas, envases y botes eran la representación misma de mi vida. Al envejecer te ibas desintegrando, y los objetos, baratos sucedáneos del sujeto que fuiste, iban suplantando tu existencia cada vez más rota y fragmentada" [All of those jars, little jars, big bottles, tubes, cases, boxes, pomes, vials, con-

---

*Javier Escudero comments on Montero's use of "excremental images" in her novels: "La falta de confianza en esos valores vitales exaltados por el modernismo se refleja en el continuo triunfo de la anti-vida, en la paradójica presencia del no-ser. Las abundantes imágenes excrementales que aparecen en estas novelas — residuos corporales, desperdicios, malos olores — asociados a la vejez y a la muerte, al deterioro y a la descomposición, refuerzan en un plano simbólico la visión pesimista que preside la obra de Montero, la percepción de una realidad corporal y de un cosmos en continua degradación." [The lack of confidence in those values that modernism exalted is reflected in the continuous triumph of the anti-life, in the paradoxical presenica of the not-being. The abundant excremental images that appear in these novels — corporal residues, waste products, bad smells — associate with old age and death, with deterioration and descomposition, strengthen on the symbolic level the pessimist vision that presides in Montero's works, the perception of a corporal reality and of a cosmos in continual degradation] ("La presencia del no-ser," 24–25).

tainers, and pots were the exact representation of my life. As you got older, you started disintegrating, and objects, cheap substitutes of the subject you once were, kept supplanting your existence, an existence that was more and more broken and fragmented] (210). The list recalls those of classic 19th-century naturalist novels. Nevertheless, the insertion of "mi vida" [my life] establishes the reflection of the female self that is absent from most of the novels of the late 19th century. Furthermore, the rapid transition to the use of "tú" [you, informal] generalizes the experience for all middle-aged women, who experience that preterit sense of that which they were [fuiste] and the corporal fragmentation [tu existencia cada vez más rota y fragmentada] visible in their real and metaphorical mirrors. The overall effect allows for a concretization of environment and an exploration of the angst of the ages.

The combination of the generalized woman's search for self with a naturalist depiction of environment appears clearly in the following quote:

> Ahora comprendía por qué no me había separado de mi marido: aunque me aburriera con él, aunque me exasperara, Ramón era el aliento animal de mi guarida, el cobijo elemental del otro de tu especie, unos ojos que te ven y una presencia cómplice frente al terror de la intemperie, frente a ese mundo exterior lleno de tormentas, violentos huracanes y cataclismos. Por entonces la soledad me daba pánico.
>
> [Now I understood why I had not separated from my husband: although I was bored with him, although I found him exasperating, Ramón was the animal breath of my lair, the elemental shelter of the other of your species, eyes that see you and a complicitous presence against the terror of difficult weather conditions, against that external world full of storms, violent hurricanes, and cataclysms. Back then, being alone made me panicked.] [64–65].

The reader experiences again the narrator's move from a specific "yo" [I] to a more generalized, but personal and intimate, "tú" [you]. The naturalist references to "breath," "animal," "species," and "difficult weather conditions" paint a fatalistic picture of the environment, as the protagonist considers her own existence and loneliness. The narrator's description of her and her companions' purchase of a suitcase to pay the ransom during the post–New Year's discount season in the department stores, compared to war in Sarajevo (70), also highlights elements of painstaking naturalist detail, detective fiction, and tongue-in-cheek humor.

Montero's narrators in *La hija del caníbal,* and Lucía in first-person in particular, pay careful attention to what they consider to be natural elements of their environment: sexual attraction, sexual acts, masturbation, desire, even love. In one section, Lucía clinically comments upon the sexual power that older women have over younger men and suggests that it is part of "a natural stage in the process of amorous maturation" (212). Exemplary lovemaking, combined with actual love, is thought to "detener el tiempo," [stop time], a moment in which "vencemos a la muerte" [we conquer death] (214). The frank comparison between this type of experience and that of masturbation advances the naturalist description of the environment, combined with an examination of the emotional and physical development of the female self.

Félix puts forth the idea of determinism and the environment, thus allowing the characters to examine their roles in their own surroundings and their fear of nothingness. Félix simplifies the concept of determinism by setting up two poles — that of naturally evil, cruel human beings and that of naturally virtuous human beings — populated by few people who will be unchanged by their environment. Nevertheless, in the middle, Félix claims, "la masa viva, criaturas bien intencionadas pero débiles; seres normales, esto es, dubitativos y confusos, que serán buenos si el entorno es favorable, y malos si el medio en que viven se pervierte" [the live masses, well-intentioned but weak creatures; normal human beings, that is, doubtful and confused, who are good if the surroundings are favorable, and bad if the environment in which they live is perverted] (81). In a sense, Félix becomes the naturalist narrator of the novel as he examines and comments upon human behavior as influenced by physical surroundings. In Félix's absence, when he is hospitalized and Lucía and Adrián are hot on the trail of Ramón's kidnappers, Lucía is able to hear echoes of Félix in Li-Chao's words: "Llamamos vida al complejo equilibrio que nace del choque entre contrarios. La realidad es siempre paradójica" [We call life that which is the complex equilibrium that is born out of the clash between contraries. Reality is always paradoxical] (230).

The theme of the fear of death is prevalent in many of Montero's novels, and *La hija del caníbal* is no exception.* Lucía regards her dog and wonders if he is exempt from the "la prerrogativa y el tormento de la autoconciencia" [the prerogative and the torment of self-awareness] (95). She determines that all living creatures in this "mundo salvaje" [savage world] (95) are vulnerable to fear and death. Montero's female protagonist anticipates her "cicatrices del porvenir" [scars of the future] (164) as she begins to understand the process of living life and maturing. By the end of the novel,

---

*See Escudero ("La presencia del no-ser," 21–22) for a more complete examination of this theme in Montero's novels.

Lucía is able to understand Félix's sage words: "En realidad, no morimos de algo exterior y ajeno, sino de nuestra propia muerte" [In truth, we don't die from something external, but from our own death] (319). From a naturalist perspective, the "external something" has a profound effect on the way we see and prepare ourselves for "our own death." Again, the external elements influence the internal definition of self.

The second tenet of Taine's and Zola's naturalism, emphasized in particular by Pardo Bazán in *La cuestión palpitante*, is the historic moment. In *La hija del caníbal*, the "moment" appears at first to be the late 1990s. The initial meticulous description of Lucía Romero, apparent contemporary protagonist of the novel, reflects one of the core techniques of both realism and naturalism: "Menos mal que en esos casos cabe recurrir a las señas de identidad, siempre tan útiles: Lucía Romero, alta, morena, ojos grises, delgada, cuarenta y un años, cicatriz en el abdomen de apendicitis, cicatriz en la rodilla derecha en forma de media luna de una caída de bicicleta, un lunar redondo y muy coqueto en la comisura de los labios" [At least in those cases it makes sense to use signs of identity, always so useful: Lucía Romero, tall, brunette, gray eyes, thin, 41 years old, scar on the abdomen from appendicitis, scar on the right knee in the shape of a half-moon from a bicycle fall, one round and very coquettish mole at the corner of the lips] (12). This detailed description, with its emphasis on physical details and its clipped phrases, could resemble a police rap sheet, thus revealing Montero's compelling mix of genres — the detective novel meets the search for self, with a naturalist bent. Nevertheless, the quote of the clipped phrases reveals as well Montero's consistent reliance on humor — the "extra" detail of the "coquettish" mole by her lips.

Other elements of this apparently simple introductory description demonstrate Montero's existentialist tendencies — what will the physical scar on Lucía's knee tell the reader about other, perhaps unseen, scars? In fact, the reader later learns of Lucía's car accident and resultant loss of a child: "Todos los hierros del mundo se metieron en mi boca. Todos menos uno, que me agujereó el vientre. Yo estaba embarazada de seis meses. Era una niña. Las piernas, la cabeza, las manos de deditos enroscados. [...] Y ahora estoy *vacía*. Así lo dicen las mujeres que han sido sometidas a la misma operación que yo: *Me han vaciado*" [All of the iron pieces in the world went into my mouth. All but one, which punctured a hole in my womb. I was six-months pregnant. It was a girl. The legs, head, hands with the little fingers all curled up. [...] And now I am empty. That's what women who have had the same operation I've had say: *They have emptied me out*] (314).

Self-admittedly influenced by postmodernism, Montero establishes an omnipresent historic unfolding, which complicates the traditional naturalist definition of historic moment (as shaped by chronology) defined by Hippolyte Taine. In her interview with Escudero and González, Montero states:

> La posmodernidad critica la respuesta de la modernidad anterior y afirma que el mundo es fragmentario, inconexo, plural, que no hay una sola respuesta al mundo. Yo soy hija del posmodernismo y considero que esa es una visión más acertada de la realidad. [...] Sin embargo, no me considero en absoluto escéptica — en el sentido de escéptica pasiva — y creo que no son incompatibles las dos cosas. Al contrario, creo que se puede vivir la vida con pasión, con utopías, luchando por un futuro mejor, sin estar obligada a creer en una respuesta total de la existencia. Así es como está ocurriendo también en España ahora.
> [Postmodernity critiques previous modernity's answer and affirms that the world is fragmentary, unconnected, plural, that there is not just one answer to the world. I am a daughter of postmodernism and I consider it to be the most correct vision of reality. [...] Nevertheless, I don't consider myself at all skeptical — in the sense of passive skepticism — and I believe that the two are not incompatible. On the contrary, I think that we can live life with passion, with utopias, fighting for a better future, without being obliged to believe in a total response to existence. That is how things are happening in Spain now.] [220–21].

In this quote, Montero speaks the language of a contemporary Zolian naturalism, that is, she conveys that an active consciousness about the way the world is — whether through a negative lens or not — allows an individual to envision and work towards a better world, and this view is often heavily influenced by a rejection of totalizing beliefs in one superior being.

Not only are the events of Lucía's life narrated in both first- and third-persons, thus revealing an internal unfolding, but they are also juxtaposed to and intercalated with the narration of the events of the life of Lucía's 80-year-old neighbor, Félix, and with the actions and opinions of their 20-year-old companion, Adrián, as all three characters attempt to solve the mystery of Ramón's disappearance. This triangular narrative configuration allows each of its inhabitants — Lucía, Félix, and Adrián — to recount life experiences as if they were happening in the moment and, through the lessons learned by others, to reshape their world views. Each of their perspectives is transformed and amplified by having listened to and learned from the others, and each comes away from the adventure of the kidnapping with a more sophisticated understanding of Spain's 20th century — the Spanish Civil War (Félix), the post–War (Lucía), and the post–Transition (Adrián).

As a result, Lucía develops a more expansive view of herself and her own historical circumstances through the temporal split towards Spain's past

and future. Moreover, the intimate friendship she develops with Félix and the amorous relationship she undertakes with Adrián permit her to come to terms with mores of sex and gender that have affected her since her rejection by means of years of inattention on behalf of her "Cannibal Father."*
In effect, the reader is unable to know Lucía truly until she has discovered herself through the split into Félix and Adrián and the increased knowledge of her own nation's development. At the beginning of the novel, several narrative segments vacillate between a "yo" and an "ella." This vacillation establishes the fragmented selves of the primary narrator, Lucía. The reader learns that the narrator needs to attempt a first-person narration but seems incapable of sustaining an authentic voice without resorting to the third person. The narrator becomes more reflexive and self-critical as she separates her self as narrator from her self as actor. By the end of the novel, a full, embodied first-person narration will indicate some identity repairs that have taken place by means of the narration itself. Soon after the early first- and third-person vacillations, a new chapter begins with "Yo nací en 1914" [I was born in 1914] (54), and the reader realizes that Félix now occupies the storyteller position, which appears to have been ceded to him by Lucía. In fact, Lucía tells the reader: "Sé que yo no soy él, pero de algún modo siento parte de sus memorias como si fueran mías" [I know that I am not he, but somehow I feel a part of his memories as if they were my own] (52). Félix's narration permits Lucía and Adrián a more intimate observation of the life of the exile in post–War Spain:

> Estuvimos hablando de tardes de toros, de pases memorables, de mis propias faenas. "¿Por qué no vuelve usted a España?," me dijo el tipo, al cabo. "Es inútil que espere a que Franco se marche, porque a mí me parece que tenemos Generalísimo para rato. Además, las cosas están cambiando; y han empezado a regresar muchos exiliados." Yo le escuchaba hablar mientras me repetía mentalmente: "Soy Félix Roble, soy *Fortunita*, soy Félix Roble."
> [We were talking about afternoons at the bullfights, memorable passes, my own victories. "Why don't you return to Spain?" the guy asked me, after a little while. "It's useless to wait for Franco to go away, because it seems to me that we'll have the Generalísimo for a while. Besides, things are changing; and many of the exiles have begun to return." I was listen-

---

*Monika Wehrheim examines this phenomenon in her essay on "Lovers and Cannibals" in the works of Rosa Montero. Wehrheim carefully looks at the real and metaphorical references to cannibalism in Montero's works and relates them to the female protagonists' fear of men. Although Wehrheim views in *La hija del caníbal* the "curing" of the Padre-Caníbal of his cannibalistic nature as too pat (175), I see it as the only resolution to the multiple stories that allow Lucía to overcome her fears of intimacy, traditional relationships, and death.

ing to him talk while I repeated to myself: "I am Félix Roble, I am *Fortunita*, I am Félix Roble.] [254].

The extensive sections narrated by Félix reflect Montero's billing of him as the "co-protagonist" of the novel. Félix and Lucía rapidly form a friendship as Félix aids Lucía in her search for her husband and, by extension, for herself. Félix jokes easily about age, recounts lengthy and fascinating stories about being an anarchist and an exile during the Primo de Rivera and Franco regimes, and ruminates about the "nostalgia de sí mismo" [nostalgia for oneself] (226). This mature and replete personality allow Lucía to discover her own talents, intellect, strength, and humor. Lucía is able to laugh with Félix and then, as a result, to begin to put her own life into perspective — to be able to laugh at her own foibles and even to take her husband's kidnapping more in stride.

As Lucía listens ever increasingly to Félix's detailed anecdotes of the Civil War period, she comes to know Félix's Spain so well that she begins to be able to put into clearer context the Spain that has conditioned her generation. Félix recounts one of his numerous war stories and emphasizes the importance of the anarchist male working in the home while his wife works outside the home, "Yo limpio la casa, hago las camas y preparo la comida. Además, baño a la nena y la visto" ["I clean the house, make the beds, and prepare the meals. I also bathe and dress the baby"] (180).* When Félix complains that the members of Lucía's generation are too afraid of the abyss to live well and that they cannot commit to any real belief, Lucía responds vociferously:

> En realidad, Lucía no estaba de acuerdo con el Viejo; en realidad, pensaba que en los años de juventud de Félix el mundo estaba lleno de creencias, tal vez no divinas pero sí religiosas, creencias en la victoria final del proletariado, o en la revolución futurista de las máquinas, o en la refundación nacional-socialista; incluso el propio Félix había sido un hombre de fe, un apóstol de la buena nueva, un predicador de la humanidad feliz y libertaria. En realidad, era ella, Lucía, ella y su generación de cuarentones, quienes se habían quedado de verdad en tierra de nadie, en un mundo desprovisto de fe y de trascendencia, en una sociedad mediocre y sin grandeza en la que nada parecía tener ningún sentido. 1Qué sabía Félix de vivir en la inclemencia y sin abrigo!
> [In truth, Lucía did not agree with the Old Man; in truth, she thought that, in Félix's youth, the world was full of beliefs, maybe not divine but certainly religious, beliefs in the ultimate victory of the proletariat, or in

---

*See Phyllis Zatlin's "The Novels of Rosa Montero as Experimental Fiction" for a discussion of Donovan's concept of "women's poetics" as it relates to Montero's fiction.

> the futurist revolution of machines, or in the national-socialist rebirth; even Félix himself had been a man of faith, an apostle of the new way, an evangelizer of happy and free humanity. In truth, it was she, Lucía, she and her generation of forty-somethings, who were left for real in no-man's land, in a world swept of faith and transcendence, in a society that was mediocre and without greatness in which no one seemed to have any sense or feeling. What did Félix know about living in inclement times with no shelter!] [164].

In turn, by debunking some of the apparently monolithic certainties of the previous generation, Lucía learns to appreciate the reasons for which her own generation might experience existential angst. She also expands her view of the generation that succeeds her own through her relationship with Adrián. As Montero states in an interview with Cabañas Alemán, "cada uno de nosotros somos multitud" [each of us is a multitude] ("Entrevista con Rosa Montero," 148). Lucía explores the "multitude" through Félix and Adrián.

Lucía's relationship with Adrián allows her to release the tension, guilt, and boredom that arose from her life with Ramón and his subsequent disappearance and to embrace the *joie de vivre*, openness, and physicality of Adrián. Lucía puts into perspective the elements that influenced her to marry Ramón — familial and societal expectations about the ways in which she would fulfill her role as a woman — and recognizes the boredom that arose out of their monotonous, unimaginative relationship. Adrián's is a post-*movida* generation, one that reflects a relative ignorance of the post–Civil War angst and of the giddy, almost desperate sense of liberation of the years of the *movida*.* Adrián is young and moves in a sphere that is at once more social, more mobile, and more influenced by globalizing norms — rapid communication, predominance of the visual, emphasis on travel and international exposure — than any that has preceded him. He moves fluidly from his own realm to those of Félix and Lucía and appears not to question or even to need to question the difference in age between Lucía and him. Lucía describes her growing attachment to Adrián and mentions in clinical language that "she thought she could smell his pheromones in the cold wind of the January night" (76). Eventually, Lucía admits to herself that she fears Adrián. Hers is a fear of his youth, of what he still might become, of the open horizon before him: "De modo que los jóvenes eran una especie de emboscados de sí mismos, identidades camufladas que se iban construyendo con los años, hasta llegar a la culminación final del ser, que es la vejez. Por eso Félix no

---

*See Escudero's "Rosa Montero y Pedro Almodóvar: miseria y estilización de *la movida* madrileña" for a thorough analysis of manifestations of a *movida* ethos in works by Montero.

asustaba a Lucía: el anciano ya había demostrado lo que era, había completado la metamorfosis" [And so the young people were somehow lying in ambush for themselves, camouflaged identities that they were constructing through the years, until arriving at the final culmination of their being, which is old age. That's why Félix didn't frighten Lucía: the old man had already demonstrated what he was, he had completed his metamorphosis] (154).

The ebb and flow of emotions surrounding the kidnapping case, the anecdotes shared by Félix, and the lovemaking with Adrián allow Lucía to realize that all ages continue to experience metamorphosis, and that such gradual change need not be feared, but rather esteemed. Later in the novel, Lucía thinks about what a strange man Félix is, but then corrects herself as she says, "qué estrambóticos éramos todos, qué trio tan absurdo" [how freakish we all were, what an absurd trio] (184). It is significant that Lucía comes to see herself as that strange character, "la peor de todos [...] justo en la edad del ser y del estar" [the worst of all [...] exactly between the age of existence and the age of just being] (184), who does not yet know or understand what she is or in what stage she finds herself. This examination of self and recognition of self-doubt are restorative steps along Lucía's "camino de vida" [life path] (316).

These questions of identity through the generations are consistently punctuated throughout the novel by the narrators' disquisitions on the passage of historic and personal time. In particular, Félix the narrator, as extension of Lucía the narrator-protagonist, comments on how biographies tend to dwell on the younger years of their subjects and then almost to dismiss the later years. He realizes, nevertheless, that this acceleration reflects our perception of the passage of real time: "Cuanto más mayor eres, más se acelera el tiempo. Y no creo que la diferencia de velocidad sea una apreciación ilusoria y subjetiva, sino una realidad física" [The older you are, the more time accelerates. And I don't think the difference in velocity is an illusory or subjective growth, but a physical reality] (256). In many ways, women's biographies must contend both with this fixation on youth and with a tendency to mix a woman's identity with that of the family that surrounds her. The novel's title reveals the extent to which Lucía has been identified throughout her life only as the daughter of famous parents.

In effect, *La hija del caníbal*, through Félix's long stories, Lucía's adventures and ruminations, and the affair with Adrián, the female protagonist is able to decelerate the pace of her own life story, to examine more carefully her own historic moment. There is a scene towards the end of the novel in which Lucía takes out her false teeth and examines the "black hole" of her mouth (315). For the first time in the novel, she articulates the events of her severe accident, of the pain, the blood, the loss of her teeth, and the loss of her daughter. She says plainly, "Mi boca es el sepulcro de mi hija" [My mouth is my daughter's tomb] (315). This admission has come after weeks of introspection and discovery in the ostensible search for Ramón and allows Lucía to take stock of her life. Lucía narrates the following as she sees the end of her affair with Adrián: "Pero yo no era su madre, y ni siquiera puedo ser *una madre*. No soy más que una hija cuarentona y talluda, una hija a medio deshacer en el camino de la vida. Aquí estoy, inventando verdades y recordando mentiras para no disolverme en la nada absoluta." [But I was not her mother, and I can't even be *a mother*. I'm just a forty-something grown-up daughter, a daughter half undone in her life path. Here I am, inventing truths and remembering lies so as not to dissolve into absolute nothingness](316). Lucía here recognizes that her ability to "invent truths and remember lies" is precisely what saves her. She understands that the writing she has done in her professional career and the ways in which she knows she will evolve as a writer have contributed to her construction of an identity apart from the wife of Ramón or the non-mother of a lost child.

Lucía is clearly already working on issues related to the third and final tenet of literary naturalism, as put forth by Hippolyte Taine, that of familial inheritance. Many critics have also treated this theme in their examination of matrilineal roots in women-authored literature. Again, the combination of the collective, naturalist approach and the individual self-viewing herself in the mirror provides a compelling reflection of self in this novel. In *La hija del caníbal*, Lucía grapples with "la enormidad del enigma de las personas, la imposibilidad absoluta de conocer al otro" [the enormity of the enigma of people, the absolute impossibility of knowing others] (27). This challenge, this human need to try to know others, starts in the home. In Lucía Romero's case, the familial portrait is particularly complex. She is an only child, daughter of an actor father and an artist mother who have been divorced for many years. Ramón's kidnapping attracts both of Lucía's parents to her home, but the reader gets the sense that they are more interested in the titillating nature of the case than in the protection of their daughter. They express interest in taking care of Lucía, something they had rarely done in her infancy and adolescence. Lucía narrates: "Cuidarme. A estas alturas. Después de no haberme hecho el menor caso durante toda mi infancia. No sabes lo que es tener dos padres artistas" [Taking care of me. At this point. After not having paid me any attention at all in my whole childhood. You don't know what it's like to have to artist parents] (100).

Montero's humor and mix of genres appear again in her portrayal of Lucía's reaction to the news piece on Ramón's kidnapping: "Eso fue todo. Apenas cuarenta palabras y un fastidioso error, porque la autora de *Patachín el Patito* es Francisca Odón, mi más directa competidora y enemiga[...]. Y para colmo me definían filialmente, como si toda mi identidad estuviera basada en el hecho de ser la Hija del Caníbal" (That was it. Barely forty words and an irksome error, because the author of *Patachín el Patito* is Francisca Odón, my most direct competitor and enemy[...]. And to top it off they defined me filially, as if my whole identity were based in the fact of being the Daughter of the Cannibal) (28). Lucía resents that her literary career has not given her any status distinguishable either from her competitors or from her familial roots. In particular, she wishes to be viewed apart from that giant figure of the "Cannibal." Félix comments on the importance of names, again highlighting his role as naturalist narrator who understands the technique of onomastics (54). Clearly, the use of the name "Cannibal" for Lucía's father refers to a stage name and also to his willingness to use up others in his own blind ambition. The lack of name attributed to Lucía's mother highlights the extent to which Lucía would prefer not to have to imagine her:

> Lucía Romero no quería parecerse a su madre. Tampoco a su Padre-Caníbal, claro está, pero era el fantasma de su madre el que la perseguía, era el destino de su madre lo que la sofocaba, eran las mismas carnes de su madre las que descubría, con horror, en el espejo de los probadores de las tiendas, cuando Lucía se estaba embutiendo unos vaqueros o un traje de verano y de repente atisbaba sin querer su espalda en el azogue y reconocía ahí, qué escalofrío, la misma caída de hombros que su madre.
>
> [Lucia Romero didn't want to look like her mother. Or like her Father-Cannibal, clearly, but it was her mother's ghost that pursued her, it was her mother's destiny that suffocated her, it was her mother's very flesh that she found, in horror, in the dressing-room mirrors, when Lucia was squeezing herself into a pair of bluejeans or a summer suit and suddenly caught a glimpse of herself from the back and recognized there, with a shudder, the same fall of the shoulders of her mother.] [115].

The view of the female self in the mirror recalls quite clearly the images in many female-authored novels, such as *Nada*, *Memorias de Leticia Valle*, *Primera memoria*, *La plaza del diamante*, *El Sur*, and *Recóndita armonía*, to name just a few, of the need to break with the image of the mother and the difficulties in effecting such a break. Again, Montero's humor and frankness permeate the narration in an effective, cross-genre mix that provides an ever-unfolding view of the female main character. At this point in the narration, Lucía has not yet come to terms with her parents as parents, as a former couple, or as individuals. It is significant to Lucía's maturation process that, by the end of the narration, she is able to love and laugh with her parents and to appreciate those parts of herself which come from them: "Así es que, después de todo, mi padre no era un caníbal, sino un tipo normal, lleno de miedos, de debilidades y de errores" [That's how, after all, my father wasn't a cannibal, but just a regular guy, full of fears, weaknesses, and flaws] (334). She recognizes that her penchant for "lying" and "inventing" comes from her artist-parents and is natural. In fact, it is what allows her to be a writer and to exist as a professional.

Ultimately, Lucía's observations of couples and her gradual acceptance of her parents allow her to navigate through her own feelings about Ramón and the surprising liberation she enjoys when he disappears. The reader becomes acquainted with Lucía only through Ramón's disappearance, and it is as if he had occupied too much space for the reader to see beyond him to the narrator-protagonist. As Lucía begins to act and speak on her own, she becomes more adept at recognizing people's roles as individuals and as part of a collective, even if that collective is that intimate unit that we call "family."

The naturalist elements of environment, historic moment, and familial inheritance function together to shape Montero's world view in *La hija del caníbal*. In particular, they allow Lucía, the female co-protagonist, to understand various periods of Spain's twentieth century, the everchanging surroundings of Madrid, and the family portrait composed of her parents and her and of her absent husband and her. The poetics of unfolding influences the depiction of the three naturalist elements: the environment — always Spain, but a changing Spain — transforms according to historic moment and literary genre (detective moments versus existential inquiries versus tropes of women-authored fiction), the historic moment shifts according to changing narrators, and family members and roles are clarified through the superficial plot structure of the detective novel.

These techniques provide a forum for discovery of self in both public and private spheres, which is effected through first- and third-person narrations that, by the end, meld largely into one, whole Lucía who is able to narrate fully from a first-person point of view. This is the character who, early in the narration, was alone and uneasy about her solitude and who, at the end of the narration, is alone and is quite satisfied with herself and her life. The transferal from a "yo" to an "ella" over the course of the novel is both amusing and effective. It allows the narrators several winks with the reader, for example, with the humorous mention of Rosa Montero (42). More importantly, this shifting from first to third person introduces the rich array of themes and techniques of the novel of self-discovery: writing as salvation; self-evaluation through an actual mirror; the metaphorical use of the mirror; the view of oneself in another in an amorous relationship. The unfoldings in *La hija del caníbal* serve to foreground the dignity of human life and the fear and beauty that exist in everyday reality, as detailed by Félix:

> Eso de que para qué servía conducirse con dignidad. Sirve para darnos la medida de lo que somos. Mire, los humanos somos incapaces de imaginarnos lo que no existe; si podemos hablar de cosas tales como el consuelo, la solidaridad, el amor y la belleza es porque esas cosas existen en realidad, porque forman parte de las personas, lo mismo que la ferocidad y el egoísmo. En situaciones extremas esos ingredientes se precipitan, y por eso hay de todo, comportamientos grandiosos y actitudes mezquinas.
>
> [That bit about why it made sense to conduct oneself with dignity. It makes sense to allow us to measure what we are. Look, we humans are incapable of imagining what doesn't exist; if we can talk about things like consolation, solidarity, love, and beauty, it is because these things exist for real, because they form a part of people, just as do ferociousness and selfishness. In extreme situations those ingredients come out, and that's why there's a bit of everything, grandiose behaviors and wretched attitudes.] [287].

The naturalist narrator, Félix, summarizes:

> Lo que te quiero decir con todo esto, Lucía, es que lo que llamamos el Bien está ya presente en la entraña misma de las cosas, en los animales irracionales, en la materia ciega. El mundo no es sólo furor y violencia y caos, sino también esos pingüinos ordenados y fraternales. No hay que tener tanto miedo a la realidad, porque no es sólo terrible, sino también hermosa.
>
> [What I'm trying to tell you with all of this, Lucía, is that what we call Goodness is already present in the core of things, in irrational animals, in raw material. The world is not only furor and violence and chaos, but is also those orderly and fraternal penguins. We don't have to be so afraid of reality, because it is not only terrible, but also beautiful.] [321].

Rather than dramatizing the negative elements of humankind's environment and inheritance, this brand of naturalism seeks to balance the negative with a depiction of some of the positive elements of the world — the orderly, the beautiful, the simply human.

The naturalist techniques that drive the novel include some third-person narration (juxtaposed to first-person narration, which recalls more explicitly the novels of formation that depict women in Spain), the use of onomastics to make characters symbolic of their vital circumstances, careful descriptions of both positive and negative aspects of physical surroundings, and the employment of medical, technical, and police language. The novel combines these naturalist techniques with narrative strategies that recall many of those that appear in other works about women, such as narration in first person, multiple unfoldings within characters, attenuation of the mother figure, and specific allusions to the novel's author. This combination allows the novel to read not as an explicitly naturalist novel, but rather as a unique blend of the public and the private, the literary and the "real," and the destruction and construction of self. Indeed, Lucía becomes the full author and actor of her own life story as she understands her multiple selves — her present and past, her familial obstacles and triumphs, new friendships that speak to a fuller life story, and a redefined approach to the self as writer. It is precisely this intersection of naturalist and more "contemporary" themes and techniques that makes Montero's *La hija del caníbal* a fascinating read and a compelling object of study.

Works Cited

Cabañas Alamán, Rafael. "Entrevista con Rosa Montero. En torno a la biografía de la mujer: *Historias de mujeres*." *Inti* 48 (Fall 1998): 148–56.

Escudero, Javier. "La presencia del 'no-ser' en la narrativa de Rosa Montero." *España contemporánea* 12:2 (Autumn 1999): 21–38.

_____. "Rosa Montero y Pedro Almodóvar: miseria y estilización de la *movida* madrileña." *Arizona Journal of Hispanic Cultural Studies* 2 (1998): 147–61.

_____, and Julio González. "Rosa Montero ante la creación literaria: 'escribir es vivir.'" *Arizona Journal of Hispanic Cultural Studies* 4 (2000): 211–24.

Grillo, Rosa Maria. "Rosa Montero tra autobiogria, narrativa e giornalismo." *Maschere: le scritture delle donne nelle culture iberiche*. Eds. Susana Regazzoni and Leonardo Buonomo. Rome: Bulzoni, 1994. 25–35.

Kakutani, Michiko. "Virginia Woolf: Every Last Bit of Her." *The New York Times*. April 18, 1995. Accessed online December 8, 2006.

Montero, Rosa. *La hija del caníbal*. Madrid: Espasa, 1998.

Pardo Bazán, Emilia. *La cuestión palpitante*. Ed. José Manuel González Herrán. Barcelona: Anthropos, 1989.

Postlewate, Marisa. "The Use of the Detective Story Framework as a (Pre)Text for Self-Realization in *La hija del caníbal*." *Letras femeninas* 28:1 (Summer 2002): 131–46.

Taine, Hippolyte. *Histoire de la littérature anglaise*. Paris: Hachette, 1885.

Wehrheim, Monika. "De amantes y caníbales: divagaciones en torno al concepto del amor en la obra reciente de Rosa Montero." *'El amor, esa palabra ...' El amor en la novela española contemporánea de fin de milenio.* Eds. Anna-Sophia Buck and Irene Gastón Sierra. Frankfurt: Vervuert, 2005. 169–83.

Winter, Ulrich. "From Post-Francoism to Post-Franco Modernism: The 'Powers of the Past' in Contemporary Spanish Narrative Discourse (1977–1991)." *Traces of Contamination. Unearthing the Francoist Legacy in Contemporary SpanishDiscourse.* Eds. Eloy E. Merino and H. Rosi Song. Lewisburg: Bucknell University Press, 2005. 177–98.

Zatlin, Phyllis. "The Novels of Rosa Montero as Experimental Fiction." *Monographic Review/Revista Monográfica* 8 (1992): 114–24.

Zubiaurre, Maite. "Heterotopia and Female Identity in Speculative Fiction: the Case of Gioconda Belli and Rosa Montero." *Ixquic: Revista Hispánica Internacional de Análisis y Creación* 4 (February 2003): 90–11.

Women, War, and Words in *La voz dormida* by Dulce Chacón

Kathryn Everly

> Woman un-thinks the unifying, regulating history that homogenizes and channels forces, herding contradictions into a single battlefield. In woman, personal history blends together with the history of all women, as well as national and World history. As a militant, she is an integral part of all liberations.
> — Hélène Cixous

Dulce Chacón's *La voz dormida* (2002) unearths the legacy of unsung female heroes of the Spanish Civil War. Encased within a larger historical framework, the novel relies on multiple layers of language that express sophisticated concepts of the female self. The language in the novel appears in two different registers in order to reflect upon wartime experience and to cross traditional narrative boundaries. Female experience emerges in the narrative in the form of letters, diaries, and oral testimony while official government papers document both women's and men's situations during and after the war. The author compares and contrasts traditional forms of female expression, such as the epistolary and diary, with the patriarchal, dominant discourse of state issued documentation resulting in the commingling of two distinct versions of the same events. The many details and contradictions of these disparate versions reveal that the "truth" of the events can never really be known. Contemporary notions of women's identity and purpose during the Civil War are reshaped in a narrative that questions not only women's participation in history but also her influence on writing and memory.

The novel inserts women's experience into the official discourse of history yet at the same time questions the validity of any "official" discourse and in the way suggests that words and language can only represent a limited view of past events. But Chacon's narrative insists that these multiple versions of history are innumerable and must be taken into account in order to move toward a more encompassing comprehension of the past. Despite the dismal setting, pending firing squads, and debilitating isolation of the Ventas prison in Madrid where much of the novel transpires, female solidarity emerges as the key to survival. Furthermore, Chacón skillfully juxtaposes locations in the novel to highlight the sense of imprisonment even outside the Ventas prison walls. The novel links the feelings of abandonment and suffering of women inside the prison to those of women hiding out in the mountains with other militia who also feel the very real constraints of political oppression. As Héléne Cixous has observed, the shared raw emotion provoked by war binds women together in a unique, historical way. Although Antonio Gómez López-Quiñones has recognized the utopic rendition of history in Chacon's novel that romanticizes the past (205), the text celebrates the role women play in the many versions of history. I maintain that the text presents a complex rendering of male and female roles in the historical development of women's liberation and in Spanish political and literary history. Chacon's novel romanticizes the past in an effort to challenge our notions of how language and writing represent historical events.

Women's suffering in the novel becomes a metaphor for the national and cultural struggle of Spain during and after the Civil War. Unlike other novelistic accounts of women's experience of the Spanish Civil War, such as Mercè Rodoreda's *La plaça del diamant*, for example, *La voz dormida* does not try to tell the other side of history, or the *her*story of war, but rather Chacón implicates women directly in the political and social activity of the time. Women not only bond together with each other but also bond with men for personal and political survival and to nurture a very weak and dying liberal Spain. Through torture and death as gender equalizers, Chacón weaves a complex tale of how women help each other overcome physical and emotional distress and support the Republican ideology even while in prison and isolated from loved ones. Imprisonment, depression, starvation, and death did not discriminate between the sexes during the aftermath of the war and Chacón bridges the personal and the political in her novel through different forms of the written word that represent both women's and men's experience. One objective of this novel is to record an alternate history and not allow women to fade into oblivion, therefore the typically feminine discourse of diaries, journals, letters, and dialogue are complimented by government-issued documents often typeset in a font resembling an "old-fashioned" typewriter. The inclusion of both private and public documentation creates a multi-layered, more complicated representation of the Spanish Civil War.

History, in the novel, is constructed from private letters and journals, traditionally considered female forms of expression, juxtaposed with the government's official documents. Chacón breaks the barrier between these traditionally masculine and feminine forms of writing by showing that content can be manipulated and molded to appeal to differing audiences when expressed in different forms. The language, style, and structure of the documents are diverse, yet the information regarding prisoners' sentences, long awaited prison releases, and political manifestations is the same. The government-issued documents following dramatic narrative scenes echo and confirm the personal histories in the novel establishing a symbiotic relationship between "masculine" and "feminine" language. While the government documents confirm the reality of the narrated events, the letters and personal testimonies stand out against the stiff prose of official state records.

The novel combines two types of discourse: the officially historical and the historically personal. The novel defies genre because Chacón melds narrative, poetry, and history as a means of creating a unique literary voice. *La voz dormida* is perhaps her most accomplished work and is a powerful testament to her dedication to unearthing information about women's wartime experience.* The four years she spent researching the novel and interviewing survivors of Franco's jails stands as evidence of her interest in how the individual lives of the women portrayed in the novel fit into and resist traditional historical accounts (Pratt 9).

The political nature of Spanish feminism is at the forefront of Chacón's novel, albeit at times in the form of disillusion with the failed promises of

---

*Dulce Chacón was born in 1954 in Zafra, Badajoz. Her poetry collections include: *Querrán ponerle nombre* (1992), *Las palabras de piedra* (1993), *Contra el desprestigio de la altura* (Premio de Poesía Ciudad de Irún 1995), *Matar al angel* (1999) and an anthology that includes the aforementioned texts, *Cuatro gotas* (2003). Her novel *Cielos de barro* (2000) won the Premio Azorín de la Diputación de Alicante and *La voz dormida* was awarded the Book of the Year 2003 by the Gremio de Librero de Madrid. Other novels by Chacón are: *Algún amor que no mate* (1996), *Blanca vuela mañana* (1997), and *Háblame musa de aquel varón* (1988). Chacón collaborated with Cristina Sánchez to write *Matadora* (1997), the autobiography of the bullfighter. She also wrote a play in 1998, *Segunda mano*, and was preparing the script for a stage version of her 1996 novel, *Algún amor que no mate* when she died [Fallece]. It was a shock to the academy and to her readers when Chacón died at the height of her success as a novelist on 3 December 2003 from pancreatic cancer.

the Republic.* Female camaraderie emerges as a motivating force behind the survival of both men and women during the long post-war years. This feminine solidarity arose in part from favorable conditions the war produced for Spanish feminism and as Geraldine Scanlon has observed female workers and soldiers were not only an ideal, but also a necessity (291). The progressive nature of wartime dependence on the female workforce at home and on the front gave way to bitter disappointment with the loss to the Nationalist forces. This unique moment of women's liberation in Spanish history is the focal point of Chacón's novel and the motivating force behind the narrative. The courage and independence that the chorus of women protagonists shows defines the vision of wartime Spain. In an effort to record this history, language becomes crucial in its tenuous, and often problematic, relationship with the truth.

The difficulty of incorporating women's experience into official history using language becomes tantamount when Hélène Cixous questions women's writing and talks "about *what it will do*" (245) that is, what ends it will achieve. She struggles with the idea of history as a monolithic ideology that excludes women yet at the same time she insists that women bring themselves to understand "their meaning in history" (245). The apparent contradiction of writing women into a formal History that has systematically excluded female experience can only function if the language used to describe female experience breaks with traditional modes of historical writing. Chacón uses, for example, oral testimony, letters, and diaries in an effort to incorporate a distinctly female voice and identity into her narrative. John Beverley addresses testimonial literature in much the same way as Cixous ponders women's writing by questioning what it "means or does for us" (266). Beverley equates testimony with the subaltern and points out that the stories of "real" experience reject the "claim of any particular form of cultural expression" (273). Therefore, the dominant testimonial tone of Chacón's novel reveals the importance of the oral history passed down through women. Women are included in the recounting of past events and taken into consideration in the study of cultural development, but how can she emerge from behind the shadow of male-centered discourse? How can she avoid always falling into the category of second in command or the dedicated spouse or partner always working in

---

*When King Alfonso XIII quickly left Spain in 1931 after municipal elections revealed his widespread unpopularity, leading figures of the Republic were ready and waiting to take over the government. However, they would soon deal with deep, violent conflicts between the Catholic Church and liberal party policy. Furthermore, incongruous ideologies of key political figures would prove detrimental to the Second Republic.

support of phallic progress? Cixous proposes that women look to the future in order to understand the past and that women must write "to break up, to destroy, and to forsee the unforseeable, to project" (245). *La voz dormida* is historical fiction that combines genres retelling and reinventing a past that has to be reconsidered from a female viewpoint in order to move toward a notion of equality. The fusing of literary and non-literary languages produces a unique experience for the reader; we are faced with several levels of "reality" within the novel. On one level, the novel is a fictional account of people and events based on years of research and interviews with women who experienced first-hand the circumstances in the Ventas prison. Yet the government-issued documents confirm the narrative in a detached, emotionless way. The two versions of history collide thus creating a fuller, more detailed picture of that particular time in Spain and of historical writing in general.

Women's role in historical events becomes tantamount to understanding the circumstances of postwar Spain. Chacón breaks up traditional modes of story-telling and historical writing in order to project an inclusive version of history that places women at the forefront of politics and war. One of the young protagonists, Elvirita, forms part of the militia hiding in the mountains and "se ha puesto los mismos cojones que el hermano" (Chacón 285). Women are compared to men in a favorable light and the individual women in the novel develop confidence and a strong sense of belonging to a larger political and moral cause. The following examples of parallel representations of events through traditionally feminine modes of writing and then through traditionally masculine modes of discourse show the nature of Chacón's project as to vindicate the experience of women and place them beside the men who fought and suffered as well. Throughout the narrative the concept of the female self grows and develops into a meaningful component of Spanish Civil War history, and more importantly, of our contemporary reading of it.

The novel describes the historic assassination of thirteen young women in the Ventas jail. Las Trece Rosas were marched out of the chapel, across the patio, loaded onto vans and taken to their deaths. Another inmate describes the scene as she peers though a window of the prison: "Salieron de la capilla de dos en dos, sin humillar la cabeza ... Algunas cantaban, Julita Conesa siempre cantaba" [They left the chapel two by two, without lowering their heads.... Some were singing, Julita Conesa always used to sing] (198). A letter written by Julita Conesa on 5 August 1939 appears after this narrative account in the novel. It is the last in a series of letters the young woman wrote to her mother and in it she says: "Besos a todas, que ni tú ni mis compañeras lloréis. Que mi nombre no se borre en la historia" [Kisses to you all, I don't want you or my friends to cry. Don't let my name fade into history] (199). Julita combines the personal and the political in her letter in an attempt to leave her mark in History. The privileging of female perspectives in the letter creates a feminist connection between the words and the events as Julita relies on her mother to tell her story and insists that the female experience not be lost in the more official versions of history. The letter is a private document yet it has found its way into a novel and gives the young victim a voice and identity upon her death.

This mingling of testimony and fiction becomes even more acute when we realize that the letter is a document that Chacón had access to while researching the novel. Julita Conesa, a flesh and blood political prisoner, wrote the letter word for word as it appears in the novel and was executed along with the other twelve women of the Trece Rosas. The letter is reproduced in Fernanda Romeu Alfaro's study in a facsimile written in pencil on worn, crinkled paper (285). Chacón does not reveal to her reader that this letter is a document she found, but she does thank Romeu in the acknowledgements "porque hizo posible que yo tuviera en mi casa las cartas originales de Julita Conesa" [because she made it possible for me to have in my home Julita Conesa's original letters] (386). The handwritten words of the letter reprinted in Romeu's study cross the textual boundaries and infuse Chacon's novelistic episode with a sense of self and a "real" personal identity. The reprinting of the letter, first appearing in Romeu's book in its original form and then in a dramatic context in Chacon's novel, fulfills Julita's wishes. Her name has not been erased from history but moves through an intertextual discourse that draws from historical document, fact, and fiction.

Several of the characters in the novel are based on real people and Chacón gratefully acknowledges them in the epilogue to her book. Chacón was not the first person to narrate the suffering, silence, and survival of women during and after the Civil War, however she did bring attention to the body of literature about Spanish women's condition through her narrative skill and established fame as a published author. Many other books tell the women's story in the Ventas jail creating an intertextual flow of characters and events that familiarize the reader with the plight of the Trece Rosas and the unflinching camaraderie that held these women together.* However,

---

*Juana Doña's testimonial novel, Tomasa Cuevas's three volumes, Sara Berenguer's and Dolores Medio's novels and the aforementioned study by Romeu are examples of the body of work that provides insight into women's situation during and after the war. The names of the women incarcerated, the group of young girls executed known as the Trece Rosas, details of infant mortalities, and the squalid conditions of the jails appear in several of the texts, including Chacón's.

many of the autobiographies that recount events in Franco's prisons lack narrative structure and flow. Chacón takes this body of information and the courageous words of the brave women that struggled to tell their stories and writes a dramatic history that incorporates their words and experiences in an stylistically accomplished historical novel.* By mingling real events and people with fictional characters, Chacón adds a distinctly literary dimension to the construction of the civil war female self.

One particularly disturbing account published in Paris in 1967 by Mercedes Núñez recounts torture methods used in the Ventas jail. She describes how the authorities tortured older women, beat pregnant women so they would miscarry, and used genital mutilation to torture and humiliate prisoners (39–40). The stark, journalistic narrative of Núñez's personal account haunts the imagination in its effort to reconstruct the atrocities of the Ventas prison. The authors of these testimonies and novels are, in most cases, women with minimal education and minimal experience in the craft of narrative. Dolores Medio's novel, *Atrapados en la ratonera*, for example, is heavy with political jargon and names of regiments and generals. Sara Berenguer admits in her introduction to *Entre el sol y la tormenta*: "Mi léxico será restingido y, a buen seguro, carente de estilo. Sólo fui a la escuela hasta los doce años" [My vocabulary surely is restricted and lacks style. I only went to school until I was 12 years old] (11). What Medio and Berenguer lack in refined prose they make up for in sheer bravery of writing down their difficult experiences. Chacón uses their texts, their stories, letters, diaries, and memories to create a polivocal narrative that incorporates fact and fiction.

A large part of the narrative tension relies on the fictionalization of actual events yet Chacón invents purely dramatic situations as well. As a counterpoint to the incorporation of Julita Conesa's letter in the novel, the narrative describes the execution of a fictional prisoner, Hortensia Rodríguez García whose name "no consta en el registro de fusilados del día seis de marzo de mil novecientos cuarenta y uno. Pero cuentan que aquella madrugada, Hortensia miró de frente al piquete, como todos.—¡Viva la República!" [was not in the oficial register of those shot on the sixth day of March nineteen hundred and forty one. But they tell of that night, when Hortensia looked straight ahead at the firing squad, like they all did. Long live the Republic!] (220). Without the proof of an actual letter written by the vic-

---

*For an overview of more canonical Civil War novels written by women see Carolyn Gallerstein's article in which she describes novels by authors such as Ana María Matute and María Teresa León.

tim, this narration gives all of the "undocumented" women a voice. Hortensia is jailed while pregnant with her daughter and she spends her pregnancy knowing that she will be killed once the child is born. The novel opens with the declaration "La mujer que iba a morir se llamaba Hortensia" [The woman who was going to die was named Hortensia] (13) immediately naming and thus identifying the character. With this bold affirmation, the narrative metonymically names all of the forgotten women that died in the prisons and in battle.

As a means to further universalize Hortensia's character, the text incorporates photography as an interpretive tool that solidifies the female identity in the novel. The narrative describes a popular photo of a *miliciana* that has been published elsewhere and serves as the cover of *La voz dormida*.*
A young, smiling militia woman gazes straight into the camera as she holds a laughing baby. In the novel, Chacón decides to reinvent this woman's identity as Hortensia holding someone else's baby. The woman's dangling earrings that seem a bit out of place alongside her military garb become a focal point in the narrative. Mateo, Hortensia's husband, gave her the earrings as a gift and she wore them all the time even when dressed in uniform with her rifle strung across her back as the photo proves. As Hortensia awaits the delivery of her child in prison she prepares a packet of things for the authorities to give to her sister who will take care of the baby. In this bundle she has hidden her notebooks full of writings and the earrings for her baby (220). The appropriation of certain details of the photograph for narrative purposes is yet another example of how the novel crosses genre boundaries.

The photograph tells a story of women in the militia and Chacón furthers her literary agenda by naming the woman and giving her a multidimensional personality. The photographic image evokes its own narrative suggesting the bittersweet success of the *miliciana* as she clearly plans to participate actively in the Republican cause but must leave her child behind. The discourse of women at war in the photograph is transformed into a narrative tool for recreating a certain historical moment from a female point of view. The identity of the *miliciana* in the photograph is transposed to the narrative as that of Hortensia for the sake of emphasizing the crucial role women played in the war. Female identity here is proactive and participatory in the making of history just as Julita's letter brings a touch of authen-

---

*This photo, "Miliciana with her child before she leaves for the battlefront," also appears in Shirley Mangini's study.

ticity to the novel, the interpretation of the photograph lends a sense of historicity to a fictional rendering of the events.

Hortensia's death by firing squad is the dramatic climax of the novel. She cries "¡Viva la República!" [Long live the Republic!] (The woman who was going to die was named Hortensia) and after she is shot "dicen, y es cierto, que una mujer se acercó a los caídos y se arrodilló junto a Hortensia. [...] Y le cerró los ojos. Y le lavó la cara" [they say, and it is certain, that a woman approached the fallen and kneeled down beside Hortensia. [...] And closed her eyes. And washed her face] (220). The narrative device of creating and propagating an oral testimony by using "dicen, y es cierto" [they say, and it is certain] unbinds the events from the text. This implies that many people have talked about the execution for "they" have told and retold the events. More importantly, our narrator assures us that the testimony of the witnesses is true: "es cierto." The oral tradition that sustains subaltern memory provides an alternative perspective to the cruel killings. Even though testimonial literature itself is a construct, it often counters official historical authority (Beverley 281).

In stark contrast to this scene, the official document sentencing Hortensia to death immediately follows. The jarringly different typeset from a typewriter notifies the reader that the information is official archival material that exists outside of the women's narrative discourse. The change of font suggests not only a different tone but also a different time and space. The typewritten document and official language stand out against Hortensia's valiant and poignant narrative death. For example, the parallel moment of Hortensia's death in the government-issued document reads: "condenamos a la procesada, como autora del delito de AHDESIÓN A LA REBELIÓN, con las agravantes de trascendencia y peligrosidad, a la pena de MUERTE y accesorias legales correspondientes, para caso de indulto, debiendo ser ejecutada la procesada por FULSILAMIENTO" [we condemn the accused, as guilty of the crime of SUPPORTING THE REBELLION, with the added aggravations of subversion and dangerous behavior, to the DEATH penalty and the corresponding legal implications, in the case of a pardon, to be executed by FIRING SQUAD] (222). The lack of emotion, the capitalized words that seem to jump off the page in a shout, and the convoluted sentence structure provide a completely opposite rendering of Hortensia's death. In this way, the novel presents two different versions of the same event. The linguistic and stylistic contrasts force the reader to piece together a new reality and question the roles of official documentation, testimony, and oral tradition. In this case, the death sentence document confirms the facts while the personal observations and word-of-mouth testimony give Hortensia's death a unique and human element.

Hortensia's memory dominates the thoughts of many of the survivors in the novel as well as her husband's experience while hiding out in the mountains after the Nationalist forces have seized control of the government. Another character, Elvirita, escapes from the Ventas prison and joins the men in the mountains functioning as a narrative link between the women in the jail and the men in action. Elvirita joins her brother and other militias in Cerro Umbría symbolizing the permeation of boundaries as she moves from the enclosed all-female space of the prison to the male-dominated, active space of the war. Her convictions, however, never waver from the importance of community that Gómez López-Quiñonez has observed in the novel "tiene un valor superior a la suma de todos sus miembros" [has a superior value in the sum of all its members] (214). In order to contribute to this sense of community, Elvirita has to prove to the men that women do have a place in the mountain and on the front lines. The importance of a female wartime identity and sense of belonging link the women in the Ventas prison to the few women hiding out in the mountains.*

In contrast to the emotional suffering of both men and women described in the novel, the declaration of political intent seems to justify the sacrifices of those loyal to the Republic. The creation of the "Agrupación Guerrillera de Cerro Umbría" appears as a separate type-written document in the novel (288–89) declaring that all present serve "bajo la dirección estratégia de la Junta Suprema de Unión Nacional Española, que dota al pueblo español de una dirección nacional de combate antifranquista por la salvación de España" [under the strategic direction of the Supreme Council for Spanish National Unity, that provides the Spanish people with an anti–Francoist national agenda for the salvation of Spain] (289). The terse language rings of authority in its detached declaration of intent.

However, following the document declaring the unification of the guerillas appears: "La Agrupación la componían sesenta y dos guerrilleros. Uno de ellos era Elvira" [The Association was made up of sixty-two guerrilla soldiers. One of those was Elvira] (289). The narrative then jumps to a conversation between Elvirita and her brother: "¿Cómo estás, chiqueta?—Yo estoy bien, no toso ni siquiera cuando corro" [How are you, kid?—I'm fine, not coughing at all, even when I run] (289). The jump from the official

---

*Female presence on the front lines was actually rare during the war and not always a popular decision (Scanlon 295).

language of the political manifesto to the easy, family chatter brings the reader back to the narrative present. Words such as "chiqueta" and the preoccupation with Elvirita's health give the reader insight into the close sibling relationship. The result of this sequence both in content and in structure is a mixing of two distinct types of discourse. The document juxtaposed with the conversation jolts the reader out of a particular comfort zone where we know what to expect and who is speaking. In this case, the male writers of the official sounding document exhibit elsewhere in the narrative nurturing, contemplative, and other more traditionally female characteristics. On a narrative level the jump from the formal tone of the declaration to the conversation breaks with conventional modes of linear storytelling. Just as Hortensia's death sentence becomes more brutal when read in the detached tone of the state, the failure of the militias in Cerro Umbría to defeat fascism becomes more devastating given the narrative importance of the familial bond.

After officially declaring their position as an organized group, the militia's hideout is ambushed by the Guardia Civil. Mateo, Hortensia's husband, is at the river away from the camp and when he sees himself surrounded by the enemy he fires his pistol in a final act of solidarity to warn the others. His act saves lives yet he is another casualty in the ongoing Civil War conflict. Six men and one woman are killed in the mountains and the police photographs of the cadavers are displayed in the shop windows of a nearby town. The grotesque display attracts viewers who are questioned by the suspicious police, for any association with the rebels is grounds for arrest. Susan Sontag analyzes the power of war photographs that "turn an event or a person into something that can be possessed" (81). In this case, the authorities appropriate death in order to display their persistence and to discourage further subversive activity. The male and female cadavers are symbolic to the extent that they are nameless and represent the equalizing nature of death. They also represent hope and affirm that some militias escaped and are still active in the mountain. The photographs convey the impossibility to separate the personal from the political because they represent a selected moment deemed important by the photographer. As Sontag points out, every photo frames the action or subject thus leaving something out. Therefore, even a photograph that supposedly represents a "real" moment in history represents only one limited perspective.

Reme, a woman released from prison, takes a train to the town in order to check if one of the photos is of her friend Elvirita. She breathes a sigh of relief and repeats "No es Elvira, no es Elvira" while her husband lifts his eyes in horror as he recognizes his friend's daughter (306). The photographs' ability to reconstruct the events of the ambush leads to a more universal interpretation of how images construct memory. Sontag points out that photographs can only selectively represent history: "collective memory is not remembering but stipulating that a certain image or event is important while another is not" (86). What is framed in the picture necessarily excludes some information and therefore photography is as representational as writing. The image evokes a mental narrative for the viewer to reconstruct events that lead up to the photographed moment. In this way both writing and photography elicit a response from the reader/viewer. The gaps in the written text between official language and narrative prose require the reader to make the connections between official and personal history. The image framed by the edges of the photograph works in much the same way. The viewer must create a situation that leads to a comprehensive interpretation of the image. Therefore, both written and visual narratives represent only a part of history. Language and photography confirm through their limits that we will never know what really happened and that the "truth" cannot neatly be defined. In the case of the photos of the dead rebels in the novel, truth ceases to be an issue. Identity, family, and voice all fall into oblivion as the purpose of the photos is to officially comment on the success of Franco's government in suppressing the insurgents. By reminding us of the scare tactics used by the police and of the manipulation of the image for official means, the photos emphasize the importance of the larger narrative project that gives voice to previously silenced history.*

Nevertheless, the novel ends on a positive note with the long-awaited marriage of one male prisoner, Jaime, to his girlfriend of more than 40 years, Pepita. After the devastation, death, and loss that drive most of the previous narrative, this quiet moment at the end of the novel brings a sense of peace and closure. Chacón includes a short paragraph at the end of the narrative and before the acknowledgments that firmly grounds the story in a historical space. She separately thanks Pepita for her contributions to the story and adds that Jaime died in 1976 in Córdoba. She explains that the authorities would visit their house every year on 1 May to assure that Jaime had no intentions of participating in an annual Republican demonstration. They arrived ironically on the day after Jaime's death and Pepita led them to his body and told them that now they could take him away (281). This poignant

---

*See Sontag's book *Regarding the Pain of Others* for an illuminating analysis of war photography as fabricated history.

moment provides an example of peaceful death in contrast to the torture and suffering in prison but also serves an important structural purpose in the novel. By bringing the characters out of the fictional reality and placing them squarely in this biographical anecdote, the author once again decidedly crosses the genre boundaries of fiction and fact. This short epilogue that stands outside of the fictional space but relates intimately to it attests to the nebulous nature of historical writing in general. We have been reading a fictional account of real people's lives mixed in with created characters and invented situations. Chacón suggests that the "real," the remembered, and the speculative all contribute to forming a more complete story and fuller picture of how things were.

In the longer list of acknowledgements that appears at the end of the book, Chacón reveals her sources. She thanks the many people she interviewed and mentions the women who have authored testimonies and studies of the war and specifically of the Ventas jail. This tribute to other texts and other voices augments a truly intertextual and cross-disciplinary project. As Gómez López-Quiñones notes, the novel "atiende a un principio de respeto y cuidadosa atención a lo contado por Pepita y otros" [maintains a principle of respect and careful attention to what Pepita and the others tell] (215). However, the narrative voice in Chacón's novel is not the only representation of the female experience during those difficult decades in Spain. She purposefully includes the voices and testimonies of many other women and she explains: "Lo que he buscado es la memoria colectiva, sobre todo de las mujeres, pero también de los hombres, que perdieron la guerra y que fueron represaliados" [I have searched for a collective memory, mostly that of women, but also of the men who lost the war and suffered retaliation] (Crespo 1). In this way, her work is not creative fiction but a unique hybrid of testimony, documentation, and extrapolation that encourages other voices, all voices, to play a part and be heard in Spain's collective memory.

Chacón's use of language in *La voz dormida* pushes issues of personal and collective memory to the forefront of the narrative discourse. Julita Conesa's letter and Hortensia's death sentence represent specific events told in multiple versions highlighting the impossibility to ever know the "truth" of those days during and after the Spanish Civil War. Instead of separating language into "fact" and "fiction," Chacón has melded private and state discourses in one historical novel that points toward the fusion of individual and collective memory. The stark contrast between the intimate, narrative recollections and the government-issued documents referring to the same events suggests that personal and national memory can be in conflict and, perhaps more importantly, that all versions of past events must be taken into account in order to understand what constitutes our notion of history. Photography as a selective science omits information that lies beyond the camera frame just as language implies another silence. By weaving together the personal and the public language, the novel points to that which is left out. The contrast in language suggests confusion and error and this becomes an integral part of the novel's purpose, which is to unearth the silences, the omissions, and the constructedness of history. The feminine voice of the novel creates a specific reflection on women's role and participation in the Spanish Civil War and this contributes to our understanding of Spanish history and of historical writing in general and of historical language in general. Through words and writing about the traditionally masculine space of war, Dulce Chacón succeeds in creating a novelistic project that challenges notions of history and memory. She has woken the sleeping voice of women's experience and identity during and after the war but also challenges absolute notions of history and documentation.

Works Cited

Berenguer, Sara. *Entre el sol y la tormenta*. Barcelona: Seuba ediciones, 1988.
Beverley, John. "The Real Thing." *The Real Thing. Testimonial Discourse and Latin America*. Ed. Georg M. Gugelberger. Durham: Duke University Press, 1996, 266–86.
Chacón, Dulce. *La voz dormida*. Madrid: Alfaguara, 2002.
Cixous, Hélène. "The Laugh of the Medusa." (1975). *New French Feminisms*. Ed. Elaine Marks and Isabel de Courtrivron. New York: Schocken Books, 1981. 245–64.
Crespo, Martín. "Entrevista con Dulce Chacón II." *La mujer actual*. 19 January 2006 <www.mujeractual.com/entrevistas/chacon/index.html>.
Cuevas, Tomasa. *Testimonios de mujeres en las cárceles franquistas*. (1982). 3 volumes. Huesca: Instituto de Estudios Altoaragoneses, 2004.
Doña, Juana. *Desde la noche y la niebla (mujeres en las cárceles franquistas)*. Madrid: Ediciones de la Torre, 1978.
"Fallece en Madrid a los 49 años la escritora Dulce Chacón." Elpaís.es/cultura. 4 December 2003. 23 February 2006. <http://www.elpais.es/articulo.html?xref=20031204 elpepucul_1&type=Tes&anchor=elpporcul&d_date=20031204>.
Galerstein, Carolyn. "The Spanish Civil War: The View of Women Novelists." *Letras Femeninas* 10.2 (1984): 12–18.
Gómez López-Quiñones, Antonio. "*La voz dormida*: El personaje como utopía política y literaria." *La guerra persistente. Memoria, violencia utopía: representaciones contemporáneas de la Guerra Civil española*. Madrid: Iberoamericana, 2006. 203–17.
Mangini, Shirley. *Memories of Resistance: Women's Voices from the Spanish Civil War*. New Haven: Yale University Press, 1995.
Medio, Dolores. *Atrapados en la ratonera*. Madrid: Editorial Alce, 1980.
Nash, Mary. *Defying Male Civilization: Women in the Spanish Civil War*. Denver: Arden Press, 1995.
Nuñez, Mercedes. *Cárcel del ventas*. Paris: Editions de la Librairie de Globe, 1967.

Pratt, Joaquín. "*La voz dormida*: entrevista con Dulce Chacón." *Puerta del sol* 12.1 (2004): 8–11.
Romeu Alfaro, Fernanda. *El silencio roto*. Oviedo?: J.C. Producción, 1994.
Scanlon, Geraldine M. *La polémica feminista en la España contemporánea (1868–1974)*. Trans. Rafael Mazarrasa. Madrid: Ediciones Akal, 1986.
Sontag, Susan. *Regarding the Pain of Others*. New York: Farrar, Straus and Giroux, 2003.
Velázquez Jordán, Santiago. "Dulce Chacón: La reconciliación real de la guerra civil aún no ha llegado." *Espéculo* 22 (2002) 26 September 2005. <http://www.ucm.es/info/especulo/numero22/dchacon.html>.

The Wounded Self and Body in Dulce Chacón's *Algún amor que no mate:* A Haunting Discourse*

Esther Raventós-Pons

Jacques Lacan has infamously argued that "woman does not exist," she is a "symptom" for man as she becomes a fantasy object *[objet à]*, a cause of his desire (167–170).† In *A Room of One's Own*, Virginia Woolf tries to understand the incongruities of a culture in which women become fantasy objects both elevated and denigrated — a culture that emphasizes their nonexistence, their absence from history, yet at the same time is capable of creating a literature in which women are portrayed as strong and eloquent individuals such as "Clymenestra, Antigone, Cleopatra, Lady Macbeth, Phèdre, Cressida, Rosalind, Desdemona, the Duchess of Malfi" (55). Woolf concludes:

> A very queer, composite being [...] emerges. Imaginatively she is of the highest importance; practically she is completely insignificant. She pervades poetry from cover to cover, she is all but absent from history [...] It

---

*An English translation of the title of this un-translated novel might be *Looking for a Love That Doesn't Kill*. All translations of Spanish passages into English, unless otherwise noted, are by the editors.

†Lacan discusses the simultaneous elevation and degradation of women through the trope of courtly love, in which the knight's "lady was entirely, in the most servile sense of the term, his female subject" (141). Lacan, according to Jacqueline Rose, views "courtly love as the elevation of the woman into the place where her absence or inaccessibility stands in for male lack, [...] just as he sees her denigration as the precondition for man's belief in his own soul" (48–49).

was certainly an odd monster that one made up by reading the historians first and the poets afterwards — a worm winged like an eagle; the spirit of life and beauty in a kitchen chopping up suet [56].

These contradictory depictions of women, that according to Woolf emerge by reading historians first and poets afterwards, are rooted in the very basis of western culture. Woman has become a "symptom" not only for man, but also for the culture itself: simultaneously a haunting absence, while paradoxically a presence both elevated by male desires — since she becomes a fantasy object — and degraded by male fears of women's self-empowerment.

In the novel *Algún amor que no mate* (2002), Dulce Chacón captures the consequences of these cultural assumptions where woman as a "symptom" fades into invisibility and silence. The writer articulates these very issues by depicting literally and metaphorically, a wounded female self, coerced into a nondesiring state of inertness and melancholia and lost in the invisible and silent domestic sphere. This wounded self acts as a kind of rip in the narrative, making the invisible and hidden forces visible, reminding us of what is not represented, and exposing to us the world of women's discarded and excluded bodies. The reader is thrust into a haunting discourse where the body becomes full of signification in its denied meaning.

The novel *Algún amor que no mate* tells a present-day story of a traditional patriarchal marriage that has gone wrong. After taking an overdose of pills, the protagonist, Prudencia, narrates the story of her past and the violent failure of her marriage from her deathbed in the hospital. Remembering her life, she opens up her emotional wounds to the reader. She depicts her suffering and her jealousy when she discovers letters addressed to the husband from his lover (26). The text also shows the devastating effects of physical and psychological abuse, which renders the character powerless to leave her abusive husband and the character regrets her existence despite admitting the difficulties she experienced to change her path (106).

Leonor E. Walker, who introduced the concept of "battered woman syndrome," describes a three-phase cycle model of domestic violence, to explain the inability of women to rebel against maltreatment: the first phase is characterized by mounting tension, leading to the second phase of the battering episode, which occurs without warning, and followed by the third phase of kind, loving, contrition and reconciliation. Walker states that it is the third stage that provides reinforcement for the woman to stay in the relationship, since she is led to believe that she is needed, that the man loves her, and that he will change (278–79). This cycle will reproduce itself repeatedly, diminishing the woman's motivation to respond; feeling powerless, she becomes more and more passive. As a result, she falls into what Walker calls "learned helplessness" (2). The battered woman becomes accustomed to being dominated and comes to believe that she cannot function without the abusive partner.* This is the case of Prudencia, where her physical and psychic injuries wound her body and impair her self-esteem so seriously that she falls into destructive emotional patterns.

The French phenomenologist philosopher Maurice Merleau-Ponty says, "My body is what opens me out upon the world and places me in a situation there" (165). The body in and of itself has no meaning; it takes meaning through its relations with the world and with others. It is socially and culturally articulated. Culture delineates, delimits and encloses women in a prison house of gender, where the body does not belong to her; it belongs to a patriarchal society and a culture that dictate women's behavior. John Berger, in his book *Ways of Seeing*, describes in the following way: *"men act* and *women appear*. Men look at women, women watch themselves being looked at. This determines not only most relations between men and women but also the relation of women to themselves" (47). Women, as Laura Mulvey explains in her essay "Visual Pleasure and Narrative Cinema," "stand[s] in patriarchal culture as a signifier for the male other, bound by a symbolic order in which man can live out his fantasies and obsessions [...] by imposing them on the silent image of woman still tied to her place as bearer, not maker, of meaning" (15). The female body becomes an object, tied to her place as bearer, silent, construing herself as a passive possession. In the novel, Prudencia follows the traditional role of housewife in a male-defined world (71). She is trapped in a traditional patriarchal marriage that dictates against female autonomy and affirmation of selfhood. She accepts her role as a housewife and becomes a passive possession, emotionally and economically dependent on her violent husband. The character falls into the stereotypical expectation that "a woman's place is in the home" (107). Her existence has no meaning or purpose outside of her marriage: she accepts society's tra-

---

*Other reasons that make women "accept" the situation of abuse are explained in *Mujeres víctimas de la violencia doméstica* [*Female Victims of Domestic Violence*]. They are: "falta de medios suficientes para mantenerse a sí mismas y a sus hijos, la opinión de los demás, la vergüenza, el miedo, los sentimientos de culpa [...], las conductas de arrepentimiento del marido, la ignorancia de sus derechos, el aislamiento al que están expuestas, su religión, etc. Las mujeres maltratadas no experimentan placer en la situación de abuso, los sentimientos más comunes son el miedo, la impotencia y la debilidad" [lack of sufficient means to maintain themselves and their children, the opinion of others, shame, fear, feelings of guilt [...], the husband's display of regret, ignorance of their rights, the isolation to which they are exposed, their religion, etc. Abused women do not feel pleasure in the abusive situation, the most common feelings are fear, powerlessness, and weakness] (Labrador 33).

ditional mandate that her place is at home, as a housewife and nothing else. She fades into the emptiness and invisibility of her domestic life.

Betty Friedan argued in the early 1960s the harmful consequences of a woman deriving her identity only by being a housewife: "The very condition of being a housewife can create a sense of emptiness, non-existence, nothingness, in women. There are aspects of the housewife role that make it almost impossible for a woman of adult intelligence to retain a sense of human identity, the firm core of self or I without which a human being, man or woman is not truly alive" (293). Prudencia, in yielding responsibility for her identity to her husband, is unable to develop an autonomous self capable of action and becomes an unintentional complice in her own imprisonment: "El hombre tiene el poder. Y la mujer debe aceptarlo así" [The man has the power. And the woman should accept that] (102).* She is a victim of the logic of the male gaze, in which women are relegated to a passive and silent position, a position of invisibility, to the point that she is reduced to nothing (65). The protagonist relies on her husband to assure her sense of identity and lacks other expectations for herself outside the boundaries of marriage. Her life depends totally upon her husband's wishes (54). After her husband loses his job and Prudencia tries to help the household by finding a job for herself, her husband denies her self-assertion, and goes into one of his rages (105). The marriage becomes a destructive force that will lead Prudencia to a feeling of increasing dissatisfaction and anxiety, leaving a legacy of vulnerability and muteness: "Se fue dando cuenta de su propio vacío, cada vez más grande, de los huecos que su marido no llenaba. Siguió entregándose, sin saber que así buscaba justificarse" [She became aware of her own ever-increasing emptiness, and of the voids her husband wasn't filling. She continued to give of herself, without knowing that in this way she was trying to justify herself] (99).† Chacón, by creating a character that complies fully to the very modes of passivity and objectness proposed by patriarchy in marriage, exposes to the reader the destructiveness unleashed when an

---

*As noted by Walker, many battered women, after experiencing powerlessness and falling into the phase of "learned helplessness," give up any resistance to abuse and, as a result, they withdraw into silence and passivity. Over time, they learn that they have no control over their circumstances and, as a result, their motivation to respond in an active way decreases, thereby "accepting" the situation by default.

†The effect of domestic violence on women is devastating. Francisco Javier Labrador, Paulina Paz, Pilar de Luis y Rocío Fernández state that this devastation affects "no sólo en la salud física, sino también en la salud mental de sus víctimas" [not only the physical health, but also the mental health of its victims]. The victims of violence tend to be depressed and suffer from low self-esteem, and anxiety. As a result, they are unable to develop healthy interpersonal relationships, and often tend to abuse themselves or others (63–73).

intelligent woman is confined, even if originally by her own choice, in the role of wife and housewife, a role that denies her an outlet for her talents as well as her passions.

Feminist myth critic Annis Pratt explains that "marriage as archetypal enclosure" is a recurrent pattern in fiction by women (45). In Chacon's narrative, "home" becomes for Prudencia not a place of security and self-realization, but a place of imprisonment and confinement, where aggressiveness and violence prevail. In *Conjugal Crime,* the psychologist Terry Davidson indicates that married women take abuse from their husbands because society teaches them to respect the institution of marriage. Marriage imposes limitations on women and a sense of duty, so that, when women are abused, they feel guilty, wonder what they have done wrong, and become passive trying to understand their maltreatment. When they do not rebel, their husbands continue the domestic abuse and "a pattern is set. All the evidence is that when the first or second assault is not firmly dealt with, there will be more" (51). Prudencia, both bound by and dependent on the structures of matrimony, rather than confront her husband, swallows her own anger: "Te has limitado a aceptar tus desgracias" [You've done nothing but accept your bad luck] (75). This emotional repression leads to a progressive failure of her will, and to a wounded body as a consequence of her husband's cruelty and violence.

The marital abuse in *Algún amor que no mate* manifests itself physically, sexually, and emotionally. Physical violence appears only in a few incidents throughout the text. However, the various types of violence play a central role in the narrative as a whole. Jacqueline Cruz considers that "aun cuando se presentan pocas escenas de violencia, la protagonista presenta un cuadro extremo de malos tratos: el marido le prohíbe salir de casa sin él, la aísla por completo de su familia y sus amigas, y exhibe sin ningún pudor su relación con 'la otra'" [even though there are only a few scenes of violence, the protagonist presents an extreme picture of abuse: her husband does not allow her to leave the house without him, he completely isolates her from her family and her friends, and he shamelessly flaunts his relationship with "the other woman"] (3). The emotional cruelty is not reflected in the body; there is no palpable evidence left of the lacerations to the heart caused by her husband's unkindness, infidelity, and absence of love.* On the other hand, physical and sexual violence leave a mark on the body; however, the victim is unable

---

*Walker considers that "psychological abuse create[s] longer-lasting pain than [do] many [...] physically induced injuries" (202).

to express it publicly and as a result, this also remains invisible. One of the most violent incidents occurs when Prudencia confronts her husband about his infidelities and tries to leave him. The violence unleashed by her husband renders her powerless (73). Then, he was sorry:

> la acurrucó en su hombro y se puso a besarla en la boca. Ella se resistía y le decía que no, que no, que por favor la dejara. Pero él siguió sin escucharla, le secó las lágrimas con la lengua. Déjame, aparta, gritaba Prudencia. Se revolvía asqueada. Entonces la miró como un poseso y se le encendieron los ojos. Quieta, nena, quieta, le decía entre dientes mientras la sujetaba. Y allí mismo, en el comedor la violentó dos veces.
>
> [he cuddled her on his shoulder and he began to kiss her on the mouth. She resisted saying no, no, please leave her alone. But he continued without listening to her, he dried her tears with his tongue. Leave me alone, get away, shouted Prudencia. She turned away in disgust. Then he looked at her as if he were possessed and his eyes were aflame. Keep still, little girl, keep still, he said between his teeth while he held her down. And right there, in the dining room, he forced himself on her twice.] [73–74].

Prudencia is hurt, despised, beaten and raped. Physically and sexually assaulted and neglected psychologically, she is placed in a situation of utter domestic horror. Her rape is a consequence of the physical violence to which her body is subjected, and emphasizes her husband's power and total control. Marital rape is the ultimate of the many humiliations that the protagonist suffers. She admits: "Y también me enseñó un dolor más negro" [And he also showed me the blackest pain] (73). These words convey powerfully to the reader the intensity of her abuse. She feels that she has lost all control over her life, and exists in what Walker called "learned helplessness," in which she gives up any resistance to abuse.* This sense of powerlessness affects her decisions; for example, in another incident, when her husband gets upset because she did not wash his shirt on time (50). Trapped in a loveless and violent marriage, sexually abused and estranged from her husband, Prudencia feels reduced to nothing.

The reader is confronted with a fearful woman, relegated to a life of domestic terror. Her husband furthers her state of mental distress by isolat-

---

*María Herrera-Sobek considers that victims of domestic abuse become invisible, voiceless, worthless and devaluated objects. "They are silent entities dominated by ingrained patriarchal vectors where the Name of the Father is Law, and years of socialization to obey the Father's Law transforms the female subject into a quavering accomplice in her own rape. That is to say, women are socialized into being participants in their own oppression" (218). According to her, women in our patriarchal society are considered holes that men are supposed to fill in. Social practices enhance women's sense of powerlessness or "learned helplessness" that will affect her decisions when faced by abuse. In this context, to break the habit of silence, invisibility, worthiness and self-doubt is extremely difficult.

ing her from friends and family.* First, he isolates her from her parents (77). Then, Prudencia rejects her friends because he does not like them (66). This behavior of accepting and validating the decisions and actions of the aggressor, according to Miguel and José Antonio Lorente Acosta, is common among battered women: "el aislamiento de las víctimas respecto a anteriores fuentes de apoyo (ej. amigos o familia) y a las actividades fuera del ambiente hogareño conllevan a una dependencia al agresor y la aceptación o validación de las acciones del agresor y de sus puntos de vista" [the victims' isolation from previous support systems (e.g. friends of family) and from activities outside the home bear a dependence on the aggressor and the acceptance or validation of his actions and points of view] (100). Consequently, Prudencia becomes more and more emotionally dependent on a husband who physically entombs her in the restricted space of home. Overwhelmed by loneliness, she completely isolates herself from the world (75). Alienated and imprisoned by the very relationship that defined her sense of security and identity, she fades into blankness. As noted by Walker, many battered women then give up any resistance to abuse, and retreat into silence and passivity. The marriage becomes a prison of habit, obligation, and fear. Enclosed in the prison of her house, the battered woman occupies no position in the social world. Prudencia becomes a transient self which walks inexorably towards death.

The depth of damage generated by the abuse has concrete and major consequences for the protagonist. Violence, isolation, and self-denial place Prudencia in a marginal and dangerous place, where the loss of selfhood carves intense pain in her body (31–32). Consequently, she looses her emotional equilibrium and fragments, talking to herself. The use of the pronoun "tú" [you, informal], while at the same time emphasizing a split self, also becomes a defense mechanism to cope with her overwhelming pain of being abused. Elaine Scarry considers that "it is the intense pain that destroys a person's self and world. [...] Intense pain is also language-destroying: as the content of one's world disintegrates, so the content of one's language disintegrates; as the self disintegrates, so that which would express and project the self is robbed of its source of its subject" (35). Intense pain dismantles the victim's capacity for language and therefore her capacity to speak the unspeakable and voice her suffering. Prudencia, unable to find a language

---

*This behavior of isolating the victim seems to be common with abusive husbands, as observed by Marjorie Homer, Anne Leonard, and Pat Taylor: "the husband's control within the marriage often manifested and reinforced by his ability to forbid wife contact with family and friends" (94).

to communicate her intense pain in face of her abuse, deprivation, and loss, disintegrates and fragments herself in a desolate, incommunicable, and isolated world, exemplifying the stark truth in Scarry's statement. However, another case of violence appears in the novel through the letters written by the husband's lover, that function loudly as a voice of the unspeakable in Prudencia's life. These seven letters, interpolated in the narrative and addressed to her husband, appear after the middle of the book and explicitly depict the increasing cruelty and violence experienced by Prudencia's husband's lover. They describe chronologically the changes of the husband's behavior towards the lover, the development of the violence, and the response of his lover towards his abusiveness. In the first letter, we notice how the husband begins to control his lover by isolating her (91–92). The third letter presents the first battering incident and her lover's forgiveness (112). Other letters continue describing the extent of his violence and the terror that she experiences: "Ayer sentí terror cuando me escondí debajo de la mesa de la cocina. Estaba temblando, recordaba la última vez que me pegaste con el cinturón. Debajo de la mesa me tapé la cabeza como entonces, agachada me protegía con las rodillas y los brazos y era incapaz de gritar" [Yesterday I felt sheer terror when I hid underneath the kitchen table. I was shaking, remembering the last time you hit me with your belt. Under the table I covered my head like before, crouched down I protected myself with my knees and arms and I couldn't shout] (132). The openly described attacks on the other woman's body signify that which has been shut out of Prudencia's discourse. The protagonist is unable to articulate her husband's assaults in the same way as the lover does; only a few incidents are depicted in the narrative, which have been already previously mentioned.

In an interview, Dulce Chacón states that "en una carta es donde más libremente expresamos nuestros sentimientos. Una carta es una forma de expresión que nos permite ser impúdicos al mostrar lo que sentimos, sin temer al rubor. Quizá por eso, porque a mí me interesan los sentimientos, el género epistolar me permite que los personajes se muestren desde lo hondo" [in a letter is where we most freely express our emotions. A letter is a form of expression that allows us to openly show what we feel, without feeling ashamed. Perhaps that's why, because I'm interested in emotions, that the epistolary genre allows me to let the characters reveal themselves profoundly] (Villalba 142). In the letters, his lover opens up her wounds to reveal a discursive realm of aggression and fear that contrasts with the partially concealed discourse of Prudencia. The increasing violence, depicted in the letters, mirrors the protagonist's own reality, and provides an insight into the horrors of Prudencia's life; it is a repetition, an inevitable recurrence of what has happened to her. However, the lover, at the end of the narrative, is able to reject the violence in her life and escape from her abusive partner: "Todo tiene un final. [...] Me pediste tiempo y yo te di toda la vida. Todo lo hice por amor, te quise hasta ese punto, hasta éste. Ahora ya no. Voy a aprender a quererme de nuevo, lejos de ti, lejos" [Everything comes to an end. [...] You asked me for time and I gave you a lifetime. Everything I did, I did for love. I loved you that much, this much. Not any more. I am going to learn to love myself again, far from you, far] (146). The lover's ability to break free from a destructive relationship emphasizes Prudencia's failure and perhaps, more disturbingly, projecting to the reader a powerless self that exists only as an object defined and controlled by the husband. The juxtaposition of the two stories not only points out the gaps in the protagonist's narrative, i.e. her inability to voice her suffering, but also creates a sense of the extremity of Prudencia's experience and of her terrible isolation, conveying powerfully to the reader the intensity of her abuse.

Scarry explains that pain is difficult to express, unlike other feelings, such as love, fear, hatred and so on, since it does not have any referential content in the external world (35). However, the unspoken and unrepresentable manifest themselves by what Steven Marcus defines as the "deformed language of symptoms, the untranslated speech of the body" (196); through "a deformed language of symptoms," we can apprehend the physical and mental pain of Prudencia that leads to her suicide: "Pero no me des más pastillas, porque me hacen recordar tu vida, la mía. Y en medio de este sueño ya no sé cuál estoy perdiendo" [But don't give me any more pills, because they make me remember your life, mine. And in the middle of this sleepiness, I don't know anymore which I'm losing] (31). Prudencia's suicide becomes an injunction to silence. Furthermore, we encounter throughout the text "the untranslated speech" of a disintegrated self that splits and yearns for wholeness. Prudencia's split-self manifests through the interplay of several narrative voices. When the character uses the first person narrative voice, she portrays herself as a helpless woman with low self-esteem, withdrawn, lonely, passive and "prudent" (as her name points out) (49). The dramatized third person narrative voice allows Prudencia to disassociate and to observe the incidents from outside, as we have seen in the example when she explains her husband's rape. According to Lucía Llorente, this third person "se sale de sí misma para hacer un recorrido por su historia pasada en tercera persona, tratando de buscar una cierta objetividad" [steps out of herself to go on a journey through her past in third person, trying to find a certain objectivity] (1), and she concludes that "si Prudencia, en primera persona es 'la mujer física,' sacrificada, sometida a los deseos de su marido y su familia, dispuesta a excusar cualquier tipo de conducta por extraña que parezca, este narrador en tercera persona representa su desdoblamiento, su conciencia. Es la faceta de Prudencia que ve las cosas con distancia, con una cierta objetividad, y que, si predominara, podría sobrevivir" [if Prudencia, in first person is the "physical woman," sacrificed, subjected to the wishes of her husband and her family, ready to excuse any type of behavior for us strange as it may seem, this narrator in third person represents her splitting in two, her conscience. It is the aspect of Prudencia that sees things with distance, with a certain objectivity, and that, if it were to prevail, she could survive] (5).

On the other hand, with the pronoun "you" Prudencia dialogues with herself, criticizing her behavior while voicing her suffering: "Deberías haberte rebelado contra tu marido, no contra el mundo. Sí que hay sitio para ti, lo que pasa es que no lo has buscado..." [You should have rebelled against your husband, not against the world. Yes there is a place for you, but you haven't looked for it...] (75). The interplay between the first, second, and third person dramatizes Prudencia's divided self, yet simultaneously exposes and disguises her fears, and denies and asserts the subject in her search to find a language that expresses the terror she experiences and the physical assaults to her body. She exposes and disguises her fears by juxtaposing a critical second person narrative voice with a passive first person narrative voice. Against the passivity of the "yo" [I] that denies the subject, the third person voice searches to assert the self. By juxtaposing several narrative voices and an internalized narrative perspective to an externalized, almost objective, perspective, the narrative sets the reader on a psychological journey into Prudencia's life while she struggles to regain control of the self, and overcome her physical and psychological trauma. However, her efforts are unsuccessful. Despite this splitting and dissociation, she cannot protect herself from either her husband, who through objectification and assault strangulates her individuality, or from cultural inhibitions. The character keeps taking up provisional speaking positions in her futile efforts to yearn for wholeness and to obtain a voice to express her intense suffering.

The capacity that pain has to destroy the sufferer's language and its non-referentiality, makes it impossible to transform it, and hence, pain stays in the body. Consequently, the sufferer of physical pain reverts back to a prelinguistic state of incomprehensible wailing, inaudible whispering, inarticulate screeching, and primal murmuring, which destroys language and all that is associated with language: subjectivity, civilization, culture, meaning, and understanding (Sáez 137). Since pain resides in Prudencia's body, she reverts back to a pre-linguistic state of incoherent screaming, that we can hear through the gaps of the different narrative voices, from which Prudencia's "robbed" self returns to speak the unspeakable: the dreadful dilemmas faced by the battered woman trying to remain true to her own sense. Moreover, the text dissolves the dominant signifying practice of character representation, when it breaks the rational unity, which represents the ego as a unified and indivisible unit, and offers a refusal of the structures and language of cultural order. According to Allon White, "Corporal disintegrations is the verse of the constitution of the body during the mirror phase, and it occurs only at those times when the unified and transcendent ego is threatened with dissolution" (qtd. in Jackson 90). The linguistic order that promotes a language of unified and rational selves, a total body, disappears in *Algún amor que no mate*. The text erodes the supports of the symbolic order and in its rift opens the way to the imaginary through Prudencia's unintelligible and voiceless screaming that materializes from her corporal disintegration. Lacan places the imaginary in a stage that developmentally precedes language and dominates in the earliest stages of human life, the time of the infant-mother dyad that Freud labeled pre–Oedipal. During that stage, the child makes no differentiation between itself and the maternal body. The child's earliest identity comes from its identification with its own image in a mirror. As a result, the child enters the symbolic order where the ego becomes a social and psychical entity through the unrecognized effect of the image of its own body and the bodies of others (734–738). Kristeva calls "semiotic" the pre–Oedipal state of Lacan's imaginary. In this stage, the child experiences the rhythms, sensations and pulsations of the maternal body. The semiotic mode is repressed when the child enters the symbolic order and language, but is not forgotten. The suppressed energies appear in the language through rhythm, syntactic irregularities and linguistics distortions (125–147). In *Algún amor que no mate*, Prudencia is unable to speak her physical pain, but we hear her silent scream through the fissures of the narrative, opening its way to the semiotic of imaginary stage. Chacón, by inserting the nonexistent language of pain, removes the wraps of the symbolic order and challenges not only language, but the conventional structures of meaning. Prudencia's life story unfolds with digressive stories about herself and her past that break the chronological narrative order and mirror her fragmented self.

The psychiatrist R.D. Laing, in his book entitled *The Divided Self: An Existential Study in Sanity and Madness,* believes that some individuals placed in impossible situations suffer from "ontological insecurity" that can create psychotic behavior and a schizoid personality, which becomes an expression of their distress. He describes the "divided self" as:

> an individual the totality of whose experience is split in two main ways; [...] there is a rent in his relation with his world and ... a disruption of his relation with himself. Such a person is not able to experience himself "together with" others or "at home in" the world. [...] [Instead], he experiences himself in despairing aloneness and isolation; moreover, he does not experience himself as a complete person but rather as split [17].

He concludes that once the fragmentation into "true" and "false" selves happens, "the self is extremely aware of itself and observes the false self, usually highly critically" (74). Although, Prudencia does not have a schizoid personality — she is neither afraid of the world nor fears people —, the state of distress that she is placed in creates an "ontological insecurity" that leads to a divided self. She recognizes that her struggle is leading her to madness (126). For Prudencia the other — the "false" self — is like a mirror that becomes a trope to reflect inner-self discrepancies. The mirror provides another version of the self transformed into another, becoming something or someone else. Thus, the double permits Prudencia to distance herself from her weak personality that shows through her lack of will power required for change: "Prudencia, hija, qué mal lo has hecho todo. Y ahora ya no tiene remedio. Siempre quisiste cambiarte por alguien, y nunca supiste por quién. Pero contigo misma no has estado a gusto en la vida" [Prudencia, dear, how poorly you've done everything. And now there's no solution. You always wanted to be someone else, and you never knew who. But you've never been happy with yourself in your whole life] (52). In differencing herself from such unruly otherness, the protagonist seeks to regain some control over her disorderly self. However, Prudencia has to see her own image reflected in the mirror to establish a conscious self-recognition and to gain a sense of self. It does not happen. She is unable to see in the mirror her "real" self, instead she finds a distorted image in which contradictory sites juxtapose in the same reflection. While the pronoun "you" serves to distance herself to criticize Prudencia's behavior for her lack of will power to act, at other times the same pronoun encourages her to comply with society's rules: "Debiste hacer todo lo que él te dijera, que para eso te casaste, para ser una esposa sumisa" [You should have done everything he told you, that's why you got married, to be a submissive wife] (144–145). As a result, doubling and dividing does not become an exchanging experience that leads to insight and strength to change her life. Prudencia's highly critical and contradictory self furthers her submissiveness and reduces her already low self-esteem. The mirror image validates her position in the world, and as the classically abused spouse, Prudencia feels responsible for her husband's action and takes the guilt upon herself. The reflection that could have provided a fragile sustenance for the self in her attempt against her mental disintegration, becomes empty: "Demasiado te miraste, Prudencia, pero no te viste. Hay huecos que tenías que haber llenado tú misma, y otros que no se llenan nunca. Eso deberías haberlo sabido" [You looked at yourself too much, Prudencia, but you didn't see yourself. There are holes that you should've filled yourself, and others that never get filled. You should've known that] (99). Prudencia fails to distinguish within the specular self the masculine power structures that rule her life, what Hélène Cixous describes as, "the uncanny stranger on display — the ailing or dead figure, which so often turns out to be the nasty companion, the cause and locations of inhibitions" (250). Prudencia finds no rest in her reflection, and becomes a transient self unable to occupy a station in the social order other than her position of passivity, dependency and social conformity.

Prudencia's self vanishes through empty reflections, portraying the "absence" of woman's corporeality when becoming a reflection of the "masculine" self. Luce Irigaray in her first work, *Speculum, de l'autre femme*, considers that the flat lacanian mirror denies the existence of women, since it reflects only the order associated with masculine law. Instead, she presents a concave mirror, or speculum, which reflects the light inward with such force that it eliminates the masculine subject and restates female subjectivity. The speculum allows for women's position to see and be seen. Although Prudencia's rhetoric presents one message — a mirroring relation that leads to absence — the novel becomes like a concave mirror that restates women's corporeality. Chacón, by reflecting in the speculum the violent reality of the protagonist's life, transforms the character's subordination, invisibility and absence into affirmation and the divided self appears in its most radical and powerful form. As Prudencia dialogues with herself, observes herself, criticizes herself, or simply narrates the events of her life, disturbed feelings bounce back and forth, de-stabilizing her self, while at the same time opening her physical and emotional wounds to herself and to the reader. As she moves in and out between almost "objective" analysis and subjective position, moving easily in and out of pronouns, shifting from the personal I to the inclusive you, the text places the reader within the distorted mirror of the speculum. Moreover, the pronoun "you" becomes a direct invitation to identification with the character, positioning the reader as an intimate and privileged observer of Prudencia's wounds and drawing him/her into self-consciousness. Prudencia keeps us very close to her. We dialogue with her as she moves disconcertingly through her life, dissipating into darkness. This intimacy is based less on fusion or even identification than on proximity. As a result of the discrepancies, contradictions, and rifts that appear in the narrative, her wounds split open to reveal the inarticulate scream of pain and despair. Reading how she explains, watches, or criticizes her reactions, produces an emotional reaction within the reader towards the violence in the novel, and even though Prudencia's physical and psychic wounds still leave her powerless, the specular text renders corporeality and visibility to the body and encourages a continual rewriting of bodily identities. Janet Wolff has argued that reinstating corporeality is "based on a recognition of the social and discursive construction of the body, while emphasizing is lived experience and materiality" (138). With the reader's awareness, the corporeality of the body is reinstated and the lacanian mirror shatters.

Prudencia is unable to inhabit in a monadic voice. To assume one voice would reveal a speaker who knows, who assumes her own authority, and who interprets her life for the reader. She cannot do that because she cannot find a coherent point of departure; therefore, she keeps disappearing and affirming through the different speaking positions. No single speaking position is definitive or completely truthful.

Furthermore, instead of the story unfolding in a chronological narrative, the linear time-sense is displaced by another more abstract, where time is broken up, placed and displaced, moving forward and backward, reflecting Prudencia's contradictory and fragmented sense of herself. Linear time is constantly confused and unwound as the narrative voices create a sense of the synchronicity of past, present, and future that structurally reflects the narrator's inner division. The chronological movement is broken with digressive stories about her in-laws, letters from the husband's lover, anecdotes, dreams, flashbacks, and fast-forwards in her constant pursuit of establishing a coherent self. Rosemary Betterton says: "The stories we tell ourselves about who we are — the half-remembered events and places which shape our lives — are the foundations on which we build up a sense of self. Re-working what that already happened, we also give it current meaning, for history always represents the present as much as the past" (173). However, Carolyn Steedman explains that when we return to our memories and dreams again and again, "the story we tell of our own life is reshaped around them. But the point doesn't lie there, back in the past, back in the lost time when they happened; the only point lies in interpretation" (5). Remembering the past, the incidents, the dreams, and the places, can give shape and meaning to the events of one's life, but this depends on how we reinterpret them. Unfortunately, Prudencia only remembers her past when she is on her deathbed in the hospital. The reader finds out that she tried to commit suicide, almost at the beginning of the novel (30). Therefore, remembering and retelling the past, to reshape the present in order to make some sense of her life, does not happen and it cannot happen for the protagonist. Prudencia is dying in the hospital. When she recounts or recriminates to herself key events from her life, her past is framed by the present, in the hospital, and also by the future, her imminent death. She recognizes, "Ahora sé que vas a morir. Y tú lo sabes también. Por eso me distes las pastillas para que muriera contigo" [Now I know you're going to die. And you know it too. That's why you gave me the pills, so that I would die with you] (158). Remembering and reinterpreting do not only remedy the problems she suffers, in fact, they exacerbate these problems and further her agony. Her psychic pain is relived, and her desire to dissolve the boundary between life and death becomes stronger: "Qué hacer cuando sólo se desea morir. Prudencia deseaba morir. [...] Ella sólo quería morir. Morir de una sola vez" [What to do when you only want to die. Prudencia wanted to die. [...] She only wanted to die. Just die once and for all] (123). The trajectory of the narrative becomes a closed circle when finally Prudencia dies, underscoring the image of imprisonment that characterizes her life. Past, present, and future lock in a riveting discourse, at once revealing and concealing Prudencia's rifts between mind and body, self and other, love and despair, life and death.

Prudencia lives in the excluded world of the marginal throughout her married life. Totally removed from her family and her community, she becomes so drawn into herself that the outside world ceases to exist and she becomes more and more embryonic (40). Her feeling of grief is an accurate depiction of her existential state. The loss of her selfhood consumes her. She is inwardly tormented in body and mind, estranged from herself and from the world. At the heart of her self-perception and self-characterization, emerges in the protagonist a constant melancholia and despair that can be associated with depression. Alice Miller considers that "depression can be understood as a sign of the loss of the self and consists of a denial of one's own emotional reactions and feelings" (45). This mental disease can blur dangerously the boundaries of the self. When Prudencia takes the physical and psychological abuse without acting, the self disintegrates, and as a result, she turns aggression against herself, sinking into depression and, ultimately suicide. The clinical psychologist Yvette Flores-Ortiz states that women victimized by violence often internalize blame for the abuse and "punish" themselves, attacking what they perceive to be the cause: the body. The attacks on the self can take the form of self-denigration or hatred, physical maladies, depression "and the ultimate assault on the self: suicide" (351–52). In Prudencia's inability to react, she rejects her own body since it becomes a source of shame and alienation. The degree of rejection is revealed through her active quest for death. Her only power is to destroy herself.* She is living out her life as if she were already dead. As a result, she chooses finally to silence herself, but not before leaving a powerfully moving record of a woman in search of selfhood. She concludes in the last pages:

> He tenido que vivir con la compasión, como si fuera un vestido que llevara puesto por dentro y no me lo pudiera quitar. Ahora sé que vas a morir. Y tú lo sabes también. Por eso me diste las pastillas, para que muriera contigo. A mí no me importa. Si con eso logro no verte más. No ver nunca la amargura de tus ojos, siempre tristes, siempre. Estoy cansada. Deja que me desnude de ti. Déjame descansar. No quiero que me confundan contigo nunca más.
>
> [I had to live with compassion, as if I were a dress that I wore on the inside and couldn't take off. Now I know you're going to die. And you know it too. That's why you gave me the pills, so I would die with you. I don't care. If that's the way I manage to not see you anymore. Not see the bitterness in your eyes, always sad, always. I am tired. Let me undress myself of you. Let me rest. I don't want anyone to confuse me for you ever again.] [158].

The profound sense of alienation and despair that emerges through the narrative enacts a message, but it is not a plea for help or understanding. Suicide not only provides a solution to her painful life but also becomes a form of self-assertion, and paradoxically, an attempt of life affirmation, as it points out the importance of being true to oneself. This act of self-destruction, a radical violation of social and bodily boundaries, elicits a strong emotion in the reader. The beginning of the narrative points to death, to the impossibility of Prudencia to be herself. In a sense, suicide is an attempt to reclaim herself for herself. Her disappearance paradoxically gives her visibility. Even

---

*Labrador, Rincón, de Luis and Fernández consider that "La ideación suicida y el suicidio se explicarían en las mujeres maltratadas como la única alternativa que ven para terminar con la situación de inmenso sufrimiento que están viviendo, como la única estrategia de solución para su problema" [The formation of the idea of suicide and suicide could be explained in abused women as the only alternative that they see to end the situation of extreme suffering that they are living, as the only strategy of a solution to their problem] (72).

though she attains with her death a self that vanishes, her elusive shadow strongly remains in the reader's mind.*

Virginia Woolf in her essay on "Being Ill" written in 1930, points out, "Considering how common illness is, how tremendous the spiritual change that it brings, [...] it becomes strange indeed that illness has not taken its place with love and battle and jealousy among the prime themes of literature" (193). Disease in Chacón's novel takes an important place. It appears through the character's suffering, which leads to moods of dissolution, anxiety, despair, self-doubt, loneliness, alienation, and loss of identity. The sense of doom dominates and increases throughout the novel, as Prudencia emerges psychologically naked and plunges deeply into a melancholia leading to self-destruction. Battered women are coerced into this condition of depression, melancholia and abjection. While it cannot be denied, as Scarry elaborates, that pain eludes language, Chacón manages to articulate through Prudencia's wounded body her pain and the pain of battered women, at the same time censuring a society that allows this to happen. For the writer: "Conocer al enemigo es empezar a combatirlo. La literatura es una forma de mirar. Posee la capacidad de abrirnos los ojos, y de formularnos cuestiones que, por el mero hecho de ser formuladas, abren el camino hacia el campo de batalla. La palabra es un arma muy poderosa" [To know the enemy is to begin to conquer it. Literature is a way of looking. It has the ability to open our eyes, to formulate questions that, by the very act of being formulated, open the way towards the battlefield. The word is a very powerful weapon] (Villalba 142). *Algún amor que no mate* opens our eyes by tackling directly the ethical and moral questions raised by the reality of gender violence. Depression, self-destruction, and the death of Prudencia, work as signifiers for the unacknowledged, unrecorded and unresolved violence against women in our culture.

---

*Jeffrey Berman in his book *Surviving Literary Suicide* discusses reader-responses towards suicidal literature. He claims that few attempts have been made to discover how suicidal characters and themes affect the readers. After gathering data from students who took the course on literary suicide and colleagues who taught some of the texts analyzed in his book, he concludes, quoting Kafka's letter to Oskar Pollack: "'the books we need are the kind that act upon us like a misfortune, that make us suffer like the death of someone we love more than ourselves, that make us feel as though we were on the verge of suicide, or lost in a forest remote from all human habitation — a book should serve as the ax for the frozen sea within us' (Kafka 16). Literature has a transformative power, for good and for ill, and nowhere is this better seen than in suicidal literature, which records the roar that lies on the other side of silence" (261–62).

Works Cited

Berger, John. *Ways of Seeing.* New York: Penguin, 1977.
Berman, Jeffrey. *Surviving Literary Suicide.* Amherst: University of Massachusetts Press, 1999.
Betterton, Rosemary. *Intimate Distance. Women, Artists and the Body.* New York: Routledge, 1996.
Cixous, Hélène. "The Laugh of the Medusa." *New French Feminisms.* Ed. Elaine Marks and Isabelle de Courtivron. New York: Schocken, 1981. 245–264.
Cruz, Jacqueline. "Amores que matan: Dulce Chacón, Icíar Bollaín y la violencia de género." *Letras Hispanas: Revista de Literatura y Cultura* 2.1 (2005). 23 January 2006 <http://letrashispanas.unlv.edu/Vol/12/JacquelineCruz.htm>.
Chacón, Dulce. *Algún amor que no mate.* Barcelona: Planeta, 2002.
Davidson, Terry. *Conjugal Crime.* New York: Hawthorne, 1978.
Flores-Ortiz, Yvette. "Re/membering the Body. Latina Testimonies of Social and Family Violence." *Violence and the Body. Race, Gender and the State.* Ed. Arutoro J. Aldama. Bloomington: Indiana University Press, 2003. 347–359.
Friedan, Betty. *The Feminine Mystique.* New York: Dell, 1963.
Furman, Nellie. "The Politics of Language: Beyond the Gender Principle?" *Making a Difference; Feminist Literary Criticism.* Ed. Gayle Greene and Coppelia Kahan. New York: Methuen, 1985. 59–80.
Herrera-Sobek, María. "The Politics of Rape: Sexual Transgression in Chicana Fiction." *Beyond Portia. Women, Law & Literature in the United States.* Ed. Jacqueline St. Joan and Annette Bennington. Boston: Northeastern University Press, 1997. 216–225.
Homer, Marjorie, Anne Leonard, and Pat Taylor. "Personal Relationships: Help and Hidrance." *Marital Violence.* Ed. Norman Johnson. Boston: Routledge, 1985. 93–108.
Irigaray, Luce. *Speculum, de l'autre femme.* Paris: Minuit, 1974.
Jackson, Rosemary. *Fantasy: The Literature of Subversion.* New York: Routledge, 1986.
Kristeva, Julia. *Desire in Language. A Semiotic Approach to Literature and Art.* Ed. Leon S. Roudiez. Trans. Thomas Gora, Alice Jardine, and Leon S. Roudiez. New York: Columbia University Press, 1988.
Labrador, Francisco Javier, Paulina Paz Rincón, Pilar de Luis y Rocío Fernández-Velasco. *Mujeres víctimas de la violencia domestica. Programa de actuación.* Madrid: Piramide, 2004.
Lacan, Jacques. *Feminine Sexuality: Jacques Lacan and the école freudienne.* Ed. Juliet Mitchell and Jacqueline Rose. New York: Norton, 1985. 733–738.
———. "The Mirror Stage as Formative of the Function of the I as Revealed in Psychoanalytic Experience." *Critical Theory Since 1965.* Ed. Hazard Adams and Leroy Searle. Tallahassee: Florida State University Press, 1989.
Laing, R.D. *The Divided Self: An Existential Study in Sanity and Madness.* England: Penguin, 1965.
Llorente, Lucía. "Voces narrativas en *Algún amor que no mate.*" 57th Kentucky Foreign Language Conference, University of Kentucky, Lexington. 15–17 April 2004.
Lorente Acosta, Miguel, and José Antonio Lorente Acosta. *Agresión a la mujer: maltrato, violación y acoso.* Granada: Comares, 1998.
Marcus, Steven. "Freud and Dora: Story, History, Case History." *Freud: A Collection of Critical Essays.* New Jersey: Prentice-Hall, 1981. 183–210.
Merleau-Ponty, Maurice. *Phenomenology of Perception.* 1945. Trans. Colin Smith. New York: Routledge, 1962.
Miller, Alice. *Prisoners of Childhood.* Trans. Ruth Ward. New York: Basic Books, 1988.

Mulvey, Laura. *Visual and Other Pleasures*. Bloomington: Indiana University Press, 1989.
Pratt, Annis. *Archetypal Patterns in Women's Fiction*. Bloomington: Indiana University Press, 1981.
Rose, Jacqueline. "Introduction — II." *Feminine Sexuality: Jacques Lacan and the école freudienne*. Ed. Juliet Mitchell and Jacqueline Rose. New York: Norton, 1985. 27–57.
Sa'ez, Nacuñan. "Torture: a Discourse on Practice." *Tattoo, Torture, Mutilation and Adornment: The Denaturalization of the Body in Culture and Text*. Ed. F.E. Mascia-Lees and P. Sharpe. Albany: University of New York Press, 1992. 126–144.
Scarry, Elaine. *The Body in Pain: The Making and Unmaking of the World*. Oxford: Oxford University Press, 1985.
Steedman, Carolyn. *Landscape for a Good Woman: A Story of Two Lives*. London: Virago, 1986.
Villalba Álvarez, Marina. *Narrativa española a finales del siglo XX. 62 escritoras de actualidad*. Badajoz: Abecedario, 2005.
Walker, Leonore E. *The Battered Women's Syndrome*. New York: Springer, 1984.
Wolff, Janet. *Feminine Sentences*. Cambridge: Polity Press, 1990.
Woolf, Virginia. *A Room of One's Own and Three Guineas*. Ed. Morag Shiach. World's Classics. Oxford: Oxford University Press, 1992.
_____. "On Being Ill." *Collected Essays*. Vol. 4. Ed. Leonard Woolf. London: Hogarth Press, 1966–67.

Female Characters in the Novels of Clara Sánchez: Reflection and Mirage

Mary Ann Dellinger

Clara Sánchez was born in 1955 on the cusp of Spain's debut into the 20th century international community and, by chronological fate, into a unique generation of Spanish women who would be raised in the shadows of the *Sección Femenina** yet principally define the new role of women in a post–Franco Spain. They represent, in sorts, the first generation of Spain's 21st century; women whose visibility in societal spheres has transcended the millenary paradigms of feminine space and gender roles.

Until the end of the Franco dictatorship (1939–1975), except during the brief historical parentheses of the Second Spanish Republic (1931–1936), women's role in Spain remained subject to a static patriarchal model of binary opposites: man/woman, exterior/interior, public/private, intellectual/emotional. Voice and visibility pertained to man's domain: in the workplace, the university, and public gathering places. Clearly delineated females spaces included the home and those directly related to homemaking, such as shops, public laundry facilities, or the seamstress's workshop Mothers served as the role model for their daughters for generations within these spaces, making a daughter's life the continuation of her mother's and so successively throughout the centuries.

---

*The *Sección Femenina* was the women's section of the Phalange, the Spanish fascist party headed by Francisco Franco.

During the 1960s era of the "economic miracle" (Graham 971),* however, the hordes of tourists into the Spain (DOS), together with the experience of Spanish immigrants beyond the Pyrenees (Risi), exposed Spanish women to a very different image of woman, and they clearly took note. Indeed, perhaps the only phenomenon more astonishing than Spain's rapid and virtually seamless transition to democracy (Bruneau 5) has been the redefinition and visibility of women within Spanish society (UWE).

Traditionally the mother-daughter relationship in Spain developed within domestic spaces, where young women learned about home economics, child care, home nursing: "all the activities that women engage in to advance the success of their households" (Kelley 200). Mothers kept vigil over the maidens' purity, mindful of ubiquitous warnings relayed in such publications as *Higiene sexual expuesta a los adultos ilustrados*, by Dr. Antonio Box M. Cospedal (1948) who states: "El himen representa para la mujer un triunfo sobre la tentación, y un orgullo para el hombre poseedor" [A woman's hymen represents her triumph over temptation and the pride of the man who possesses it] (quot. by Otero, *Española* 166).

In today's Spain, where women's visibility in society is perhaps best symbolized by an all female presidential cabinet, the mother-daughter relationship extends far beyond family recipes, the abnegation of motherhood, and the from-birth preparation of a trousseau, and it was the women of Clara Sánchez's generation who first guided their daughters into the new society that lay beyond the front door. Women's image, imposed by the Spanish patriarchy and best portrayed in the Manichean Eve/Virgin Mary iconicity of Christianity (Dellinger 33), has been recast by woman herself within spaces previously inaccessible to her.

The present study examines the female characters in three of Sánchez's novels: *Desde el mirador* (1996), *Últimas noticias del paraíso* (2000), and *Un millón de luces* (2004) from psychological perspectives of image/self-image and the physical concepts of reflection and mirage. Critical studies on women protagonists in the Spanish novel written by women, along with psycho-sociological analyses of identity, provide the theoretical framework for this essay that traces the trajectory of Clara Sánchez as a novelist and the portrayal of Spanish women in her work to show how Sánchez uses her writing to unveil

---

*Spain experienced an economic boom in the 1960s thanks to tourism and the thousands of emigrants employed in Northern Europe who not only created a better job market nationally, but helped to boost the economy through the money they wired home. The Franco government quickly coined the term "economic miracle" crediting the *Generalísimo* for the new-found prosperity.

the face of her generation and their legacy by revealing not only her perception of their collective self-image, personal frustrations, and common tribulations, but more importantly the re-defined dynamics of woman's inter/cross-generational relationships in a society that has so dramatically changed over the course of her lifetime.

Clara Sánchez's generation grew up during the more forgiving second half of the Franco dictatorship, ushered in by the 1953 signing of the Pact of Madrid between President Eisenhower and General Franco and the end of the brutal post–Civil War period referred to as the *primer franquismo* (1936–1952). Two years later the United Nations admitted Spain to the world organization and Franco finally received unilateral recognition as the Spanish Head of State, confirming that a new era had, indeed, begun.

The *segundo franquismo* (1952–1975), sometimes euphemistically called the *dictablanda*,* would bring significant changes not only to the political situation of the nation, but more importantly to day-to-day life. Pressure from the international community, especially the United States, as far as the regime's blatant disrespect for human rights resulted in a more lenient censorship of the press and the arts, greater mobility for Spaniards and non-Spaniards in and out of Spain, and greater consideration — albeit limited — as far as the individual rights of Spanish citizens.

Daily life did not change quickly or even notably for women, however, until well into the 1960s. The 19th century concept of woman as the "*ángel del hogar*" [angel of the home] continued to define woman's role as it had always done, and the teachings of the *Sección Femenina* persisted in reminding young women that:

> El destino de la mujer es ser esposa y compañera del hombre, formar con él una familia y educar y cuidar bien a sus hijos. El lugar donde la mujer desarrolla sus actividades es la casa, porque allí vive la familia.
>
> [Women's destiny is to be man's wife and companion, to form a family, and to nurture her children. Women's place of work is the home because it is there where the family lives.] [*1957 Enciclopedia Elemental*, quot. by Otero, *Sección Femenina* 183].†

Those women employed outside the home worked in jobs centered on caregiving, primarily nursing, teaching (elementary and preschool), or sewing, although by end of the 1960s considerably larger numbers of single women had begun to enter the work force in more diverse trades and professions.

---

*Dictablanda is a play on words derived from the Spanish word for dictatorship: *dictadura*. The Spanish adjective *dura* means hard or unyielding; *blanda* is its antonym.

The ultimate goal of woman, however, awaited her at the altar. A woman's success was measured by the way her family looked, her meticulous attention to their clothes, the neatness of her home and her physical appearance. Likewise, a man's reputation within society hinged on her morality and the image projected through the observable success in her feminine roles of wife, housekeeper, and mother. In 1968, while American women were publicly burning their bras and their European counterparts beyond the Pyrenees were devouring *The Feminine Mystique*, Spanish girls learned:

> Cuando estéis casadas, pondréis en la tarjeta vuestro nombre propio, vuestro primer apellido y después la partícula "de," seguida del apellido de vuestro marido. Así: Carmen García de Marín. En España se dice señora de Durán o de Peláez. Esta formula es agradable, puesto que no perdemos la personalidad, sino que somos Carmen García, que pertenece al señor Marín, o sea, Carmen García de Marín.
>
> [When you are married, you will write your name, your first last name followed by "*de*" and your husband's last name; for example, Carmen García de Marín. In Spain we say *señora* of Durán or of Peláez. This is an agreeable formula because we don't lose our own personality, but rather we remain Carmen García who belongs to Mr. Marín. We are, therefore, Carmen García of Marín.] [*Economía doméstica* quoted by Ortiz, *Sección Femenina* 183].

Feeble attempts such as these to create a Spanish brand of feminism failed dismally at keeping women in their traditional roles or at least stuck in the chasm of the epistemological rupture within the established social order. The growing number of Spanish women in the universities, the more widespread and certainly public opposition to the Franco regime, and the writings of French feminists of the late 1960s and early 1970s would be contributing factors in forming a new feminine psyche. It came as a surprise after Franco's death, especially for Spanish men, when women moved to the forefront of Spanish political and culture life where they have remained ever since.

The image of self in Spanish novels written by women between 1955 and 1996, reflect the paradigm shifts in women's roles, affected in part by the feminist macro culture worldwide, but most importantly by European and American societal models. As in real life, however, fictional representations of the changing self/collective image of the *española* as perceived by women writers would evolve slowly, albeit traceably.

In the introduction of her book, "*The Strange Girl" in Twentieth Century Spanish Novels Written by Women*, Ellen Mayock observes:

> Whether consciously or not, Spanish women writers of the post–War and post–Franco periods are culturally conditioned by [...] anti-feminist ide-

ologies [such as the *Sección Femenina*]. Their narratives therefore respond always directly or indirectly to the declaration that the creative realm is reserved for men (20).

The creative response — rebellion as the case may be — is embodied in the protagonist of the Spanish novel written by Spanish women during the Franco era, who the novelist Carmen Martín Gaite identifies as *la chica rara*— the "strange girl" (quot. by Mayock 21). The *chica rara*, notes Mayock, mature into the "strange woman" (*mujer rara*), during the Post-Franco period, although not totally replacing her younger version (221). The "strange girl/woman" dares to overstep the physical boundaries of feminine space into the "life of the street. Her actions demythify typical feminine stories of the past, her physical appearance takes on a secondary or non-existent role, she eschews flirting and very self-consciously examines her own 'interior' spaces" (21).*

Much like mirror images projected in fun houses, the *chica rara* and the mature *mujer rara* represent a distorted image of the traditional Spanish woman. The distinctive feminine characteristics reflected in the mirror remain the same, but her image appears warped or deformed as per the model imposed by the patriarchy and assumed with little resistance by Spanish women throughout the centuries.

These protagonists, "strange" in their image as transgressors of male spaces and societal roles, have little in common with the women portrayed in Clara Sánchez's three novels who transcend both the millenary paradigm of the Spanish woman and that of the "strange girl/woman." These women move in new architectural spaces, such as the *urbanizaciones* (gated communities), the *Híper* (big box store), and skyscrapers on Madrid's elegant *Castellana* boulevard. Unlike the street the "strange girl/woman" had to command for herself, these generic spaces are not defined by gender†, but rather reflect the expansion of socioeconomic classes within contemporary Spanish society.

The female characters in Sánchez's three novels, *Desde el mirador*, *Últimas noticias del paraíso*, and *Un millón de luces*, reflect different stages in the re-formation of women's collective identity in Spain as Spanish women

---

*While "the strange girl" is a pivotal idea in her study, Mayock underscores the many different faces and sexualities of "strangeness" and "interior spaces" as it is manifested in women's writing during the Post-War and Post-Franco periods as well as a discussion of contemporary works.

†By saying that these spaces are not gender-specific, I do not suggest that women necessarily share the same prestige or privileges within them. I refer only to access.

moved from traditional social paradigms to modernity, and finally to postmodernity, neither of which evolved casually or by chance.

> Collective identity is not naturally generated but socially constructed: it is the intentional or non-intentional consequence of interactions, which in their turn are socially patterned and structured. [... they are] images of similarity and dissimilarity constructed by human beings as they interact. [Roninger and Herzog quot. by Bill Richardson 47].

Thus progressing from the very private space of the mother-daughter relationship within domestic spaces in which a woman's self-image is a reflection of her mother's — as defined by Spanish millenary tradition — to the public sphere of the workplace and through the interactions of her characters among themselves and in relation to others, male and female, Sánchez reflects the process by which the identity of today's post-modern Spanish woman has evolved. All three novels are first-person narrations, each encompassing different and progressive stages of this evolutionary process from private to public spaces, traditionally considered masculine domain.

Desde el mirador, the most introspective of the three novels, centers on the illness and consequent hospitalization of the narrator/protagonist's mother over the course of four seasons, which she observes from a glass window —*el mirador*— at the end of the hospital hallway. But the novel is really about the narrator herself as she deals not only with her mother's affliction, but her own identity by coming to terms with the relationships closest to her and the mother-daughter bond, in her dual role as her mother's daughter and her daughter's mother.

The teenage male protagonist of *Últimas noticias del paraíso*, Fran, narrates his own story in this *Bildungsroman* set within the societal framework of *pasismo*, the term popularly used to describe the ubiquitous pessimism and malaise of Spanish youth caused by the worsened socio-political situation of the nineties and the overall disillusionment with the Socialist government (1982–1996) of Felipe González (David Knutson 91–92). Nonetheless, as Knutson notes in his analysis of *Últimas noticias*, Sánchez de-emphasizes violence, drugs and sex associated with *pasismo*, thus ensuring Fran more meaningful relationships with those whose lives cross with his (94). These characters include the key female figures in Fran's life: his mother, his best friend's sister, Tania, and Yu, the woman he follows to the end of his world.

The writer never fully develops the female characters in *Últimas noticias*, however, which along with male narrator/protagonist makes the novel particularly interesting in terms of female identity; but only within the context of the three novels. It is not the fact that she chooses a teenage male to narrate the story, but that she doesn't choose a female voice as she does in the other two novels. Nor is it important that the only developed character is Fran, but rather that she avoids development of the female characters in *Últimas noticias*.

The diametrical opposite occurs in the third novel. Sánchez returns to the first-person woman narrator/protagonist in her latest novel, *Un millón de luces*, in which many women's stories unfold and intertwine within the multi-story glass walls of the glass tower, the skyscraper/office building of the company for which the protagonist works. Although Sánchez touches on different maternal issues — including infertility and single parenthood — the mother/child dynamic is just one of many different personal and social relationships among women she explores in the novel. These are today's women in a European Spain; women who interact and react within a more complex and dynamic society symbolized architecturally by the postmodern structure of her *torre de cristal*.

As previously stated, the reality of Sánchez's characters has little in common with that of their "strange" predecessors, much less the traditional Spanish woman of 19th and early 20th century novels. By the same token, the dynamics between the principal female characters in *Mirador*— mother, daughter, and best friend — differ considerably from those in *Luces*, who are all co-workers or partners/lovers of co-workers, while the cast of women in *Noticias* either do not interact with one another at all or interact only through Fran. Their role in the narrative therefore is limited, especially in comparison with the female characters in the other two novels.

Reflection in *Mirador* is contemplation, as the protagonist struggles to define herself only for herself within the context of family and in juxtaposition to her best friend, Cati, whose life represents the antithesis of her own, while in *Noticias,* Sánchez stands back to observe women from a third-person perspective, as if she were still negotiating the meaning of women's new collective identity at the turn of Spain's 21st century. The image of woman is only mirage, an undefined "maybe" on the horizon of what might be or is possibly not. A definable image of the postmodern Spanish woman does not emerge until *Luces,* manifested through Sánchez's confident exploration of self-cognition and interaction between women in the formation of a collective identity and psyche. From *Mirador* to *Luces,* the image of woman progresses from self-perception to mirage — deflection of woman's image — to reflection of the new Spanish woman in her multiple roles in a postmodern society. Sánchez projects, re-evaluates, and reveals an ever-changing collective identity through reflection and mirage.

Life has taken one of its characteristic turning points for the narrator/protagonist in *Desde el Mirador* when the narration begins. She has turned forty, her mother has just recovered from a long and critical illness, her daughter has matured, her best friend has committed suicide, and she and her husband have gone their separate ways. Sánchez weaves in and out of temporal spaces past and present through flashbacks and flash-forward, as her protagonist scrutinizes the choices she has made in life and, more importantly, those she did not. She agonizes about imminent shifts in her reality, watching the seasons turn from the look-out window at the end of the hospital hall where her mother fights for her life, and realizes after a few months that she, for the first time in her life, is in the throes of a mid-life identity crisis:

> Todavía no había entrado en la vida en su "sentido más profundo" ni estas palabras significaban nada. No podía saber si esa profundidad de verdad existía. Porque no existe hasta que no toca el cuerpo.
> [I hadn't yet entered into life as far as its "deepest meaning," nor did these words mean anything. I couldn't know if that so-called depth even existed. Because it doesn't exist until your body can feel it.] [113].

The sudden rupture of her routine, marked by train trips to and from the hospital and the endless hours waiting in the hallway serve as a catalyst for the existential odyssey that she undertakes in which she comes to terms with her changing role identities and the emergence of a new conception of self.

Psychologists define role identities as designations we give to ourselves based on our interactions with others and our roles in relationship to other individuals in our lives. Michael Hogg et al explain:

> Role identities provide meaning for self, not only because they refer to concrete role specifications, but also because they distinguish roles from complementary or counterroles. For example, the role of mother takes on meaning in connection with the role of father, "doctor" in connection with "nurse" and so on. Ultimately it is through social interaction that identities actually acquire self-meaning; they are reflexive [...] [256–57].

Up to the point where her mother falls ill, the protagonist's role identities have defined her as daughter, wife, mother, and office worker, always in relation to the other people in her life. Then suddenly her life is turned upside down. Her spouse, Mario, has left, leaving her without husband to her wife. Her teenage daughter no longer depends on her — no child to her mother — and with the distinct possibility of no mother to her daughter, she feels she needs to remake herself within the context of a definitive "philosophy of life" (120).

Her self-exploration begins with her mother, which in turn leads her to the re-evaluation of her relationship with her own daughter and the contingent role as wife/partner. Thinking that perhaps she may find her "philosophy of life" in her mother's example, she reminisces about her idyllic childhood, only to realize that her progenitor's self-definition stemmed solely from her role as mother:

> Cuántas veces he oído a mi padre gritarle: "¡Disfruta!." Y cuántas veces la he visto a ella mirarle sin poder disfrutar, porque lo que había afuera, nosotros [sus hijos], estábamos en su cabeza no simplemente como éramos en ese instante, sino con nuestras enfermedades pasadas y nuestros problemas y con toda una gran incógnita de futuro y también estaba ella que no miraba con todo su pasado, con todo lo que ya había visto y padecido. No podía disfrutar si su pensamiento no se lo consentía.
> [How many times have heard my father yell at her: "Enjoy yourself"! And how many times I have seen her look at him without being able to enjoy herself, because of what was going on around her, us [her children], we were in her head not only as we were at that moment, but all our past illnesses and our problems and the great unknown that was the future, and she was also there with her own past, with all she had seen and suffered. She could not enjoy herself if her thoughts did not allow it.]
> [145–46].

It soon becomes clear to the reader and the narrator herself that her mother had led the archetypical life of the traditional Spanish woman, in which everything was more important than she and suffering was woman's lot. Hoping to receive guidance and comfort, the protagonist tries several times to explain her marital problems to her mother, but to no avail: "Y mi madre me susurró casi al oído: 'Hay que aguantar mucho en esta vida. Y siempre se puede aguantar un poco más'" [You have to put up with a lot in this life. And you can always put up with a bit more] (18). Abnegation and woman are synonyms in the lexicon of the Spanish patriarchy; the protagonist's mother sees herself only in her children as had her mother, and her grandmother before, and so on through the generations of the Spanish millennia. The protagonist's inner conflict—her identity crisis—is both the aspiration and the fear to change the course of her own destiny according to her own needs and desires, beyond or in addition to the daughter-wife-mother roles of the generations before her.

Mothers and daughters remain nameless in *Mirador,* in contrast to the protagonist's husband, Mario, and her best friend, Cati, the only two persons who the protagonist believes have any real sense of what life is all about. Both resist routine, repelled by responsibilities and what they see as mundane obligations, such as full-time jobs and domesticity. The protagonist sees them as free spirits, people whose lives she should perhaps emulate in order to give meaning to her own. She explains her admiration for them:

> Me atraía la gente así y siempre acababa relacionada con ella. Gente que tendía a vivir una historia más que una vida, con esa inclinación de la historia por interesar a los demás, en tanto que la vida no le interesa más que a uno mismo y en este sentido ninguna vida vale más que otra.
>
> [I was attracted to people like that and I always ended up in a relationship with them. People who live a story instead of a life, because a story is more interesting to others and a life is only interesting to the person living it, making no one's life any more valid than another's.] [42].

The protagonist's angst is characterized by the *vida/historia* [life/story] binary she has formed in her mind and to which she makes constant reference when comparing her own existence to that of Cati or Mario. She views their lives as a story—*una historia*—guided by a "philosophy of life," which basically consists of doing what they want, where they want, and when they want. She, to the contrary, does what she is supposed to do. Her existence consists of a repetitive cycle of actions, day in, day out, week in, week out, year in year out. Life's obligations, not a definable personal philosophy, mandate her existence and restrain her from creating her own life story, similar to those she believes others around her enjoy.

Cati's *carpe diem* "philosophy of life" seems to especially gnaw at the narrator's self-consciousness, as her narration flashes back to their summer trip to the beach, discussions of motherhood, and their job experiences. But even memories are extraneous to Cati's philosophy of life, to her "story," constantly in fluctuation and revision. She reminds the protagonist about the months they worked together in the same office: "este tiempo, el transcurrido allí, no contaba y no existía" [the time passed there neither counted nor existed] (71) and insists that her friend only finds happiness in enslaving herself to her circumstances (178).

The final flashback takes the reader to Cati's suicide, as unexpected by the reader as to the protagonist herself. Jolted by the end of Cati's "story," the narrator experiences an epiphany about her own existential struggle:

> No me pregunto qué le habrá ocurrido. Cierro los oídos a las palabras que atraviesan la habitación y los abro hacia dentro, hacia el paraíso de la mente donde permanece todo lo bueno presente, pasado y futuro. Allí había quedado la transparencia de una mañana pasada y también por llegar que entra en los pulmones y me lava los ojos. Los cierro un instante.
>
> [I don't wonder about what had happened to her. I close my ears to the words crossing the room and I open them inwards, towards the paradise

of the mind where all the present, past, and future good remains. The transparency of a morning past and that of one yet to come enters in my lungs and cleanses my eyes. I close them for an instant.] [220].

The resolution of forty-year old narrator/protagonist identity crisis comes as no surprise, however; we have known of her recovery since page twenty. The unfolding of the story has traced the process, but never quite made sense until Cati's suicide and the protagonist's ensuing epiphany. It is only then when the reader can completely comprehend the protagonist's conclusions, stated at the beginning of the novel: "Estoy segura de que uno de los mayores riesgos psicológicos y emocionales que corremos los seres humanos consiste en mezclar nuestra persona con otra persona y entrar así en la extraña dimensión" [I am sure that one of the greatest psychological and emotional risks human beings face consist in confusing our own persona with that of another, entering thereby in a strange dimension] (20).

This "strange dimension" seemingly refers to the identity crisis the narrator has suffered. From it she has learned she is a person for whom routine is a "philosophy of life." More importantly, she realizes that the roles she plays while carrying out the various activities in relationship to others in her life that make her who she is: this is her identity, different than anyone else's and unique in its own right. Self-definition does not necessarily depend on gender roles or biological definition, but the way the individual conceives him/herself; hence, her use of "seres humanos" [human beings] instead of "men" or "women."

The forty-year old protagonist in *Desde el mirador* could be Clara Sánchez or any woman of her age, if it were not for chronotope of the Spanish Civil War. The narrator's mother, she tells us, was three years old when the war began (1936) and lived in fear for three years—until the end of the war. This reference not only sets the novel in Spain, establishing the ages of the characters, but serves as a generational marker. It distinguishes the mother's generation, children of the Spanish Civil War (85) who would not live in a free nation until late in life. It also establishes the protagonist as a member of the Sánchez's in-between generation of women—born during the Franco era, but coming of age after his death—the first generation of Spanish women who would take the first step beyond the threshold, while not quite daring to plant both feet beyond the front door. Although Cati might be considered a "strange girl" according to Martin Gaite's description because "her desires are not those of the girls and women who surround her" (Mayock 21), but Sánchez neither makes the "strange girl" her protagonist nor does she resolve her issues as she does those of her narrator. Thus she initiates Spanish woman's journey from the traditional to modernity and ultimately to post-modernity.

In *Desde el mirador*, Sánchez projects woman's self-image in the intimacy of her own conscience, asking first "Who am I?" before addressing the issue of a collective identity or determining her place within a public community. This image becomes mirage in *Últimas noticias del paraíso* where Clara Sánchez goes beyond the intimacy of the mother-daughter bond to other cross-generic relationships straddling domestic and public spaces.

Mirage is not the reflection of an image, but rather an optical effect caused by bending or reflection of rays that make distant objects seem inverted (Merriam-Webster), "distorted" or "wavering," "displaced from its true position" (Heidorn). Much like a mirage, the women in *Últimas noticias del paraíso* seem displaced, their image redirected from their development to Fran, the novel's protagonist-narrator. This is not to say that they play a trivial role in the story; to the contrary, the plot develops through the interactions between Fran and the female characters, the most important being his mother.

As is the case in *Desde el mirador*, Sánchez gives no name to the maternal character, both are *Jedenfrauen* of their particular generation. But in *Últimas noticias,* she forms a clear image in the reader's mind of the mother through Fran's detailed descriptions of this suburban housewife who shares her life with her only child, a husband who is out-of-town most of the time, and her friendship with the cleaning lady. She enjoys the benefits her middle-class life affords her and as her son becomes a teenager and her husband's absences increase, she even dares to step out, having an affair with her aerobics teacher — Míster Piernas, as Fran calls him.

Their affair does not last, however, nor does the domestic bliss of suburban life financed by the absent money-maker. Fran's father ultimately files for a divorce, and his wife returns to her former job as a dentist's assistant in order to maintain the lifestyle she and her son had always enjoyed. Her early exit from their home on her first day back at work marks a turning-point in Fran's life, an imposed coming of age, far earlier than he had expected or wanted: "Con ella se alejaba toda la rutina de una vida. Se alejaba mi niñez, mi adolescencia, lo que se me había dado sin que lo pidiera. Me encontraba muy deprimido" [With her went the routine of my whole life, my childhood, my adolescence, all that I was given without having asked for it. I felt very depressed] (131).

Like her son, Fran's mother finds the situation unbearable and decides to marry her dentist/employer in order to return to her financial worry-free life. Marriage, she decides, will allow her to quit her job and Fran his at a local video rental shop. She explains: "Porque no tengo otra cosa que hacer. Ésa es la realidad. Me paso casi todo el día en esa consulta. Qué más me da casarme con él" [Because there isn't anything else for me to do. That's the reality. I spend my whole day in that office. Why not just marry him?] (190).

Like a mirage, the liberated woman initially projected in the person of Fran's mother is a misplaced, distorted, inverted image of Spanish woman who, according to the patriarchal architype, should be married and at home. She does not contest the divorce and willingly returns to the workplace, determined to take-over all responsibility as the head of the family. But she is not a risk-taker. She goes back to her job as a dental assistant because it is familiar, and when the pay does not afford them the lifestyle she and Fran had come to expect, she chooses the only sure-thing option she believes remains: marriage.

Fran's mother avoids a loveless second marriage, however, when her son unexpectedly comes into a huge inheritance from a neighbor. This money allows him to buy her an expensive flat overlooking Madrid's Retiro Park and to hire the cleaning lady as a full-time employee to take care of the home and his mother as he leaves for China to start a new life with his exotic lover, Yu.

The third female character of importance as far as the plot development and also relevant to Fran's romantic life is Edu's sister, Tania. Fran recounts how a boyhood crush has turned into sexual yearning with the coming of adolescence, although nothing beyond a trusting friendship ever comes of their relationship. As a teenager, Tania plans for a new independent life in the city, but this, too, is just a mirage. After her marriage to the Mexican gangster, she disappears from the story, making short entrances and exits throughout the rest of the novel. But Sánchez never defines her character, shrouding her in mystery, as she does Yu, and Edu's mother, who also appears sporadically throughout the novel. She does not provide enough information about these women to invoke an image of them, collectively or individually, in the reader's mind.

Who is this emotionally and physically weak woman, wife of the veterinarian, mother of Edu and Tania? Who is the adult Tania? Who is Yu? These are the questions Sánchez leaves her readers asking themselves, even at the conclusion of her novel. We know her female characters only through their relationship with Fran, and even then, their image constantly morphs into another or into oblivion as Fran matures and his world expands from the suburbs, to the city, and finally to China. They are distorted images, deflected against the backdrop of a post–Franco Spain, illusive images of a new, yet still undefined Spanish womanhood.

Collective identity and women's multiple roles simultaneously played in domestic and public spaces remain undefined in *Noticias*, in which the writer has begun to break woman loose from the centuries-old three-faceted identity of daughter-wife-mother, but stops of re-defining her within the context of a new postmodern society. Woman's image remains a mirage, something "illusionary," perhaps even "unattainable" (Merriam-Webster). Sánchez does not delineate the new roles in interaction with the old in the formation of a new female identity — p erhaps because she has not yet defined them in her own mind — but rather forces her readers to fill in the gaps both within Fran's story and extratextually, consequently piecing together for themselves an image of the contemporary Spanish woman, an image which Sánchez clearly defines in her latest novel: *Un millón de luces*.

The first-person female narration of *Un millón de luces*, tells a story not unlike that of *Mirador* in its revelation of one woman's exploration of self-identity. This time, however, Sánchez distances her protagonist/narrator from the immediate family, removing her from domestic spaces and placing her within the very public sphere of a large corporation housed in its company-owned skyscraper. The protagonist herself establishes her break-up with a long-time live-in boyfriend as the beginning point for her story: "Todo comenzó cuando Raúl y yo nos separamos tras ocho años de convivencia" [Everything began when Raúl and I separated after eight years of living together] (10).

The author disassociates her protagonist from any relationships at the onset of the narration; she stands alone or — better said — she enters alone through the revolving doors of the glass tower; all former associations remain in her unrevealed past. We learn little about her family, especially her mother. In fact, very early on in the novel, the reader surmises that maternity will remain a marginal issue as far as the protagonist/narrator is concerned: "Vértigo y seguridad al mismo tiempo. Más o menos ésta ha sido siempre la sensación que me inspiraba mi madre y la maternidad en general" [Vertigo and security at the same time. This has always been more or less the sensation inspired by my mother and maternity in general] (17). Unpleasant childhood memories, we later find out, revolve around her mother, but her mother was not the perpetrator in these incidents, and the reader easily discerns that these recollections do not plague the character as ongoing psychological issues of this type might cause in others. She describes the "three most disgusting women" she remembers: the first, a teacher who asked her if the woman with the loud voice was her mother; the second, a doctor whose carelessness almost killed her mother; and the third, a babysitter who played with her by making her suck on her nipples, adding: "He conocido a unas cuantas más, que en el fondo son versiones de las anteriores" [I have known a few others, but they are basically different versions of these three] (51).

This description serves as the final description of past events centered on protagonist's mother, emphasizing the security of the mother/daughter relationship already stated (17), from which the protagonist has been able to separate in a healthy, non-traumatic manner. She honestly notes her mother's shortcomings — her loud voice. She recognizes that she might have lost her mother through a doctor's negligence, but doesn't dwell on the incident. There is no blame for her mother hiring a babysitter who sexually abused her. Vernacularly commented, she "has moved on."

Mark W. Baldwin and John G. Holmes state that "Individuals process self-relevant information according to patterns established in the context of significant relationships" (1096). Obviously, the most universally significant relationships are affective ties fostered by family in childhood and romance in later life, but Sánchez avoids descriptions of her protagonist's familial bonds and romantic liaisons, concentrating on her inter-office relationships with both men and women — all professional and/or platonic. She does not discount mother/daughter relationships, maternity, or childhood memories, but rather marginalizes them within the plot.

Establishing her protagonist as both the narrator and narrative focal point, Sánchez weaves, ricochets, and deflects her story with and from those of the women whose lives cross hers either directly through her day-to-day interaction within the glass tower or indirectly via the extra-office associations and relationships of her co-workers. For example, the protagonist's brief encounter with maternal instincts involves the caretaking of a gay co-worker who has been physically and emotionally assaulted.

Her close relationship with the CEO's personal chauffeur reveals a tale of two women who are the chauffeur's wife, mother of his children who struggles to make ends meet, and his barren lover — his boss's wife — whose economic status allows her indulge the chauffeur's children with lavish gifts and weekly excursions to places their parents are unable to afford.

Highly educated women wield power in the glass tower, while some men in similar positions owe their success to the economical support or — more ironically — the extra-marital affairs of their wives. Ríos, the CEO, maintains Vice-President Sebastián on the payroll for the sake of his lover, Trenas's wife, even though the Vice-President has duties. Ríos himself owes much of his success to his independently wealthy wife, Hanna. Indeed, *Un millon de luces* could be easily converted into a soap opera, were it not the writer's delicate and broadminded treatment of subjects heretofore considered taboo, such as adultery, incest, and a mother's abandonment of her children.

It is in this careful treatment of these topics where the face of today's Spanish woman emerges, a composite of the principal female characters that interact within the glass tower. Certainly such issues as women's infidelity, incest, and child neglect have always existed in Spain, but any public representation has been traditionally motivated by moral judgment, parables, and *dichos*.

But the women in *Luces* belong to a very different society than that from which all these cultural artifacts were born. Teresa, the wife of the vice-president, Sebastián Trenas, and CEO Ríos's lover, married to be free of a dead-end job in a pastry shop, and ultimately has to deal with her husband's suicide. Lorena, a Ph.D. in economics, fights her way to the boardroom and succeeds, while anorexic Vicky, a meager administrative assistant and never-wed single Mom, abandons her dreams of a *House Beautiful* type home in favor of the best education her money will afford her son. Anabel, Teresa's daughter, has an affair with her mother's lover, is later rejected by him, and gains an unhealthy amount of weight as she seeks solace in food.

Eating disorders, a consumer economy, the glass ceiling clearly pertain to a postmodern society, one where women moves physically in and out of exterior and interior spaces as freely as men, although their status may not necessarily be the same as men's within all. Divorce, so traumatic for the *Mirador* protagonist, is merely one more facet of co-existence in *Luces*. Fathers play maternal roles and women manage corporate budgets and, more importantly, no one thinks twice about either situation.

In her role as author, Clara Sánchez merely recounts the stories that unfold in and around the glass tower. We find no true resolution, except the bankruptcy of the firm and the sale of the company, when everyone goes their separate, unrevealed ways and the novel ends. There is no tidy happily-ever-after insinuated, as is the case in the other two novels, but there can be no doubt about the women of the glass tower. Each has her own identity based on the consequences of her own decisions, actions, and mistakes, all of which she takes full responsibility. Collectively they are today's Spanish woman: professional, mother, daughter, boss, co-worker, and friend, as much a vibrant contributor to societal welfare and economic prosperity as man without denying her biological circumstances.

As women's role identities have expanded from the organically-defined to include the self-defined, synthesizing traditional images of mother and spouse with professional and public roles, the collective identity of the Spanish woman has been re-formed within new architectural spaces and a restructured, less classist society in which her upward mobility no longer need depend on "a good marriage." Psychologically and emotionally prepared to question patriarchal authority, she has evolved from "the strange woman" of her grandmother's generation, through the intimate and communal struggles of her mother's in-between generation.

In her three novels, *Desde el mirador, Últimas noticias del paraíso,* and *Un millón de luces,* Clara Sánchez traces the psychological and sociological processes that have molded the psyche of today's *española* (Spanish woman). She begins in the traditionally female spaces of home and the hospital as an extension of the home—in the protagonist's role as caretaker—then takes her female characters to public spaces, still predominantly dominated by women, like the *híper* and aerobic classes. Finally she removes them almost entirely from the domestic environment into the modern work-place, into spaces defined by social and economic power. Her narrative style mirrors this evolution: from deliberation, to reaction, to interaction; from abnegation, to reassessment, to realization.

Clara Sánchez's female characters evolve from *Desde el mirador* to *Un millón de luces* in much the same way as woman herself has progressed over the course of the last half a century in Spain. It will be interesting to see where she takes them now as the women of her in-between generation return to domestic spaces as grandmothers and matriarchs. Meanwhile, these three novels of her literary production will continue to represent the psychological trajectory of Spanish women in the formation of a new collective identity through image as perception, then mirage, and finally reflection against the background of 21st century postmodern Spain.

Works Cited

Baldwin, Mark W., and Holmes, John G. "Salient Private Audiences and Awareness of the Self." *Journal of Personality and Social Psychology* 52 (1987): 1087–98.
Bruneau, Thomas C. "Spanish Case Study." Center for Civil-Military Relations. 2000. 30 Dec. 2006. <http://www.ccmr.org/public/images/download/spanish_case_study.pdf>.
Dellinger, Mary Ann. "'1Encerradla!': El espacio arquitectónico como el origen de la tragedia en la trilogía lorquiana." Unpublished thesis. Arizona State University, Tempe, AZ.
Graham, Helen. "Spain and Europe: The View from the Periphery." *The Historical Journal* 35 (1992): 969–83.

Heidorn, Keith. "Mirage." *The Weather Doctor. Exploring the Science and Poetry of Our Weather and Atmosphere*. Island Net. 2007. 3 Jan. 2007. <http://www.islandnet.com /~see/weather/doctor.htm >.

Hogg, Michael A., Deborah J. Terry, and Katherine M. White. "A Tale of Two Theories: A Critical Comparison of Identity Theory with Social Identity Theory." *Social Psychology Quarterly* 58 (1995): 255–69.

Kelley, Heidi. "Enlacing Women's Stories: Composing Womanhood in a Coastal Galician Village." *Constructing Spanish Womanhood. Female Identity in Modern Spain*. Eds. Victoria Lorée Enders and Pamela Beth Radcliff. Albany: State University of New York Press, 1998. 195–223.

Knutson, David. "A New Generation: Young Spanish Literary Characters at the End of the 20th Century." *Monographic Review* 17 (2001): 90–103.

Mayock, Ellen. *The "Strange Girl" in Twentieth Century Spanish Novels Written by Women*. New Orleans: University Press of the South, 2004.

Merriam-Webster OnLine. 2006. 28 Dec. 2006. <http://www.m-w.com/dictionary/ mirage>.

Otero, Luis. *La española cuando besa*. Barcelona: Plaza & Janés, 1999.

_____. *La Sección Femenina*. 3rd ed. Madrid: EDAF, 1999.

Richardson, Bill. "'A wound that cries out'; Trauma and Collective Identity in Buero Vallejo's *El tragaluz*." *Bulletin of Hispanic Studies* 83 (2006): 45–60.

Risi, Marcelo. "España se abre al mundo." BBCMundo.com. 20 Nov. 2000. 30 Dec. 2006. <http://www.bbc.co.uk/spanish/especiales/franco/presente.shtml>.

Sánchez, Clara. *Desde el mirador*. Madrid: Alfaguara, 1996.

_____. *Un millón de luces*. Madrid: Alfaguara, 2004.

_____. Personal Interview. 15 October 2002.

_____. *Últimas noticias del paraíso*. Madrid: Alfaguara, 2000.

Stryker, Sheldon, and Peter J. Burke. "The Past, Present, and Future of an Identity Theory." *Social Psychology Quarterly* 63 (2000): 284–97.

United States Department of State. "Background Notes: Spain." 2000. 30 Dec. 2006. <http://www.state.gov/www/background_notes/spain_0008_bgn.html>.

University Women of Europe-UWE. "Report of the UWE-European Project Meeting." 2005. 30 Dec. 2006. <http://www.ifuw.org/uwe/european-project/cork- 19jun05. htm>.

PART III. NEW WRITERS OF THE 1990s

Looking for the Other: Peninsular Women's Fiction after Levinas

Nina L. Molinaro

As Robert C. Spires has recently argued, "The change of a century, let alone a millennium, tends to inspire retrospective views in literary studies with the implication that something new must have just emerged, or is about to do so" (485). As proof of this sentiment, critics on both sides of the Atlantic have recently fastened on the emergence of a "new" generation of narrative fiction writers in Spain, born between 1960 and 1971, whose texts respond to the pressures of globalization and the consolidation of Spain's democracy, and what both might mean to and for individual Spanish citizens.* Congruently, most of these critics attach the novelty of the group, in

---

*Scholars have yet to reach consensus on the birthdates of the members of the group, as well as most other characteristics. José María Izquierdo, for example, discusses the new Spanish narrators born between 1959 and 1971; Sabas Martín, in the introduction to *Páginas amarillas*, refers to writers from "la joven narrativa española," born between 1960 and 1974; and in her 1997 essay Carmen de Urioste applies "juventud" to those writers born between 1961 and 1971, whereas in her 2001 treatment of the women writers of this same group, she identifies as members of the "nueva narrativa group" those writers born between 1959 and 1974. Although electing birthdates to distinguish generational members is always more or less arbitrary, I opt for 1960 as the opening date because, in keeping with the millennial theme, Martín suggests that "Los autores nacidos en esa fecha contarán cuarenta años en el 2000, edad más que razonable para prescindir del calificativo de <<joven>> al referirnos a cualquier escritor" [The authors born on that date will be forty years old in 2000, an age at which it is reasonable to stop using the adjective "young" when referring to writers. Trans. by editors] (x). And at the other end of the temporal spectrum, 1971 signals the birthdate of José Ángel Mañas, the unofficial *enfant terrible* of the generation. Although my essay concentrates on the novelists of the group, when discussing the emerging narrative generation it has become commonplace to include both novelists and short story writers, in part because the majority of novelists (*continued on next page*)

part or in the main, to political, economic, and technological factors that inform post-transition Spain.

The persistent abuse of generational markers to reduce, exclude, and compartmentalize authors, texts, and the literary movements to which they may or may not belong has been amply documented.* Nevertheless, people like to use monikers. José María Izquierdo, for example, assigns to the emerging group of Peninsular writers the marker "narradores españoles novísimos de los años noventa" while implementing Pedro Salinas's well-known definition of generation. In the same forum, Izquierdo simultaneously declares that Salinas's notion eschews "la dualidad diacronía/sincronía de todo fenómeno humano" [the diachrony/synchrony duality of every human phenomenon] (293).† In a similar vein, Toni Dorca identifies marketing factors in the Spanish publishing industry's push to publish young authors in order to satisfy "la demanda de protagonismo de un sector de la población que quería ver reflejadas sus inquietudes en unos relatos tallados a su gusto y medida" [the demand for centrality by a sector of the population that wanted to see their concerns reflected in stories shaped to their tastes and sizes] (309). Then, following Germán Gullón's lead, Dorca singles out the members of the Generación X as those writers who most closely comply with this demand.

Picked up by numerous commentators, the tag of "Generación X" refers to the recent group of writers because of the striking stylistic and ideological similarities between a subset of these writers, who tend to focus on Spain's disenchanted urban youth,‡ and the U.S. cultural phenomenon first identified in 1991 by Douglas Coupland in his now classic novel *Generation X: Tales for an Accelerated Culture*. Some Peninsular Gen X writers tend to employ technical strategies that echo those of hard realism or dirty realism** in order

---

(continued) in the group also write short stories, and, to my knowledge, all of the authors who are best known for their collections of short stories have also published novels. Many of these same writers have also published poetry, theatre, screenplays, literary criticism, personal essays, journalism, and travel narrative, among other genres.

*José F. Colmeiro summarizes this polemic vis-à-vis the recent group of writers.

†All subsequent English-language translations of primary and secondary texts from the Spanish original are mine.

‡Regarding other labels for the subset of writers, Izquierdo also references "Generación JASP," "Cofradía del cuero," and "Jóvenes caníbales" (296) as synonyms for Spain's Generación X. "Generación Kronen" and "la tribu del Kronen," echoing Mañas's 1994 novel *Historias del Kronen*, have also gained some critical currency. In light of my argument, I might note that this sub-group of writers tends to "universalize" Spain's youth as Euro-Caucasian, Castillian-speaking, male, heterosexual, and middle-or upper middle-class.

**See Bill Buford's "Editorial" for one of the earliest descriptions of dirty realism. Critics also apply the term "neorealism" to the sub-group of contemporary Peninsular *(continued on next page)*

to articulate the preoccupations, habits, and cultural references of a certain so-called youthful demographic of the Spanish population. It is worth noting that among the cluster of writers known as "hard realists," critical attention has regularly gravitated to the novels of José Angel Mañas and, in lesser measure, to those of Ray Loriga as standard-bearers for the concerns of the generation as a whole.* As an oft-cited example, Mañas's initial novel, titled *Historias del Kronen* shocked the literary establishment in Spain in 1994 by becoming a finalist for the prestigious Nadal Prize. The novel has since gone through multiple editions, has inspired scores of scholarly articles, and has served as the basis for a successful feature-length film directed by Montxo Armendáriz and released in 1995.

One of the primary drawbacks of the aforementioned critical elision is that hard realism represents only one of the many divergent narrative strategies of this group of writers. Within the parameters of my essay, and of the larger volume to which it pertains, the related danger is that the focus on the hard realists has all but eclipsed the women narrators of the cohort,† not to mention those who write in Peninsular languages other than Castilian, those who challenge heteronormativity, and those who claim an ethnic or racial identity other than that of the dominant Euro-Caucasian. I seek, in part, to redress this practice by discussing Marta Sanz's *El frío* (1995), Belén Gopegui's *Tocarnos la cara* (1995), and Luisa Castro's *La fiebre amarilla* (1994), three novels produced by women writers from this generation that dramatically break with the manifest tendencies of the hard realists and inquire into the ethics of otherness, as theorized by the philosopher Emmanuel Levinas. Moreover, I intend to argue that these novels call into question, to use one of Levinas's key phrases, the concerns that inhere in the generation as a whole, concerns that complicate both subjectivity and alterity.

As Carmen de Urioste has eloquently demonstrated, the concluding decade of the twentieth century in Spain is rife with fictional narrative writ-

---

(continued) novelists. See, for example, Germán Gullón's Introduction to Mañas's *Historias del Kronen*. Moreover, María T. Pao's suggestive discussion of Mañas's first novel as an example of "blank fiction" might well extend to other novels by Spain's dirty realists.

*In addition to Mañas and Loriga, the sub-group of hard realists in Spain's Generación X regularly includes Juan Bonilla, Gabriela Bustelo, Martín Casariego, Francisco Casavella, Lucía Extebarria, Ismael Grasa, Pedro Maestre, Daniel Múgica, Benjamín Prado, and Roger Wolfe.

†Whereas most discussions of Spain's newest group of narrators focus, if not exclusively then predominantly, on the male writers, the unquestionable exception is Lucía Etxebarria, whose fictional texts have garnered at least as much attention (if not more) than Mañas's novels. Gabriela Bustelo's *Veo Veo* (1996) has also been cited as an illustration of hard realism.

ten by women who pertain to one of at least two generations. The first of these corresponds to "a group of women writers whose emergence has been regarded as the 'boom' of Spanish feminine narrative," while the second pertains to "a new 'generation' of writers, the so-called 'generation X'" (Urioste, "Narrative" 279). Because she compares the two groups in order to assert a more panoramic view of the narrative production of women writing and publishing in 1990s Spain, Urioste stresses the commonalities, rather than the differences, among them. Amid these correspondences, she argues that both groups continue the efforts of a previous literary generation that included Carmen Laforet, Carmen Martín Gaite, Mercedes Salisachs and Luisa Forellad, among others. The writers that comprise the two generations have also started a tradition that will allow other women authors in Spain to follow suit. Within the context of the new generation, she foregrounds some seventeen women writers whose fiction appears in the 1990s and who were born between 1959 and 1974: Mercedes Abad (b. 1961), Enriqueta Antolín (no birth date given), Nuria Barrios (b. 1962), Lola Becarria (b. 1963), Gabriela Bustelo (b. 1962), Luisa Castro (b. 1966), Lucía Etxebarria (b. 1966), Susana Fortes (b. 1959), Espido Freire (b. 1974), Belén Gopegui (b. 1963), Almudena Grandes (b. 1960), Begoña Huertas (b. 1965), Ángela Labordeta (b. 1967), Blanca Riestra (b. 1970), Juana Salabert (b. 1962), Clara Usón (b. 1961), and Pilar Zapata Bosch (no birth date given).* These authors represent a curious, and perhaps predictable, mix of writers who had already enjoyed publishing success in the 1980s (Abad, Grandes and Zapata Bosch), writers who achieved prominence and published more than one novel during the 1990s (Antolín, Riestra, Castro, Etxebarria, Fortes, Freire, Gopegui, Labordeta, and Salabert), writers who produced one narrative text in the 1990s and did not publish another until after 2000 (Barrios, Becarria, Bustelo, and Huertas) and writers who authored their only novel to date in the 1990s (Usón). Evidently, the abovementioned women demonstrate heterogeneity with regard to productivity and longevity.

Urioste further postulates that Spain's new narrative by women, together with the fiction by those women authors whose work continues the edito-

---

*Urioste alludes to space limitations as the reason why she was unable to include an analysis of novels by other "new" women novelists, namely Cuca Canals (b. 1962), Elvira Lindo (b. 1962), Ana Rioja (b. 1962), Ángeles Caso (b. 1960), and Marta Rivera de la Cruz (b. 1970). She also notes in Table I that Martín, in his introduction to *Páginas amarillas* (1997), mentions texts by Care Santos (b. 1970), Paula Izquierdo (b. 1962), Marta Sanz (b. 1967), and María Jaén (b. 1962). I would add Carmen Montalbán (b. 1963) and Beatriz Pottecher (b. 1961) to the list of new women narrators, and there are undoubtedly others who also merit inclusion.

rial and critical successes of women's writing in 1980s Spain is recasting language, identity, and context. Moreover, women novelists of the 1990s, and the Gen X writers among them, usher in "the construction of several exemplary female subjects for women readers" (Urioste, "Narrative" 289). If by "exemplary female subjects" she includes the problematization of subjectivity, then I am in complete agreement, insofar as I would argue that the female members of the contemporary generation, along with their generational cohorts, are actually changing the face of subjectivity by means of a sustained exploration of relationality, as well as an interrogation of alterity.

I have elected to center on the aforementioned novels by Sanz, Gopegui, and Castro because, like many of their female and male generational counterparts, these authors all consistently question how human beings imagine and practice relationships, and how such "intersubjectivity" articulates ethical responsiveness and responsibility. Unlike most of their male cohorts, however, the three novelists attend to the ways in which female subjects approach, perceive, and grapple with others and the discourses of otherness. I find this especially relevant to contemporary Spain because, as Helen Graham and Jo Labanyi cogently observe, "[i]t is perhaps a measure of the success of Francoist political indoctrination that 'others' still tend to be seen as existing without rather than within" (5); and Spain's newest literary generation, by contrast, consistently directs attention to the "others" within, or alterity.* In particular, I will be analyzing *El frío*, *Tocarnos la cara*, and *La fiebre amarilla* with an eye to the startlingly disparate ways in which the texts challenge female subjectivity in relation to otherness (and vice versa), how the women characters see and speak their selves, how and why they respond to others, and, more importantly for my argument, how such recognition frames the limits, liabilities, and liberations of alterity itself.

My argument finds its theoretical grounding in the work of Emmanuel Levinas (1906–1995), a Franco–Lithuanian philosopher who dedicated his considerable career to a phenomenological exploration of alterity.† Levinas proposes that ethics, or what he conceptualizes as the primordial responsi-

---

*Elsewhere I have discussed Levinasian alterity in novels by women and men from the current generation. See my "Facing Towards Alterity and Spain's 'Other' New Novelists," in which I analyze Gopegui's *Tocarnos la cara* and Mañas's *Mensaka* against Levinas's concept of "the face." "I do not, however, take up the question of gender in that forum.

†Levinas began his career as a phenomenologist and has reiterated that the phenomenological method remained with him throughout his life. His prolific career, evidenced by an abundance of articles, interviews, public lectures and more than two dozen book-length texts, has been well-documented. His major philosophical contributions may be found in *Totalité et infini: Essai sur l'extériorité* (1961) and *Autrement qu'être ou au-delà de l'essence* (1974) and, together with his other intellectual activities, attest to his lifelong *(continued on next page)*

bility of the self to and for the Other, bears irrevocably on the construction of human subjectivity. At the core of his argument lies an extensive critique of the Western ethical tradition and the ways in which said tradition, while permitting a separation between self and Other, has consistently upheld that such separation is always necessarily superseded by consciousness, rationality, or knowledge.*

For Levinas all human identity is and has always been insoluble. Nevertheless, one of the foremost tasks of Western philosophy, he contends, has been the systematic erasure of ontological difference, or the diminution of the Other to the Same. Levinas writes the following in 1949:

> Western philosophy coincides with the unveiling of the other in which the Other, by manifesting itself as a being, loses its alterity. Philosophy is afflicted, from its childhood, with an insurmountable allergy: a horror of the Other which remains Other. It is for this reason that philosophy is essentially the philosophy of Being; the comprehension of Being is its final word and the fundamental structure of man [as quoted in Davis 32].

This "horror of the Other" has translated into the widely disseminated concept that human beings can theorize and understand ourselves only by absorbing all that is beyond or other than ourselves; in order to elaborate being, the self, or the subject we perceive what is external to us as loyal images of ourselves, as familiar, reflective, and so many versions of the Same. By contrast, Levinas maintains that ethics precedes all other claims on human subjectivity; before we can conceive of what there is in the world or how we know we must formulate ourselves, and in order to accomplish that, we must

---

(continued) preoccupation with the question of otherness as it relates to intersubjectivity, politics, and Judaism, among other concerns. Both volumes were translated from the original French into English by Alphonso Lingis. All further references to *Totalité et infini: Essai sur l'extériorité* will be to Lingis's English translation, published in 1969 as *Totality and Infinity*. Levinas's ideas are extraordinarily complex and far-reaching, and many of his commentators have guided me through the intricacies of his writing and his reasoning. I found particularly helpful the essays included in *The Cambridge Companion to Levinas*, edited by Simon Critchley and Robert Bernasconi, as well as Colin Davis's *Levinas: An Introduction*. For a relatively complete list of primary works by Levinas and secondary works, grouped by topics, on his thought see Stacy Keltner's Bibliography, included in Critchley and Bernasconi's edited volume. Any errors of interpretation are of course my own.

*Western ethics has sought to articulate and respond to the question "what should I do?" for at least 2500 years. Emerging from the philosophical activities of Socrates (469–399 B.C.) and Plato (427–347 B.C.), both of whom considered the ethical subject to be exclusively male, ethics follows the connections between discrete human actions and the communal world in which such actions arise. Founded as equally regulatory and performative, ethics typically manifests through an array of hierarchized oppositions that include good/bad, right/wrong, public/private, individual/ collective, human/divine, reason/emotion, and subject/object. And gender scholars might well suggest that male/female and its corollary masculine/feminine represent the salient conceptual and practical hierarchy among these.

establish our relationship to the Other and to others.* We do not exist without first existing for the Other, an event that thrusts responsibility upon us. And when we exist, as we must, for the Other, we inescapably evoke the terrain of the ethical.

Because Levinas is a phenomenologist, he conceptualizes ethics as an "optics" (23, 29) and a process of relational awareness, both of which he equates with a "calling into question of the Same" by otherness. Alterity disturbs subjectivity, and one of the ways that it does so, according to Levinas, lies in the feminine event of welcoming or hospitality that unavoidably accompanies eros: "And the other whose presence is discreetly an absence, with which is accomplished the primary hospitable welcome which describes the field of intimacy, is the Woman. The woman is the condition for recollection, the interiority of the Home, and inhabitation" (155). Pure erotic love may be defined, in Levinas's corpus at least, as the way in which Same and Other come upon one another, as "aspects of metaphysical desire and voluptuosity" (Hutchens 146). The ethicality of this encounter may be located in the infinitely generous reception of the feminine. Levinas writes that the embodiments of the Other, whether they be "the friend, the child, the brother, the beloved, the parents" share the status of "that to which [a being] was bound before even having taken the initiative of the search and despite the exteriority in which [a being] finds [the Other]" (254). The feminine enacts the disorder that always goes along with alterity and exposes the paradox that is the relationship between alterity and sameness, between the beloved, indispensable other who *a priori* obligates the subject to responsibility and the subject who must extend "himself" (in Levinas's formulation) beyond interiority in order to respond hospitably to an ethical obligation that precedes being.

For all of the radical potential of his thought, Levinas's work takes a curious stance vis-à-vis gender. As is frequently the case with Western philosophy, his theories showcase a supposedly universal human subject who, not coincidentally, tends to exhibit overtly masculine characteristics. When

---

*Scholars have dedicated considerable attention to Levinas's distinction between "autrui" and "autre," both of which he occasionally capitalizes. I follow Lingis's translation, in which he notes, in Levinas's preface to *Totality and Infinity*, that "[w]ith the author's permission, we are translating '*autrui*' (the personal Other, the you) by 'Other,' and '*autre*' by 'other.' In doing so, we regrettably sacrifice the possibility of reproducing the author's use of capital or small letters with both these terms in the French text" (24–25). Additionally, in the "Translator's Note" to *Ethics and Infinity*, Richard A. Cohen indicates that he has followed Lingis's convention and adds that "*Autrui*, in French, refers to the personal other, the other person; *autre* refers to otherness in general, to alterity" (17).

he purposefully incorporates gender into his discussion, Levinas does so in ways that have elicited the entire spectrum of responses among feminist philosophers, from outright rejection to cautious consideration to enthusiastic embrace. Although he seems to critique many of the same philosophical premises and conclusions that feminism finds discriminatory with regard to gender differences, the models that he proposes may in fact reproduce many of the same unequally weighted binaries that he tries to undo.*

Gender critics identify several challenges in Levinas's assimilation of femininity.† First, it often seems that he would have us consider his inclusion of the feminine as if it were entirely removed from being a woman. Second, for those such as Simone de Beauvoir who consider equality or reciprocity between women and men to be a laudable goal, as Tina Chanter comments, "Levinas fits seamlessly into a long line of male thinkers who have subordinated women to men, refused to construe the relation between the sexes as reciprocal, denied women full subjectivity, and consigned them to the rank of the inessential" (2). Third, theorists like Luce Irigaray object that Levinas instrumentalizes the feminine in order to facilitate the transcendence of the male subject. Once again, femininity is exploited in the name of sexual difference, but such difference is closed off by Levinas's own inability to fully articulate the feminine as not only representing access to the Other but as the most accessible mode of the Other. Moreover, his dependence on the heterosexual model as the closest equivalent to ontological difference traps him in metaphors that ultimately limit his logic and constrain his ability to relate sexual difference, not to mention other indices of difference, to alterity.

Those who might wish to redeem the gendered dimensions of Levinas's work, however, point to the radicality of his project, which involves nothing less than the reformulation of ontology in terms of ethics. And femininity is vital to this reformulation as "a way of rendering what cannot be reduced to beings. It is, in this sense, an elaboration, or dramatization, of the ontological difference" (Chanter 15–16). Because femininity makes available the

---

*Because philosophical language has been so thoroughly permeated by the rhetoric of sameness, critics such as Jacques Derrida have argued that Levinas himself, especially in *Totality and Infinity*, cannot successfully escape either the discursive limits of referentiality or the disciplinary requirements of Western philosophy. Any consideration of the evolution of Levinas's thought from *Totality and Infinity* to *Otherwise than Being* would go well beyond my present essay.

†For lucid analyses of the role of the femininity in Levinas's thought, I am indebted to Tina Chanter's "Introduction" to *Feminist Interpretations of Emmanuel Levinas*, as well as to the essays contained in that volume.

site and sight through which alterity is realized, it occupies a privileged position in his work. To the abiding yet unresolved question of whether Levinas continues the philosophical discourse of masculine privilege or whether he successfully resists this discourse, or perhaps more realistically, whether his work suggests unrealized avenues for critiquing this discourse, one response from philosophers such as Chanter has been to suggest that "[t]o read Levinas well would perhaps be not only to read his texts faithfully; it would be to turn away from his texts, or rather to turn his texts to what lies beyond them, and to ask what they foreclose" (6).

As one of the horizons that lies beyond Levinas's texts, narrative fiction opens up alterity to the possibilities of gender. As I intend to subsequently demonstrate, the novels by Sanz, Gopegui, and Castro take up a number of related issues that Levinas, as a philosopher, could have neither imagined nor theorized. To wit, how might the new generation of women novelists in Spain address the questions that Levinas's own texts do not resolve regarding gender and alterity? How might their novels follow "the epiphany of the feminine" (Levinas 264) towards response, responsiveness and responsibility? And finally, how do gender, alterity and eros "face" one another (to use one of Levinas's key terms) in novelistic discourse?

I begin with a consideration of Marta Sanz's *El frío* not because alterity asserts itself in and through the novel, or because an encounter with the Other is realized. Instead, erotic love fails spectacularly and repeatedly, and this failure gives way to a split narrative of the frustrated integration of the Other into the Same, and others into subjects. Sanz's novel probes the edges of subjectivity in its display of gendered selves who perform irresponsibility and unresponsiveness as the breakdown that precedes ethical alterity. However, while the erotic encounters do not result in intimacy with the Other, neither do they generate knowledgeable, coherent subjects who prevail over division. Instead, *El frío* limns the spaces between the egoism that Levinas critiques and the future extended by and to gendered alterity.

From the outset of Sanz's text the reader is confronted with two visions of the same narrative situation. *El frío* is organized around a sequence of thirty-five consecutively numbered chapters that zigzag between the perspective of an unnamed woman who speaks mostly in the first person and that of an omniscient third-person narrator whose objectivity verges on psychosis. In the odd-numbered chapters, the woman returns by bus to an unspecified geographic point of origin after having just traveled to visit her male lover, who is a patient in a sanitarium. She recounts how, upon her arrival, the man unceremoniously and inexplicably dismissed her. During the long and uncomfortable return trip, she mentally shuffles through her amorous history, only to conclude, as she steps off the bus and into the departure terminal, that she has learned nothing and feels nothing. Her final lines bear witness to the overwhelming sense of paralysis that paradoxically fuels the novel: "[n]o sé si alguna vez saldré de aquí. Tengo las suelas pegadas al pavimento. Oigo las bocinas de los coches en los pasos de cebra. Camino hacia la salida con la mente en blanco" [I don't know if I'll ever get out of here. I have my soles stuck to the pavement. I hear the cars honking in pedestrian crossings. I walk towards the exit absent-minded] (121). The narrator-protagonist's words, while firmly rooted in one human being's unsuccessful attempt to transform dependency into agency, resist any easy assignation of blame, guilt, or accountability. The woman responds to the perceived threat of persecution by inverting that threat and substituting herself in the place of her lover, but she only ends up engendering separation.

The other narrative door hinges on the actions of a sanitarium patient named Miguel who, having just discarded his recently arrived female lover, is drawn into a cat-and-mouse game of sexual domination with Blanca, a nurse at the same institution. At first it appears that Miguel, cowed by drugs and his physical environment, will thoroughly capitulate to the predatory desire of Blanca. In an unexpected twist, however, he physically subdues the nurse and, uttering his only words in the novel, graphically threatens to slit her throat with a stolen crochet hook. When he releases his prey, she runs blindly through the building and collapses in the staff lounge, while Miguel, in the final scene of the complementary narrative, calmly dons brand-new pajamas, lies down on his bed, and closes his eyes.

The distinct plotlines are bridged, on the surface at least, by two female subjects who direct their amorous attentions to, presumably, the same male object. In the first instance, the narrator and her lover exchange places across time and space; in their past relationship, according to her account, he was the intelligible subject and she the unintelligible other, whereas in the present moment she asserts subjectivity and assigns to him the place of ontological and sexual difference, an arrangement that is replicated in the second storyline. In this line, Blanca initially directs and stars in the drama of her interaction with Miguel; she dresses him, moves him, speaks for him, and interprets his actions to others. In a word, she possesses him, to the point that he gives the impression of existing solely as an extension of her will. From the interstices of the clinically detached narrative perspective, however, it becomes clear that Miguel exercises agency from the margins. He silently encroaches on the intimacies of other patients and staff members, converting private solitudes into public exhibitions. As a final indication of his triumph, after he orchestrates Blanca's terrified submission, she retreats to communal institutional spaces (the kitchen, the art room, the halls) and forced sociality with her co-worker, whereas he retires alone to his room.

Sanz's novel is not anti-relational. On the contrary, it reads as extravagantly relational, as so many examples of selves and others and the trauma that undoes complementarity. For the first-person narrator, her desire and her subjectivity crumple when her lover rebuffs her, but her narrative also begins at this same point. Although her demands for recognition intensify throughout the text, she receives recognition only from herself because her lover is conspicuously absent and because she mentally rejects the other passengers on the bus, while folding them into her emotional chronicle. As part of that process, she reminds herself (and the reader) of previous and current suffering, both of which are exacerbated by the activities of her fellow travelers. Her pain also manifests in the frequency with which she shuttles between the first, second, and third person perspectives, as exemplified in the succeeding passage:

> [y]o adivino, aprehendo sus oscilaciones bajo el agua. La veo. La radio puede explotar; está conectada a la red eléctrica y en este cuarto la humedad arde. Ten cuidado. No quiero ver tus espasmos, que me dejes sin irte, sin que la estructura blanda de mi propia voluntad decida, por fin, alejarse. A la búsqueda de un nuevo cristalino, uno distinto, otro.
>
> [I guess, I capture her movements under the water. I see her. The radio could explode, it's connected to the electric outlet and in this room the humidity burns. Be careful. I don't want to see your spasms, leave me alone without going anywhere, without the bland structure of my self-will deciding to finally go away. In response to the search for a new crystalline lens, another one, different.] [46–47].

The "I," "you," and "she" all refer to the same person, who attempts to fill the void left by her obligations to the Other. Levinas has written that "[t]he relationship established between lovers in voluptuosity, fundamentally refractory to universalization, is the very contrary of the social relation. It excludes the third party" (264–65). In the absence of the feminine welcome of alterity, conversely, the erotic encounter has diminished the female subject, provoking a chain of echoes designed to restore her to herself. In the narrative of her past, alterity was precluded by the disappearance of the female object into the male subject. In the present story, the narrator envisions excessive disorder where there once was excessive order. Her lover owes her but because she clings so desperately to her need to see herself reflected in and by him, she cordons off her access to otherness and her own possible status as an other.

In the parallel narrative, the reverse occurs. At first glance, an ethical interpretation of the relationship between Miguel and Blanca is more straightforward because the two participants seem to defy ethicality. The plot of sexual domination, so at odds with the Levinasian ideal of erotic intimacy, spells a much more intricate dance of subjection and liberation. When Blanca tries to erase Miguel's agency, she assumes that she is converting him into a wholly visible being—the antithesis of the feminine welcome. He reacts by retreating, like the "other" narrator, into himself, but unlike her he violently projects that self onto others. In each case the result is the same: Miguel and the unnamed woman end up alone and adrift. But he wants solitude, interority, and separation, while she perhaps still imagines some kind of connection as she walks literally and figuratively toward an exit.

Whereas *El frío* maps the damage that comes with the ruin and resurrection of subjectivity, Belén Gopegui's *Tocarnos la cara* proffers a partial and temporary paradigm of alterity.* The plot of the novel hangs on a quartet of actors: Ana Hojeda, Íñigo Martínez, Óscar Azores and Sandra, whose last name is not revealed. Together with their teacher Simón Cátero, they decide to create an experimental theatre group called El Probador. Sandra serves as scribe and secretary, producing the text that we read by setting down her memories, transcribing the words and actions of the participants, and "taking notes" on the training sessions, as well as on the encounters staged by the members of the theatre group. The goal of El Probador consists of presenting "[u]n teatro para que cada cliente pueda ver su fantasía sometida a las leyes de la carne. Igual que bailarines. Algo aprenderán" [a play in which each client can see his fantasy subjected to the laws of the flesh. Just like dancers. They'll learn something"] (30). In practice, a specific client declares her/his fantasy to one of the actors who then functions as a human mirror so that the client may become the desired image of herself/himself.

The professional and personal activities of El Probador are also traversed by the actions of three additional people. Pedro Alexei facilitates the preparation of the actors and mediates between teacher and students, until he reveals towards the end of the novel that he is dying. Simón's deceased mentor José Espinar supplies the concept and blueprints for El Probador in

---

*In contrast to the scant criticism that exists on any texts by Sanz or Castro, Gopegui's fiction has inspired several articles. See essays by Nuria Cruz-Cámara, Eva Leguido-Quigley, and Janet Pérez for treatments of *Tocarnos la cara*.

the form of his journals, which Sandra reads and integrates into her narrative. And Fátima Uribe, Simón's ex-wife, reappears without warning in Madrid while the actors are forming El Probador; she then establishes a well-financed theatre company of her own and contributes directly and indirectly in the dissolution of her competition. Sandra documents all of these interventions, in spite of the fact that she does not fully understand their relevance to the project at hand.

The actors in El Probador believe, to varying degrees, that they will reveal alterity in the course of their dramatic encounters. By temporarily effacing their own identities in order to extend to the desiring subject an alternative version of herself/himself, they consider their efforts to be eminently ethical. In isolation and without external confirmation, they stage the responsibility that human beings assume on behalf of the Other. The clients approach the theatre group in order to rehearse this obligation and they use the actors to personify versions of the Other, so that they may themselves be transformed in the process.

In reality, however, the concept runs aground from the start. During a practice session between Íñigo and a potential client (Pedro), the former charges "[y]o sufro, tú sufres, él sufre. ¿No ves que eso es lo único que pasa? ¿No ves que nadie sabe lo que debe hacer?" [I suffer, you suffer, he suffers. Don't you see that's all that happens? Don't you see that no one knows what he should do?] (54). To which "the client" responds by standing up, facing Íñigo [cara a cara] and uttering the following words: "[y]o miento, tú mientes, él miente. ¿Qué harías si te entregara mi admiración por ti, qué harías si tuvieras que ir con ella a todas partes?" [I lie, you lie, he lies. What would you do if I gave you my admiration, what would you do if you had to go everywhere with her?] (55). As the client, Pedro seeks to converse with a prior incarnation of himself in order to alter his vaguely articulated present circumstances. Íñigo reflects back to the client the doubts, questions, and suspicions that have arisen as the result of the distress of the latter. And Pedro, in an impromptu reversal of roles, then directs Íñigo to a hypothetical situation of welcome, couched as unconditional admiration. In this example, Pedro offers to the representation of himself a different response, one that locates otherness in infinite acceptance and generosity, which he cannot accomplish on his own behalf because he is not obligated to himself. And just as he is not ethically obliged to himself, so too do the clients who use El Probador avoid otherness.

By trying to span the distance between sameness and difference, the actors of *Tocarnos la cara* begin where the lovers of *El frío* left off, at least in theory. Relationality pervades all aspects of Gopegui's novel, and erotic intimacy regularly exceeds the relationships in a number of ways. First, Simón confesses toward the end of the novel that, unbeknownst to his students, he imagined El Probador as an instrument of revenge. The reader learns that Simón was devastated when Fátima abandoned him, and that he devoted the subsequent years to building his professional resources in order to lure her back. He knew that she would return to Madrid if she heard that he was establishing another theatre company and that she would most likely attempt to compete with him. When Fátima does return, she creates a large commercial theatre company and tries to convince all of the members of El Probador (save Simón) to join her. She succeeds only with Óscar, possibly because he suggests on several occasions that he is in love with Sandra, who does not return his affections.

As a prototypical Don Juan figure, Simón also employs El Probador to generate a series of successful seductions, first with Ana and later with Sandra. As Sandra herself comments, "A diferencia de otros donjuanes, Simón no engañaba para ocultar, sino para exhibir su engaño y que la mujer en cuestión se viera en el deseo de redimirle" [Unlike other Don Juans, Simón did not deceive in order to hide, but in order to exhibit his deceit and so that the woman in question would see herself in her desire to redeem him] (26). His exhibitions also consist of visits to a professional escort, whom he names Fátima in honor of his ex-wife. Although Sandra spends little time describing Simón's amorous exploits, as a continuation of the above quotation, the entire novel might be considered her attempt to see herself in her desire to redeem him. After all, Sandra glimpses Simón and Ana embracing in the shadows of the theatre building; Sandra listens as Ana verbally struggles with Simón's growing disinterest; and Sandra, on at least two different occasions, follows Simón to the bar where he meets "Fátima." Given that she controls the narration, it is logical to suppose that she would include some mention of her own amorous entanglement with Simón, especially since it precipitates the conclusion of her narrative.

Significantly, Simón narrates the final twenty pages of Sandra's text in order to intervene in the lofty goals of El Probador. In the place of welcome, generosity and responsibility, he inserts violence, scarcity, and liability: "Digo también que dos personas cuando se miran se enfrentan. Siempre hay violencia en el hecho de admitir a otro. Hay que violentarse, hay que hacerse fuerte, hay que obligarse a saber que ni toda la comida ni todo el sitio son nuestros" [I say also that when two people look at each other, they confront each other. There is always violence in the fact of admitting another. It is necessary to do violence to one another, it is necessary to become strong, it is necessary to obligate one another to know that neither food nor place is really ours] (213–14). In this proclamation Simón enunciates the antithesis of Levinasian alterity, but the difference between *Tocarnos la cara* and *El frío* is that his statement finalizes an otherwise ethical experience.

Although Sandra opens the novel by claiming that she is relating "la historia de un esfuerzo y una desbandada" [the story of an effort and a disbandment] (11), her phrase applies equally to several stories displayed throughout the novel. The history of El Probador certainly marks both effort and disbandment, as do all of the erotic histories chronicled in the novel. For Simón, in the constant projection and recuperation of desires and needs, alterity is merely the illusion of permanently postponing his debt to others: "Al utilizaros, yo me he endeudado hasta el cuello. He gastado por encima de mis posibilidades. [...] El orgullo, el miedo a la deuda es también el miedo a ser uno entre muchos, el miedo a formar parte de una comunidad" [By utilizing you, I have become indebted up to my neck. I have spent more than I could ever make. [...] Pride, fear of debt are also the fear of being one among many, the fear of becoming part of a community] (206). But what of the others? The efforts of the theatre group, for instance, may finally come undone but they underscore the call of being for the Other, of exceeding one's own subjectivity in order to put forward hospitality to and assume prior responsibility for the Other. Sandra perhaps comes closest to this welcome by scarcely recalling Simón's seduction of her. Her narrative welcome calls into question his egoism and suggests the prospect of intimacy, even though it is not sustained. She watches and prepares for the signs of otherness, even if those signs have already been co-opted by sameness.

If *El frío* recounts the obstacles to alterity, and *Tocarnos la cara* delves into the postponement of otherness, then Luisa Castro's *La fiebre amarilla* lyrically formulates a subject position that expansively liberates ethical obligation. In equal measure myth and ghost story, Castro's novel folds compound temporal planes into a fable on mortality as the outer reach of all consciousness. At least three discrete temporal realities interlace themselves into the action of the novel. In the first, a seventy-year-old woman named Virginia Legazpi falls down a flight of stairs on the eve of a much-anticipated church-sponsored trip to Coimbra to visit the shrine of Fátima. While in the hospital, the doctors discover that she has inoperable cancer and they send her home. She floats in and out of delirium for two weeks and then dies.

In the second enmeshed temporal plane, Virginia's father Jesús Legazpi flees to Cuba with a mysterious woman when his daughter is ten years old. Within the year, Virginia receives word that her father has died of yellow fever but she refuses to believe the telegram, preferring instead to wait for him to come home and justify his actions to her. His arrival some six decades later coincides with the onset of Virginia's self-diagnosed yellow fever, after she tumbles down the stairs. He brings with him the woman for whom he supposedly abandoned his family and he begs Virginia to meet her and to forgive them both. When she agrees, "death" enters the room and invites Virginia to accompany them to Cuba. And the third timeline is organized around Ladislao, the taxi driver who drove Legazpi and his lover to Ferrol in order to embark on their transatlantic voyage, and in the present conducts these same passengers back to Virginia's house (which is also her mother's house) so that her father might finally make amends to his daughter.

Due to the interplay of perspectives, each of which carries equal narrative authority, it is impossible to discern with any certainty which time zone predominates, the one that corresponds to Virginia's childhood, the one that trails the two weeks between her accident and her father's appearance, or all those in-between. Castro threads into the novel the temporally disjointed memories of Virginia Legazpi, her father Jesús, her mother Amadora, her husband Francisco Pena, her adult daughter Juana, the village priest, the village doctor, Ladislao, and a wandering countess into the novel. And often these memories are recounted in some sort of mental present, confounding any smooth distinctions between then and now.

Virginia has clearly spent a lifetime rehearsing the anticipated reunion with her father. After at least a sixty-year separation (if he ever existed at all), she had culled what she knows of him from her imagination and from her mother's time-bending reminiscences. As an embodiment of the Other, Jesús Legazpi is cast as an exorbitantly unfamiliar man from a distant land, who survives a massive shipwreck that washes up on the Galician shores. Within four days of their meeting, Virginia's mother and father are married, and by the fifth day the young bride begins to be afraid because "[c]ada vez que le miraba a la cara me parecía distinto" [each time that I looked him in the face, he seemed different] (115). On the sixth day Amadora locks herself in her room. When she unlocks the door the next day her husband has left her, and during the next ten years she hears reports of his constant womanizing. Her brush with one manifestation of alterity has temporarily halted, until she returns from a pilgrimage to a nearby hermitage after Legazpi has departed for Cuba. From that point onward, as her daughter grows into adulthood, Amadora becomes younger, a process that culminates when the 80-year-old Amadora dies on her birthday, but not before exacting a promise from her daughter that the latter will visit the shrine of Fátima on her mother's behalf. Amadora and Virginia exchange places literally and figuratively throughout the novel. While her mother substitutes an obsession with the Virgin for her attraction to her husband, Virginia melds her adolescent fantasy and her adult need for reconciliation into a fantastic conversation with her father. By calling into question her own being, she summons otherness in the person of her deceased father, who in turn responds by inviting death itself to their shared encounter.

La fiebre amarilla represents a long slide into the final welcome, which daughter and father reciprocally offer to one another. In a text replete with departures, denials, and delusion, the abundance of arrivals, intersections, and coincidences are remarkable. If Virginia views herself as the epitome of filial duty, she also draws on that duty to free herself and her father into absolute otherness. Alterity, as it presents in the text, surpasses consciousness, rationality, and knowledge. In the final scene, as Virginia pictures the world turning upside down, with no one to see it or hear it, she invites her father's lover into her room. Her father replies with the following: "Virginia ... sólo tú sabes que estoy aquí. He tenido que ocultarme bajo estas ropas, he tenido que engañarles a todos. Nadie sabe que existo, Virginia, y cuando nadie sabe que existes, nadie quiere llevarte a los sitios, nadie te deja entrar, nadie te deja salir" [Virginia ... only you know that I am here. I have had to hide beneath these clothes, I have had to deceive everyone. No one knows that I exist, Virginia, and when no one knows that you exist, no one wants to take you anywhere, no one lets you in, no one lets you out] (167). His words explain why the Other escapes comprehension and why recognition of the Other can provoke only an ethical response. When she, in turn, utters his name to his face, he repeats it back to her, and past and present, fantasy and chronology converge. The fundamental difference between Same and Other, self and other hesitates at the moment of intimacy and ontological generosity. And the scene spreads to embrace the arrival of the paternal beloved, "aquella mujer" to Virginia and "la muerte" to all other appearances. Virginia finds her suitcase and asks Don Pablo, her attending physician, for permission to leave with her companions. She hears words but the person who speaks them has already exited the room. At this moment, she exists solely for the Other, albeit momentarily, but that may be enough.

We have seen how the novels by Sanz, Gopegui, and Castro track Levinas's "epiphany of the feminine" differently. In *El frío* one female subject finds herself and loses the Other, while another female subject finds the Other and loses herself. *Tocarnos la cara* suggests a more hopeful scenario whereby competing human wants stifle a shared gesture of hospitality. The female narrator faces intimacy and is then eclipsed by another's competing ego. And, finally, the protagonist of *La fiebre amarilla* works her way into alterity by realizing her responsibility to the Other and by releasing her claim on the familiar. All three novels position female subjects as capable of transcendence. In all three novels those subjects are disturbed, which precludes their disappearance into sameness and intelligibility. And all three novels foreground ontology as intimacy. Ultimately, gender makes all the difference for Levinasian alterity. We are perhaps left to wonder about the role of the masculine in a feminine erotic economy, in which the loving woman responds to the beloved man. But surely that is another story, told differently by other writers of Spain's latest literary generation.

Works Cited

Buford, Bill. "Editorial." *Granta* 8 (1983): 4–5.
Castro, Luisa. *La fiebre amarilla*. Barcelona: Anagrama, 1994.
Chanter, Tina. Introduction. *Feminist Interpretations of Emmanuel Levinas*. Ed. Tina Chanter. University Park: The Pennsylvania State University Press, 2001. 1–27.
Cohen, Richard A. "Translator's Note." *Ethics and Infinity*. By Emmanuel Levinas. Trans. Richard A. Cohen. Pittsburgh: Duquesne University Press, 1985. 17–18.
Colmeiro, José F. "En busca de la 'Generación X': ¿Héroes por un día o una nueva generación perdida?" *España Contemporánea* 14.1 (2001): 7–26.
Critchley, Simon and Robert Bernasconi, eds. *The Cambridge Companion to Levinas*. Cambridge: Cambridge University Press, 2002.
Cruz-Cámara, Nuria. "Notas sobre un 'Bildungsroman' posmoderno: *Tocarnos la cara* de Belén Gopegui." *Crítica Hispánica* 26.1–2 (2004): 41–48.
Davis, Colin. *Levinas: An Introduction*. Notre Dame: University of Notre Dame Press, 1996.
Dorca, Toni. "Joven narrativa en la España de los noventa: la generación X." *Revista de Estudios Hispánicos* 31 (1997): 309–24.
Gopegui, Belén. *Tocarnos la cara*. Barcelona: Anagrama, 1995.
Graham, Helen, and Jo Labanyi. Introduction. *Spanish Cultural Studies: An Introduction*. Eds. Helen Graham and Jo Labanyi. Oxford: Oxford University Press, 1995. 1–19.
Gullón, Germán. Introduction. *Historias del Kronen*. By José Ángel Mañas. Barcelona: Destino, 1994. v–xxxviii.
Hutchens, B.C. *Levinas: A Guide for the Perplexed*. New York and London: Continuum, 2004.
Izquierdo, José María. "Narradores españoles novísimos de los años noventa." *Revista de Estudios Hispánicos* 35 (2001): 293–308.
Legido-Quigley, Eva. "La superación de una 'episteme' posmoderna saturada: El caso de Belén Gopegui en *Tocarnos la cara*." *Monographic Review/Revista Monográfica* 17 (2001): 146–64.
Levinas, Emmanuel. *Totality and Infinity*. Trans. Alphonso Lingis. Pittsburgh: Duquesne University Press, 1969.

Martín, Sabas. "Narrativa española tercer milenio (guía para usuarios)." *Páginas amarillas*. Madrid: Lengua de Trapo, 1997. vii-xxx.
Molinaro, Nina L. "Facing Towards Alterity and Spain's 'Other' New Novelists." *Anales de la literatura española contemporánea* 30.1–2 (2005): 301–24.
Pao, María T. "Sex, Drugs, and Rock & Roll: *Historias del Kronen* as Blank Fiction." *Anales de la literatura española contemporánea* 27.2 (2002): 245/531–260/546.
Pérez, Janet. "Tradition, Renovation, Innovation: The Novels of Belén Gopegui." *Anales de la literatura española contemporánea* 28.1 (2003): 115–38.
Sanz, Marta. *El frío*. Madrid: Debate, 1995.
Spires, Robert C. "Depolarization and the New Spanish Fiction at the Millennium." *Anales de la literatura española contemporánea* 30.1–2 (2005): 485–512.
Urioste, Carmen de. "La narrativa española de los noventa: ¿Existe una 'generación X'?" *Letras Peninsulares* 10.3 (1997–1998): 455–76.
_____. "Narrative of Spanish Women Writers of the Nineties: An Overview." *Tulsa Studies in Women's Literature* 20.2 (2001): 279–95.

Revaluing the Mother in Lucía Etxebarria's *Un milagro en equilibrio*

Sandra J. Schumm

The title of Lucía Etxebarria's 2004 Planeta Prize-winning novel, *Un milagro en equilibrio* [A Miracle in the Balance], brings mystical and religious connotations to the letter/journal the protagonist Eva addresses to her infant daughter Amanda.* However, even Eva's name — echoing that of the bearer of Original Sin — intimates that her writing will be a subversive counterbalance to patriarchal Catholic tradition in Spain. Eva's words to Amanda attempt to regenerate a bond between mothers and daughters, whose "relationship has been minimized and trivialized in the annals of patriarchy," according to Adrienne Rich (226). In addition to providing a written legacy for Amanda, Eva's journal explores the relationship with her own mother as a missing link in her identity.† She also directs her words to a readership

---

*Etxebarria's other novels include: *Amor, curiosidad, prozac y dudas* (1997); *Beatriz y los cuerpos celestes* (1998; Premio Nadal), *Nosotras que no somos como las demás* (1999), *De todo lo visible y lo invisible* (2001; Premio Primavera), and *Cosmofobia* (2007). She has also published a book of stories: *Una historia de amor como otra cualquiera* (2003); poetry: *Estación de infierno* (2001) and *Actos de amor y placer* (2004; Premio Internacional Barcarola); essays: *La Eva futura/La letra futura* (2000), *En brazos de la mujer fetiche* (2002; with Sonia Nuñez Puente), and *Ya no sufro por amor* (2005); and biographies: *La historia de Kurt y Courtney ¡aguanta esto!* (1996) and *Courtney y yo, memoria de un capítulo cerrado (1994-2004)* (2004). She has co-authored several screenplays: *Sobreviviré* (1999), *I love you baby* (2001), *La mujer de tu vida* (2001), and *Amor, curiosidad, prozac y dudas* (2001).

†María de la Cinta Ramblado Minero emphasizes that in *Beatriz* the protagonist's separation from her mother contributes to her identity formation. Much of the criticism about Etxebarria's earlier novels emphasizes the opening of societal barriers and exploration of identity in her work. Carmen Urioste discusses female homosexuality in *Amor* and *(continued on next page)*

beyond her familial bonds, expanding her revaluation of the maternal from the individual to the collective. Eva rejects the submissive model for women and unearths the hidden side of the archetypal mother that patriarchal religion and society condemned and silenced, setting forth a new model of openness, visibility, and strength for females.

Etxebarria's protagonist, Eva Agulló Benayas, begins writing a journal to her eleven-day-old daughter, Amanda, around the first of October and finishes in January, two months after her mother's death. Eva, a published novelist, recounts Amanda's behavior and development, as well as how she met Amanda's father. Additionally, Eva describes her reactions to the physical, mental, and emotional adjustments of her recent pregnancy and new motherhood. She also relates information about her own childhood and poor self-image, her attempts to escape the pain of her identity conflict through alcoholism, and her limited amount of essential knowledge about her own mother. According to Eva's tale, a series of acausal, seemingly coincidental, events — including readings of Tarot cards and the gift of a compass from an unknown man — lead to Amanda's conception and the end of the self-destructive, alcoholic phase of Eva's life. Her daughter's birth and her mother's subsequent illness and death guide Eva to the self-understanding that she reveals to Amanda in her journal. Eva acknowledges, however, that her writing is not only for herself and for Amanda in the future; it is also for her reading public and part of the collective wisdom about motherhood. Eva explains, "lo que escribo ahora mismo, estas palabras sólo para ti, pudieran publicarse..." [what I am writing right now, these words only for you, could be published...] (29). Eva wishes to break through the extensive barrier of maternal absence and silence.

The minimized and invisible relationship between mothers and daughters in Spanish society is evidenced by the plethora of novels by female authors that eliminate the mother. Narrative featuring young protagonists whose mothers have died are so prevalent after the beginning of Francisco Franco's dictatorship in Spain (1939–75) that Birutė Ciplijauskaitė comments in *La novela femenina contemporánea* that novels by Spanish women "se destacan por la ausencia de la madre" [stand out because of the absence

(continued) Beatriz as a counterpoint to the heterosexual role demanded of women. Also see Akiko Tsuchiya about lesbianism and gender roles in her early novels. Jessica Folkart examines discourse as a method for recreation of self in *Beatriz*, while Kathryn Everly probes the metaphysical aesthetic in the same novel. Susana Díaz writes of the intimate themes and perversion of *novela rosa* techniques in early novels. Katja Carrillo Zeiter explores Etxebarria's creation of new models for women, and Vance Holloway examines *Beatriz* as a heroic quest. Pilar Escabias Lloret's interview with Etxebarria probes her fascination with myth and Biblical references.

of the mother] (77).* Without a mother figure, there can be no matriarchal bond, no "cathexis between mother and daughter," which Rich calls "the great unwritten story" (225).

This fictional matricide in narrative by women is symbolic of the position of mothers in Spain after the Spanish Civil War (1936–39). In 1938, even before the end of the war, Franco had enacted policies limiting women's rights and making them dependent on their spouses by reestablishing the Civil Code of 1889, making the husband "el representante de la mujer" [the representative of his wife].† Women could not represent themselves in courts of law, own property, or obtain a divorce from an unfaithful or abusive husband. Wives were encouraged to procreate through monetary benefits, abortion laws were revoked, and females were discouraged from working outside the home and expected to become wives and mothers, all of which eliminated the feminist advances acquired at the beginning of the Second Republic (1931–39). Education for young women encouraged them to be wives and mothers, and Carmen Martín Gaite explains that it "[n]os enseñaba, en resumidas cuentas, a representar. No a ser" [taught us, in short, to perform. Not to be] (*Usos* 64). Women were hidden behind a mask of learned dissimulation — they frequently could not express their true feelings or personality — their real selves were invisible.

Additionally, the alliance between Franco and Pope Pius XII emphasized strict Catholic doctrine and used the image of the Virgin Mother Mary as the ideal for Spanish women. Martín Gaite explains that "el culto a la Virgen María proponía a las chicas casaderas su propio camino de perfección para el futuro" [the cult to the Virgin Mary proposed to married girls their own route of perfection for the future] requiring "la devoción incondicional a la Virgen María" [unconditional devotion to the Virgin Mary] (*Usos* 108, 110). The only sanctioned roles for women in Franco's rule were those of pas-

---

*Ciplijauskaité refers to but does not quote Silvia Truxa's *Die Frau im spanischen Roman nach dem Bürgerkrieg* (Frankfurt: Vervuert, 1982). Some of the more familiar novels that eliminate the mother include Carmen Laforet's *Nada* (1945), Rosa Chacel's *Memorias de Leticia Valle* (1945), Ana María Matute's *Primera memoria* (1960), as well as *La plaça del Diamant* (1962), *El carrer de les camèlies* (1966), and *Aloma* (1968) by Mercè Rodoreda. A few of the novels published well after Franco's death that feature female protagonists whose mothers have died are Adelaida García Morales' 1985 novella *Bene* (published as *El Sur seguido de Bene*, Madrid: Anagrama), *Las mujeres que hay en mí* (2002) by María de la Pau Janer, and *Bella y oscura* (1993) and *El corazón del tártaro* (2001) by Rosa Montero.

†See Geraldine Scanlon 122–58 regarding the legal position of women in Spain under the Civil Code of 1889 and 320–38 for an overview of the changes Franco made for women. Also see Lisa Vollendorf about the overthrow of feminist ideas during the Civil War and Franco's dictatorship, especially page 6.

sive wedlock and maternity or virginity. The Virgin Mary was the principal cultural archetype for females, but her image during Franco's dictatorship did not include any of the stronger or negative associations that C. G. Jung recognizes as integral in the "dual nature" of archetypal figures (16).

Jung enumerates the qualities of the mother archetype as being not only "maternal solicitude [...] wisdom and spiritual exaltation that transcend reason [...] all that cherishes and sustains, that fosters growth and fertility," but also negative aspects, including "anything secret, hidden, dark; the abyss, the world of the dead, anything that devours, seduces, poisons, that is terrifying and inescapable like fate" (16). Ancient myths, literature, and other religions proffer many archetypes for women that contain active and destructive qualities not seen in the contemporary view of the Mary figure. For example, Kali, Hecate, Demeter, Isis, Mary Magdalene, and others demonstrate co-existence of positive and negative traits.

Originally, the image of the Virgin Mary in Spain also exhibited some disparate qualities that fit better with Jung's description of the mother archetype. According to Linda Hall, who traces Spanish reverence of Mary from the Crusades to the Conquest of the New World in *Mary, Mother and Warrior*, adoration of the Madonna was strong in Spain beginning in the Crusades (17–44). Hall observes that in the years of the *Reconquista* of Spain from the Muslims (722–1492) Mary was "identified with war and conquest, particularly of peoples perceived as non–Christian" and "Marian devotion in Spain was related to earlier mother goddesses, often those associated with fertility and closely tied to the Spanish landscape" (18). The Virgin Mother originally inspired active, material, and even negative associations, like that of the Cross.

However, in 1950 when Pope Pius XII proclaimed the Assumption of Mary as dogma, he barred her from the possibility of death and, as Jung explains, "divested [her] of all the essential qualities of materiality" (42). (In 1854, Pope Pius IX had proclaimed the Immaculate Conception of the Virgin Mary, excluding her from all sin. In both instances patriarchal intervention defined the prototype for women as an unattainable image.) Clearly the model that the *Sección Femenina*, the branch of Franco's rule dedicated to women's issues, and the Catholic Church established for Spanish women sublimated the wisdom, strength, and arcane aspects that Jung's description of the mother archetype embodies. Etxebarria describes a contemporary feminist view of the Virgin in *La Eva futura* (2000): "María en la tradición católica es una figura estática, pasiva. Un objeto de adoración, algo a lo que mirar" [Mary in the Catholic tradition is a static, passive figure. An object of adoration, something to look at] (113).

The name of Etxebarria's protagonist, Eva, in *Un milagro en equilibrio* serves as an antithesis of the passive Marian model set forth for Spanish women. The Catholic Church stresses that Eve was the woman who committed Original Sin, while Mary saved humanity by giving birth to Christ the Redeemer. Eve and Mary together counterbalance each other. Etxebarria further explains in *La Eva futura* that "María y Eva son dos caras de la misma moneda: <Eva/avE>, de forma que el saludo a María, Ave, cierra o sana la tradición pecadora de las mujeres, puesto que si fue una mujer la que cometió el primer pecado, fue también una mujer la que concibió a aquel que lo redimiría para toda la humanidad" [Mary and Eve are two sides of the same coin: <Eva/avE>, such that the greeting to Mary, Ave, closes or cures the sinful tradition of women, given that if it was a woman who committed the first sin, it was also a woman who conceived the one who would redeem it for all of humanity] (114). Continuing this line of thinking, if Eva is the other side of Mary, Eva could redeem women from the one-sided, incomplete model that they were expected to follow that left them bifurcated, silent, and passive. Like her prototype, Etxebarria's Eva brings forbidden knowledge to the forefront and serves as a genesis. Instead of following the normal decorum of silence about her intimate thoughts, sexual activities, personal blunders, neuroses, and the like, Eva reveals all of this information to her daughter. She breaks barriers of communication between mother and daughter with her complete candor and severs Amanda from a model that demanded perfection.

One rupture that Eva explains to her daughter is the basis for naming her Amanda instead of "un nombre más normal" [a more normal name] (146), as her family suggested, or "Eva, para que fueras la tercera de la familia que lo llevaras (tu abuela, tu madre y tú)" [Eva, so that you would be the third woman in the family with that name (your grandmother, your mother, and you] (148–49). She is Amanda "porque Amanda, en latín, es la forma gerundiva dativa femenina del verbo amar, es decir, que Amanda significa 'para ser amada'" [because Amanda, in Latin, is the feminine, dative, gerund form of the verb *amar* [to love], that is to say, that Amanda means "to be loved"] (148). Eva stresses throughout her journal how important Amanda is to her. Calling her Amanda also follows the example of her atheist great-grandfather, who named his daughters Roman names and not after Catholic saints. Additionally, Eva writes, "me ha hecho ilusión darte un nombre pagano que explica que tu madre te concibió en abstracto y en concreto, como concepto y embrión, para amarte. Porque al pensarte te di forma y al nombrarte te creé: tu eres mi *logoi*" [it pleased me to give you a pagan name that explains that your mother conceived you abstractly and concretely, as a concept and an embryo, to love you. Because by thinking of you I gave you form and by naming you I created you: you are my *logoi*] (148). Eva's break from religious precedents and her thought process about naming her daughter emphasizes that she considers Amanda an individual distinct from restrictive models.

Although Etxebarria points out in *La Eva futura* that Eve is the antithesis to the Virgin Mary, the protagonist Eva tells Amanda that she does not want her daughter to have the negative characteristics associated with Eve. Eva explains that her Biblical namesake is "suplantadora, porque es la sumisa que le quitó su puesto a la primera esposa, a aquella Lilith que no nació de la costilla de Adán, la que fue creada a la vez que su compañero y modelada a partir del mismo barro [...] a la que un Dios padre masculino y vengativo expulsó del Paraíso..." [a fraud, because she is the submissive one who took the place of his first wife, the one named Lilith that wasn't born of Adam's rib, but was created at the same time as her companion and modeled from the same clay [...] the one who a masculine and vengeful God the father expelled from Paradise...] (149).* According to Erika Bornay, who documents socially induced misogyny through the *femme fatale* figure in art, Lilith is the "iconografía del deseo y la misoginia masculinos, el papel relevante del arquetipo de la *femme fatale*" [iconography of masculine desire and misogyny, the relevant role of the archetype of the femme fatale] because she was the first woman to rebel against man and God the Father (17). Lilith is the first *bad woman*, in contrast to the purity of the Virgin Mary, and Bornay points out that artistic expression often depicts Lilith with a serpent or as half woman/half serpent to show her personification as Devil. Lilith, as serpent, is the one who incites Eve to commit Original Sin. Even though Eva considers her name meek — like Eve before she eats of the tree of Knowledge — the archetypal Eve conveys rebellion just as Lilith does. But at this point in her writing process, Eva — like her namesake before tasting the apple — has not attained the wisdom or self-understanding that the closure of her journal brings.

Besides feeling that "Eva" connoted submission before Amanda's birth, Eva wanted Amanda to have a name distinguishable from hers. In contrast, Eva says that having the same name as her mother caused her to be "en per-

---

*In *Amor,* the protagonist, Cristina, says Lilith and other strong women in the Bible "demostraron que no eran el apéndice de nadie" [demonstrated that they were not the appendage of anyone] (252).

manente búsqueda de una identidad que desde el principio me fue negada pues ni mi propio nombre tenía..." [in permanent search of an identity that was denied to me from the beginning since I didn't even have my own name...] (150). Eva has read that naming offspring the same as a parent can prevent the child from developing her own personality and she tells Amanda, "quería crearte, y crearte distinta a mí" [I wanted to create you and to create you distinct from me] (149). Psychologists confirm that the bond between mothers and daughters often causes unconscious identity confusion for female children,* and novels such as Ana María Moix's *Julia* and Esther Tusquets' *El mismo mar de todos los veranos* demonstrate the daughter's inability to differentiate herself from her mother. Eva notes that her own mother was called Eva and she was Evita — a little version of her mother.

In addition to the difficulty of making herself distinct from her progenitress, Eva also had a bifurcated personality because expectations for her contrasted with the way she really was. In an attempt to please others, she had to conceal significant aspects of her essential self. Eva discloses:

> ... siempre me he sentido dos. Una, mi yo esencial, la persona que verdaderamente soy bajo todas estas capas de cebolla de disfraces y convenciones sociales que se superponen unas a otras y esconden lo que hay en el interior [...] una criatura escondida que se alza intacta desde las memorias de infancia[...]. Y la otra, la persona que no soy pero que siempre creí ser a partir de lo que los demás decían que era: un [...] desastre.
>
> [...I have always felt like two. One, my essential self, the person that I truly am beneath all these onion layers of disguises and social conventions that overlay each other and hide what there is in my interior [...] a hidden creature that rises up intact from my memories of childhood[...]. And the other, the person who I am not but that I that I always believed I was from what others said I was: a [...] disaster.] [14].

The aspiration that women and girls should be saintly caused Eva to believe any other qualities needed to be hidden. The world communicated to her that her real self was not acceptable, so Eva insulated her personality and adopted masks to hide behind. Eva's perception of the division between her real self and the one society demanded of her is reminiscent of Julia's schizophrenic division of personality in Moix's *Julia*. By writing to Amanda, Eva highlights her dangerous splitting of self and the cause of her inner separation in order that her daughter might avoid the same conflict.

Eva clarifies that she was further confused about her inner struggle because her mother's behavior demonstrated that females should react with

---

*For example, see Jung 36 and 39 and Nancy Chodorow 93.

passive compliance to the demands of others and suppress their own needs. She feels that comprehending her mother would help her know why she tried to be the person others wanted instead of her true self. Eva expresses her frustration about misunderstanding her mother's life and for imitating her exasperating conduct:

> Lloré por el amor que le había tenido y que tantas veces se había transformado en odio cuando caía en el crisol de la impotencia. Mi impotencia ante la imposibilidad de verla feliz, sana, contenta. Mi impotencia al sentir que ella no era otra cosa que un apéndice de mi padre, alguien a quien yo no quería de ninguna manera parecerme y a quien sin embargo siempre acababa imitando en mi estúpido coleccionismo de hombres que me gritaban siempre para ponerse por encima de mí, réplicas de mi padre....
>
> [I cried for the love I had had for her and that so many times had transformed itself into hate when it fell into the crucible of impotence. My impotence facing the impossibility of seeing her happy, healthy, content. My impotence upon feeling that she wasn't anything more than an appendage of my father, someone who I didn't want to resemble in any way and who, nonetheless, I always ended up imitating in my stupid collection of men that always shouted at me to get the best of me, replicas of my father....] [341].

Eva's primary model for behavior indicated by her actions that a woman should serve as silent, abnegated support for her husband, just as the *Sección Femenina* instructed. But Eva's more subtle observations of her mother's unhappiness contradicted the compliant role she played.

Jung points out that, especially for girls, the biological mother becomes the model they follow: "The carrier of the archetype is in the first place the personal mother, because the child lives at first in complete participation with her, in a state of unconscious identity" (36). Eva's lack of knowledge about why her mother tolerated a life that made her so unhappy, while she espoused subservience to her husband, led Eva to repeat the same behavior, unknowingly choosing men who treated her badly. Their lack of respect exacerbated her identity problems, leading her to drink excessively to numb the confused part of herself and, thus, perpetuated her state of unconscious identity with her mother.

In *Ya no sufro por amor* (2005) Etxebarria echoes Jung, saying that the "equilibrio emocional" [emotional equilibrium] of the daughter depends on the mother as "representante del paradigma" [representative of the paradigm] (50). Following her mother's illness and death, Eva laments that she never understood her: "Mi madre ha muerto, ya está fuera de mi alcance [...] y me he quedado sin saber la razón última de sus silencios y sus melancolías...." [My mother has died, she's out of my reach now [...] and I am left without knowing the ultimate reason for her silence and her melancholy...] (414). Part of Eva's desire to know about her deceased progenitress arises from the realization that Eva Benayas was not acting as a whole person and that she, like Eva, was hiding the part of her condemned by a hyper-patriarchal culture. Knowing that her mother was more than her father's accessory would separate Eva from a detrimentally unbalanced archetypal model that was also destructive for Eva Benayas and made it impossible for both her and Eva to live healthy lives. Eva seeks validation of the part of her self she has had to hide and of the obscured part of her mother that she perceived but could not substantiate.

In contrast to the confusion that Eva feels with regard to her mother's behavior, the path was simpler for motherless protagonists in earlier novels because they had no conflicted mothers indoctrinating them to be submissive. Martín Gaite points out that many of the protagonists in post-war novels by women, beginning with Andrea in Laforet's *Nada*, were "chicas raras" [strange girls] who did not conform to society's expectations.* These protagonists were free of the imprint of the personal mother, who becomes the unconscious prototype for her child. They acted unconventionally and served as literary models for women, giving them an alternative to the role of happy wife and mother prescribed by the *Sección Femenina*.

Ellen Mayock employs Martín Gaite's concept of the "chica rara" and elaborates that "[t]he *chica rara* evolves into the *mujer rara* in the narrative of the immediate post–Franco period. She evolves from passive observer of her surroundings to being an inherent part of those surroundings as she becomes increasingly comfortable with her role not only as voyeur/recorder but also as innovative creator of text" (231). Eva fits into the category of "chica/mujer rara" [strange girl/mother] because she has difficulty conforming to the role expected of her and because of the emphasis on her task as author. But Eva would also like to revalue Eva Benayas as a "strange mother." Revaluing her in this way would mean recognizing that her mother also had an unconventional nature, albeit a hidden one. Eva needs to know the forbidden, intimate details of her progenitress' life that belie the subservient, docile role she appeared to play.

Since the protagonist Eva symbolizes a counterbalance to the passive Marian model, Eva Benayas's name suggests that she also might have con-

---

*See *Desde* 101–22. Martín Gaite's writing is an exception to works deficient in positive mother/daughter relationships. See Emilie Bergmann about Martín Gaite's supportive matriarchal dialogue.

flicted with the expectations of society. Eva's mother's friend Eugenia reveals that Eva Benayas was practically engaged for several years to Miguel, Eva's uncle. Even though they were deeply in love, Miguel married Reme Agulló, and Eva Benayas later wed Reme's brother, Vicente. Eugenia tells Eva, "Miguel se casó con Reme porque creía que Eva no podía tener hijos, y ya ves, al final la Reme no tuvo ninguno y la tuya cuatro" [Miguel married Reme because he believed that Eva couldn't have children, and you see, in the end Reme didn't have any and your mother had four] (313). Again, the importance of motherhood in Spanish society is evident, as Miguel and his family did not consider Eva Benayas worthy of marriage since—because of a congenital heart condition—she could not conceive children without grave risks to her health and the child's. Miguel's Francoist parents also scorned the political beliefs of the Benayas family, but the most important aspect of this revelation for Eva was the hint that her mother had secret passions outside of her marriage. This suggestion of rebellion intrigues Eva.

Eugenia also unveils a surprising personality trait that Eva had not observed in her mother: "a tu madre se le veía que tenía mucha fibra [...] y la otra [Reme] parecía más fácil de llevar, poquita cosa" [One could see that your mother had a lot of strength [...] and the other one [Reme] seemed easier to persuade, a weak little thing] (316). Eugenia's comments about Eva Benayas's strength and integrity contrast sharply with the tearful, weak behavior Eva always saw. Eva hated her mother "porque no conseguía entenderla y porque me exasperaban sus suspiros, sus enfermedades, sus cansancios y sus lágrimas..." [because I never was able to understand her and because her sighs, her illnesses, her exhaustion, and her tears exasperated me...] (394). But knowing that her mother had probably been in love with her uncle for so many years partially explains her defeated attitude, the resentment of her aunt Reme, her uncle Miguel's alcoholism and death (possibly suicide), and her father's repeated words that his wife was "mercancía usada" [used merchandise] (381). If her mother had revealed all this as Eva matured, their relationship and Eva's self-concept could have been very different. However, Eva Benayas's disclosure of passions outside of marriage would have undermined the ideal of marriage the *Sección Femenina* expected of all women. It also would have transgressed the saintly archetypal role to which they conformed: the Virgin of the Assumption.

The influence of the ubiquitous Virgin archetype on Eva's parents becomes particularly evident immediately before Eva Benayas's death when she is "incapaz de moverse o incluso de sobrevivir sola" [incapable of moving or even surviving by herself] (297). Eva says that she is surprised to find a religious card with a picture of the Virgin of the Assumption on her mother's bed and asks the nurse who put it there: "[M]e ha contestado que no está segura, pero que juraría que mi padre, lo que me ha sorprendido todavía más, porque de toda la vida siempre fue muy escéptico con respecto a lo que consideraba supercherías" [She answered me that she wasn't sure, but that she would swear that it was my father, something that surprised me even more, because all of his life he was always very skeptical of what he considered superstitions] (297). Eva's father crowned his wife's bed with an image reflecting the Pope's elevation of the Virgin to a level that detached her from her human weaknesses. As his wife nears death, completely passive and dependent upon others, Vicente associates her with the mystic image he wanted her to be — the submissive Virgin that Jung says has "ethereal incorruptibility" (41). Vicente even decides not to give his wife the "cinco minutos de lucidez antes del final" [five minutes of lucidity before the end] that the doctors offer (179). In contrast to Eva's desire to revalue her mother with hidden strength and passions, Vicente would like to erase his wife's passive rebellion — demonstrated by her tears and depression — that proved he could not control her feelings.

Although Vicente links his wife to the idealized Virgin as she is dying, during most of their marriage he constantly reminded her "del favor que le hizo al casarse con ella" [of the favor that he did for her by marrying her] and "del favor que le hizo al traerla a Madrid" [of the favor that he did for her by bringing her to Madrid] (381) — possibly to get her away from the gossip related to Miguel. Vicente always said that he loved her more than she loved him, but — instead of respecting her — his efforts to win her affection echo Franco's laws that made wives and daughters nearly equivalent to property. Eva relays how she herself felt in her father's presence:

> En cuanto a mi padre, siempre sentí que asfixiaba como una planta parásita. Porque cuando él me quería yo me odiaba. Porque para que me quisiera yo tenía que fingir que no era yo, que no creía en lo que creía, que no recordaba lo que recordaba y que aprobaba unos comportamientos que no aprobaba. [...] Me quería cuando no era yo.
>
> [With respect to my father, I always felt that he asphyxiated like a parasitic plant. Because when he loved me I hated myself. Because in order for him to love me I had to pretend that I wasn't me, that I didn't believe in what I believed in, that I didn't remember what I remembered and that I approved of behaviors that I didn't approve of. [...] He loved me when I wasn't me.] [395].

The combination of the dominate legal position of men and the submissive model set forth for women caused mother and daughter to deny their true feelings and resulted in neurotically destructive emotions for both of them.

The omnipotence of the Virgin archetype for Eva Benayas is also evident. In order to fulfill the esteemed role of motherhood, she made several pilgrimages to Elche to pray to the Virgin of the Assumption. After giving birth to a child when it was believed that she could not have any, Eva Benayas named her first daughter Asunción, in honor of the Virgin. When Eva, her fourth child, was born, she depended even more on the Virgin because of her age and heart condition. Eva describes the pregnancy, "Se pasó todo mi embarazo en la cama, rezando entre susurros y manoseando una estampita de la Virgen. Y es por eso que yo me llamo Eva Asunción (agárrate)..." [She spent all of my pregnancy in bed, praying between sighs and touching a replica of the Virgin. And it's because of that that I'm called Eve Assumption — How does that grab you? ...] (299). Neither of Eva's names belongs to her — one is her mother's and one her sister's. But her name is bifurcated in another way as well because it refers both to the woman representing Original Sin and to the Virgin proclaimed without sin. Jung believes that consideration of the Virgin in that dogmatic way "does nothing to diminish the tension between opposites, but drives it to extremes" (43). The conflict Eva has felt all her life is represented by her name, and Eva wonders if her mother felt the same tension.

Eva even questions whether her mother's whole married life was a way to prove her worth in a society that honored an unrealistically sanctified concept of motherhood. Eva writes to Amanda, "yo ya nunca sabré si mi madre de verdad añoraba al tío Miguel o [...] si amó a mi padre o sólo le estuvo agradecida, o si le aguantó tantos años y tantos gritos en un esfuerzo por demostrarle al mundo [...] que valía todo lo que la familia de Miguel no supo ver" [I'll never know now if my mother really yearned for Uncle Miguel or [...] if she loved my father or was only grateful to him, or if she put up with so many years and so much shouting in an effort to demonstrate to the world [...] that she was worth all that Miguel's family refused to see] (414–15). Not understanding her mother's dedication to her conflicted marriage was crippling, but describing everything for Amanda helps Eva respect her mother and herself and recognize that they both had to conceal essential aspects of their personalities. Eva's fascination with the intimate details of her mother's life and her process of self-inquiry are not new in Spanish fiction by women. Montserrat Roig's trilogy of novels *Ramona, adéu* (1972), *El temps de les cireres* (1976) and *L'hora violeta* (1980), for example, emphasizes the importance of communicating women's feelings, and Ciplijauskaité highlights the heritage of female narrative in Spain that focuses on identity formation. But Eva's communication of matriarchal heritage to her own daughter is a genesic task: the purpose of this transmission is to begin a new era of forthright communication between mother and daughter and among women.

Eva tells Amanda that part of self-understanding and power resides in maternal knowledge: "No puedes entender tu historia si no entiendes primero la mía, aunque en principio no parezca que tengan mucha relación estas líneas que escribo con tu vida" [You can't understand your story if you don't understand mine first, although at first it might not seem that these lines that I'm writing have much connection with your life] (78). Since Eva's lack of comprehension about her mother's depression and submissiveness left her impotent and victimized, she vows to Amanda, "[N]o quiero que tengas que enterarte, confusamente y por terceros, de partes trascendentales de la historia de tu madre..." [I don't want you to have to find out, confusedly and from third parties, about transcendental parts of your mother's story...] (415). In order to learn significant details of her mother's life and make her own existence comprehensible, Eva had to loosen Eugenia's tongue with a glass of anise. In contrast, Eva freely relates intimate thoughts, sexual attractions, and other private information to help Amanda understand her maternal history. The "forbidden" knowledge Eva communicates provides a more complete legacy and counterbalances the Marian archetype that dictated that women be silent and sinless.

As Etxebarria's novel suggests, communication with daughters is relatively scarce in Spanish narrative by women. While many female protagonists highlight that they are writing about their thoughts, unlike Eva, most do not name their children as the intended readers. Etxebarria's novel is partially intended as a fictional intertext with Carme Riera's 1998 journal to her unborn daughter, Maria. In the prologue to *Temps d'una espera*, Riera explains that "un grupo de profesoras norteamericanas, interesadísimas por la literatura hispánica actual, que con el pretexto de que no existen diarios de embarazo me animaron y hasta me pidieron encarecidamente que publicara el mío" [a group of female North American professors, extremely interested in current Hispanic literature, with the pretext that journals of pregnancy don't exist, encouraged me and even pleaded with me to publish mine] (9).* Etxebarria's Eva says she bought Riera's book during her pregnancy:

---

*I quote from Riera's Castilian version, *Tiempo de espera*. *Temps d'una espera* (Barcelona: Columna, 1998), was published first.

> Lo leí — o más bien lo devoré — en menos de una hora y, cuando lo cerré, me quedé con la sensación de que un abismo se abría entre la percepción del embarazo según la Riera y la realidad que yo estaba viviendo. En aquellas páginas — maravillosamente escritas, por cierto — se describía una especie de remanso idílico de días huecos y redondos, una paz derivada de la conexión mística entre la madre y el bebé. Nada que ver con lo mío....
> [I read it — or rather I devoured it — in less than an hour and, when I closed it, I had the sensation that an abysm was opening between the perception of pregnancy according to Riera and the reality that I was living. In those pages — marvelously written, for sure — a sort of idyllic space of free and rounded days was described, a peace derived from the mystic connection between the mother and baby. Nothing to do with my pregnancy....] [37].

Riera's pregnancy seemed unrealistically agreeable, so Eva says she wrote Riera asking if she had never vomited or experienced other unpleasant effects. Eva describes topics from morning sickness to hormonal changes, again highlighting the shadow side of almost everything.

In addition to the common theme of pregnancy and the letter in diary form written to a daughter that *Un milagro en equilibrio* shares with *Temps d'una espera*, Riera's expression of the estranged relationship she had with her mother also inspires Etxebarria's work. For example, Riera laments to Maria that she knows nothing about her mother's pregnancy with her and continues, "Es posible que nunca llegue a saberlo. De mi madre no sé nada y ella parece poco propicia a las confidencias" [it's possible that I will never find out. I don't know anything about my mother, and she's not inclined to be confidential] (38). Eva further expands Riera's idea of the importance of the mother's thoughts and the wish to have established better communication with her. Several other Spanish women novelists in their publications after 2000 — including Soledad Puértolas, Cristina Cerezales, Esther Tusquets, Rosa Montero, María de la Pau Janer, and Riera herself — also express a nostalgic desire for motherly intimacy.*

Eva elaborates to Amanda the importance of understanding her mater-

---

*Puértolas laments the lack of knowledge about her mother in a book of memoirs, *Con mi madre* (2001), and her novel *Historia de un abrigo* (2005) centers around a missing fur coat that belonged to one narrator's deceased mother. Cerezales' 40-year-old protagonist, Justa, in *De oca a oca* (2000) visits her godmother, who helps her trace her origins and examine the conflicted relationship with her mother. In Tusquets' *Correspondencia personal* (2001), the writer addresses her mother in the first of four letters. Montero's *El corazón del tártaro* (2001) focuses on Zarza's forgiving her mother and herself, and Carlota in de la Pau Janer's *Las mujeres que hay en mí* (2002) is inspired by the ghosts of her mother and grandmother. In Riera's *La mitad del alma* (2003), the protagonist, C., searches for details about her dead mother after discovering that an extra-martial relationship resulted in her conception.

nal heritage, but she also emphasizes Amanda's importance for her. Eva comments — somewhat sarcastically — that a neighbor lady now respects her simply because she is a mother: "Tu presencia me legitima: ya no soy la chica de vida dudosa y mala fama mediática, ahora me he convertido en toda una madre de familia…" [Your presence legitimates me: I'm not the girl of doubtful life styles and bad reputation any more, now you have converted me into a complete mother of a family…] (292). Eva's observation that maternity validates her is very traditional, but Amanda's conception also marked the moment that Eva saw herself as "una persona entera y no como una mitad en permanente búsqueda de la otra mitad que debía completarla…" [a whole person and not like a half in permanent search of the other half who would complete her…] (311). Instead of having a child because society values motherhood, being Amanda's mother marks Eva's identity as a whole person.

Eva also stresses another creative, albeit self-serving, aspect of having a child: "si alguna vez hubo una musa interesante, ésa has sido tú, la más linda, la más dulce, la más inspiradora de todas" [If ever there were an interesting muse, she has been you, the prettiest, sweetest, most inspiring of all] (329). Amanda's role as muse connects with Ciplijauskaité's observations about the innovative novels of development dealing with fetal children written in European countries other than Spain between 1970 and 1985. Ciplijauskaité comments, "Es de notar que casi todas las autoras que se ocupan de este tema lo vinculan al nacimiento de la palabra: la gestación del lenguaje del cuerpo para unas; la posibilidad de diálogo libre para otras; la transmisión de la sabiduría primordial, eternal para todas" [it is notable that nearly all the female authors that occupy themselves with this theme link it to the birth of the word: the gestation of the language of the body for some; the possibility of free dialogue for others; the transmission of primordial, eternal knowledge for all of them] (66). Although Etxebarria's novel deals with a newborn rather than unborn child, it is about pregnancy and Eva's feelings toward Amanda before her birth as well. Eva also believes that improved communication between mother and daughter leads to greater acumen.

In addition to writing to her daughter Amanda, Eva — like the real life Riera — acknowledges other readers. After publishing *Enganchadas,* a novel about women addicted to drugs, Eva receives a letter from Nuria, a former cocaine addict. Nuria writes, "Yo tengo ahora treinta años y a veces pienso en tener un hijo, pero me asaltan un montón de dudas: ¿se me deformará el cuerpo?, ¿perderé mi libertad?, ¿sabré quererle? Por eso me parece tan importante que una mujer como tú escriba un libro sobre la experiencia, porque sé que no harás nada cursi ni lleno de tópicos" [I am 30 years old now and sometimes I think about having a child, but I have tons of doubts: Will it ruin my figure? Will I lose my freedom? Will I know how to love it? Because of that it seems so important that a woman like you write a book about the experience, because I know that you wouldn't do anything mundane or full of clichés] (35). And Eva intends to publish her diary/letter to Amanda because "todo el mundo me pedía que escribiera sobre la maternidad: porque hay muy poco escrito, y muy poco aceptable" [everybody asked me to write about maternity: because there is very little written, and very little acceptable] (43). Eva tells Amanda, "Esta carta no es sólo para ti. Puede que también sea para Nuria[...]. Puede que sea para mí..." [This letter isn't only for you. It may also be for Nuria[...]. It may also be for me...] (43). Nuria represents Eva's readers, and writing for her is Eva's (and Etxebarria's) contribution to collective wisdom conveyed in novels by women. Again, Eva includes the marginal or shadow side of culture, overturning the saintly expectations for women that Franco's rule demanded.

As noted in the beginning of this essay, Franco's dictatorship reduced women's rights, and his alliance with Pope Pius XII imposed a beatific, submissive model for women that essentially silenced any wisdom or authority they might have expressed. Women novelists symbolized the resulting lack of matriarchal communication by using motherless protagonists who broke away from the passive role demanded of women. Eva's journal, however, communicates the most intimate and controversial details of Amanda's history and insures that a new legacy of matriarchal knowledge has commenced. Eva ruptures barriers of communication between mother and daughter and breaks away from an archetype that dogmatically condemned women to neurotic behavior patterns. Etxebarria's novel — published soon after the birth of her own daughter and dedicated to her mother — also reaches from the personal to the collective. Instead of eliminating the mother, Etxebarria revalues her role in *Un milagro en equilibrio* and offers a new paradigm of openness and honesty for female communication. While diminishing the influence of the Virgin archetype augments women's individual qualities and strengths, it also promises to widen what John Ward Anderson calls a "schism" between the Catholic Church and Spanish society. Since severe conflicts have resulted from backlashes against liberal ideas in Spain, finding equilibrium between patriarchal religious dogma and female individuation may be a true miracle.

Works Cited

Anderson, John Ward. "A Church-State Schism in Spain: Socialist Leader Backs Policies at Odds with Catholic Doctrine." *The Washington Post on the Web* 1 Mar. 2006. 25 May 2006 <http://pqasb.pqarchiver.com/washingtonpost/access/995133901.html>.

Bergmann, Emilie L. "Narrative Theory in the Mother Tongue: Carmen Martín Gaite's *Desde la ventana* and *El cuento de nunca acabar*." *Spanish Women Writers and the Essay: Gender, Politics, and the Self.* Eds. Kathleen Glenn and Mercedes Mazquirán de Rodríguez. Columbia: University of Missouri Press, 1998. 172–97.

Bornay, Erika. *Las hijas de Lilith*. Madrid: Cátedra, 1998.

Carrillo Zeiter, Katja. "<<...el amor y otras mentiras>>. Mujeres, sexo y amor en las novelas de Lucía Etxebarria." *<<El amor, esa palabra...>>: El amor en la novela española contemporánea de fin de milenio*. Eds. Anna-Sophia Buck and Irene Gastón Sierra. Madrid: Iberoamericana, 2005. 41–53.

Chodorow, Nancy. *Reproduction of Mothering: Psychoanalysis and the Sociology of Gender*. Berkley: University of California Press, 1978.

Ciplijauskaité, Biruté. *La novela femenina contemporánea: Hacia una tipología de la narración en primera persona (1970–1985)*. Barcelona: Anthropos, 1988.

Díaz, Susana. *[Per]versiones y convergencias*. Madrid: Nueva, 2005.

Escabias Lloret, Pilar. "Entrevista con Lucía Etxebarria, Aberdeen, 18 de noviembre de 2000." *Tesserae: Journal of Iberian and Latin American Studies* 8.2 (2002): 201–12.

Etxebarria, Lucía. *Amor, curiosidad, prozac y dudas*. Barcelona: Plaza, 1997.

———. *La Eva futura: Cómo seremos las mujeres del siglo XXI y en qué mundo nos tocará vivir*. Barcelona: Destino, 2000.

———. *Un milagro en equilibrio*. Barcelona: Planeta, 2004.

———. *Ya no sufro por amor*. Madrid: Martínez, 2005.

Everly, Kathryn A. "Beyond the Postmodern Bodily Aesthetic in *Beatriz y los cuerpos celestes*." *Monographic Review/Revista Monográfica* 27 (2001): 165–75.

Folkart, Jessica. "Body Talk: Space, Communication, and Corporeality in Lucía Etxebarria's *Beatriz y los cuerpos celestes*." *Hispanic Review* 72.1 (2004): 43–64.

Hall, Linda B. *Mary, Mother and Warrior: The Virgin in Spain and the Americas*. Austin: University of Texas Press, 2004.

Holloway, Vance. "The Feminine Quest-Romance in Spain at the End of the Twentieth Century." *Monographic Review/Revista Monográfica* 17 (2001): 36–61.

Jung, C. G. *Four Archetypes: Mother/Rebirth/Spirit/Trickster*. Trans. R. F. C. Hull. From *The Collected Works of C. G. Jung*, Vol. 9.1. Princeton: Princeton University Press, 1992.

Martín Gaite, Carmen. *Desde la ventana: Enfoque femenino de la literatura española*. Madrid: Espasa, 1992.

———. *Usos amorosos de la postguerra española*. Barcelona: Anagrama, 1987.

Mayock, Ellen C. *The "Strange Girl" in Twentieth-Century Spanish Novels by Women*. New Orleans: University Press of the South, 2004.

Ramblado Minero, María de la Cinta. "Conflictos generacionales: La relación madre-hija en *Un calor tan cercano* de Maruja Torres y *Beatriz y los cuerpos celestes* de Lucía Etxebarria." *Espéculo: Revista de Estudios Literarios* 23. Mar. 2003. 6 Mar. 2006 <http://www.ucm.es/info/especulo/numero23/conflict.html>.

Rich, Adrienne. *Of Woman Born: Motherhood as Experience and Institution*. New York: Norton, 1976.

Riera, Carme. *Tiempo de espera*. Barcelona: Lumen, 1998.

Scanlon, Geraldine M. *La polémica feminista en la España contemporánea (1868–1974)*. Madrid: Siglo XXI, 1976.

Tsuchiya, Akiko. "The 'New' Female Subject and the Commodification of Gender in the Works of Lucía Etxebarria." *Romance Studies* 20.1 (2002) 77–87.

Urioste, Carmen de. "Las novelas de Lucía Etxebarria como proyección de sexualidades disidentes en la España democrática." *Revista de Estudios Hispánicos* 34.1 (2000): 123–37.

Vollendorf, Lisa. Introduction. *Recovering Spain's Feminist Tradition*. Ed. Lisa Vollendorf. New York: MLA, 2001. 1–27.

Negotiating Girlhood: Mediating Bodies and Identities in Novels by Care Santos

Parissa Tadrissi

> If there is something right in Beauvoir's claim that one is not born, but rather *becomes* a woman, it follows that *woman* itself is a term in process, a becoming, a constructing that cannot rightfully be said to originate or to end. As an ongoing discursive practice, it is open to intervention and resignification.
>
> Judith Butler, *Gender Trouble*, 33.

In the above passage, Judith Butler defines woman as a term, equating language with ideas and with meaningful identities. She further implicitly posits that the term woman, the idea woman and the identity of a woman are each and together a process, not a state. If this is true, how can we typify this process, how can we understand the female identity process? More specifically, how is this process represented in Spanish literature and in the work of Care Santos? Through her fiction narratives, Santos offers a specific view on the female identity process. She achieves this through both the structure of her stories and through the symbolic values of the language she uses to tell her stories.

When talking of the process of becoming or constructing womanhood, the idea of adolescence is central. Adolescence directly implies a part of a process, a particular segment of the overall identity process. It comes early in the overall life of womanhood, but neither at the beginning nor the end. In Mikhail Bakhtin's term, the process is unfinalizable (*nezavershennost*).*

---

*"Nothing conclusive has yet taken place in the world, the ultimate word *(continued on next page)*

However, adolescence is a critical aspect of the overall process — it represents an accelerated period of progression. It also creates a clear directionality of the female identity process, womanhood increases with time and increases at differential rates during different periods of that time.

This understanding of the role of adolescence in the woman process applies clearly to Santos' narratives, and to the time and place where Santos' stories take place — present day Spain. The concept of adolescence occupies a particular position in recent writing in Spain. At the beginning of the twenty-first century, stories of adolescence, some of which focus on girls, provide a platform upon which many other social themes can be addressed. These themes of social change in Spain include race and ethnicity, sexual orientation, class, female subjectivity, and nationalism. Adolescence plays a dual role here — the process of being a woman as an individual experience and the process of womanhood as a national experience.

No other contemporary Spanish writer appears to have captured all of these experiences as well as Care Santos (b. 1970). Santos herself is not solely a creator of fiction narratives. She has had success as a journalist (she is the director of the cultural section of *El Mundo* newspaper) and thus she holds an influential and relevant voice within the social debates currently taking place in Spain. She is the author of over twenty novels — including twelve *novelas juveniles* aimed at teenage readers such as the bestsellers *Okupada* (1997) *Laluna.com* (2003) and *Los ojos del lobo* (2004).

This essay focuses on two of Santos' *novelas juveniles* [young adult novels]: *Laluna.com* (2003) and *Operación Virgo* (2003). These two novels allow us to consider the role of the female identity process in Santos' works as well as how her works have been playing a role in the female identity process in Spain in recent years. This essay explicitly assumes an interplay and connectedness between Santos' narratives and the larger social narratives ongoing in Spain today. It is within this assumption that language, narrative structure, and social reality can all be seen as taking part in a single dialogue.

The analysis here is based upon the idea that the text can be understood in terms of several areas of meaning. As Roland Barthes argues:

> It is well known that a sentence can be described, in linguistic terms, on several levels (phonetic, phonological, grammatical, contextual); these levels stand in hierarchical relation to each other, for if each has its own units and its own correlations, thus making an independent description mandatory, then none can, of itself, produce any meaning. No unit per-

(continued) of the world and about the world has not yet been spoken, the world is open and free, everything is still in the future and will always be in the future" (166).

taining to a certain level can be endowed with meaning unless it can be integrated into a superior level: a phoneme, although perfectly describable, means nothing by itself; it partakes in meaning only if integrated into a word; and the word itself must in turn be integrated into the sentence [242].

For Barthes, meanings from text must be derived in terms of these several layers of linguistics for any meaning to be produced at all. What is key here is not Barthes' particular rubric of linguistic analysis levels, but the idea that meanings can be produced from a text, and that meaning must be produced from several levels at once.

This idea is similar to one in Mikhail Bakhtin's "Discourse in the Novel," "Form and content in discourse are one, once we understand that verbal discourse is a social phenomenon — social throughout its entire range and in each and every of its factors, from the sound image to the furthest reaches of abstract meaning" (259). Both Barthes and Bakhtin argue that linguistic formality must be considered as well as the content within that linguistic structure. Both theorists also imply that readings of a text are social. Reading is a social interaction among many, including the reader and the text as well as other readers and other texts. This social interaction between reading of linguistic form and content produces meanings from the text.

If meanings are produced, rather than pre-exist, then more than one production of meaning is possible. This essay represents one particular reading of Santos and of contemporary Spain, focusing on the meanings of the symbols, ideas, and concepts that are integrated through Santos' novels and recent Spanish societal changes. Santos appears to be well aware of the social side of reading. Not only is the idea emphasized in her traditional paper and ink texts, it is an integral part of her Internet World Wide Web text. She maintains an interactive website where she and her readers form an interactive community for discussions of the novels and social issues.

Santos connects the reading of her books to her web page http//:www.caresantos.com, where she provides exercises for the teaching of many of her novels in high schools. Technology and girls' issues take center stage in these novels, allowing for a two-fold analysis — the role of the Internet as community forming and the reappropriation of "girliness" as a means of empowerment. Santos' novels lead us to a few questions: How has Internet technology influenced girls' ideas about their bodies and their identities? Might the teenage girl find refuge in works that reflect her reality? Are unity, community and self-fulfillment possible for teenage girls in Spain today? In response to these questions, I analyze the many ways in which teenage girls go about becoming women in *Laluna.com* and *Operación Virgo*. These girls struggle to define themselves against the models offered by older generations and within the new definitions of identity brought about by the Internet and information and communication technology.

On her website, Santos openly addresses sex and sexuality, eating disorders, non-traditional families, and the subordination of women, offering her readers a forum wherein characters and readers are presented with specific topics for dialogue. The fact that these discussions can also be continued and carried out both in cyberspace and the classroom, further contributes to fostering a sense of community for these teenage readers. In light of this, I also pay attention to how both of these novels have been assessed on her web page by her readers. By allowing her readers to post comments about her work, Santos establishes a relationship with her young readers that needs to be considered within global-village narratives and the communities formed through the World Wide Web.

A sense of community is important for girls because they are subject to social dangers. They are vulnerable to rape, verbal abuse, violence inflicted by others and subject to diet pills, illegal substances, eating disorders and self-mutilations. Yet, on the other hand, girlish vulnerability is being reinscribed as "girl power" by popular cultural production (bands, books, magazines, films) that acknowledge the culture's violence but portray girls as in-charge, active participants and self-defenders rather than passive victims. In her article "El adolescente en la literatura juvenil actual," critic and teacher Anabel Sáiz Ripoll indicates that

> En la adolescencia, ese periodo de la vida capital en los seres humanos, se inicia el sentido histórico y la necesidad de actuar, de tomar parte de los acontecimientos, de decidir el rumbo de la propia vida. Aparecen, en consecuencia, las preguntas sobre el sentido de la existencia (¿Quién soy?, ¿adónde voy?) y se elaboran los sistemas de valores sobre los que se cimentará la personalidad adulta. Por eso es tan importante ofrecer puntos de apoyo que favorezcan el proceso de maduración, y la literatura puede cumplir, con éxito y eficacia, parte de esta tarea.
>
> [In adolescence, the period of supreme life in human beings, the sense of history and the need to act, to take part in events and to decide one's path in life are initiated. In consequence, questions about the meaning of existence [Who am I? Where am I going?] emerge and elaborate the value system which will consolidate an adult personality. For this reason it is very important to offer support that favors the maturation process, and literature can fulfill, with success and efficiency, part of this task.] [1].

Care Santos offers, through her novels, an alternative to the dominant script of how girls in Spain should become women. Her fiction enables the girl reader to identify with the self-fashioning project of the protagonist, a project that does not fit within the "traditional mold" of social subordination and domestic dependence that has hitherto been the norm for girls. She offers, and promotes, an alternative reading of the contemporary Spanish social issue of female adolescence. Her effort is to produce a new textual model of the female identity process and how girls in Spain do (and should) become women, accentuating how this particular segment of the identity process should be imbued with meaning.

This new production represents new possibilities for girls in Spain and offers potential answers to ¿quién soy? ¿adónde voy? [Who am I? Where am I going?]. These young women break away from the stereotypes and expectations previously imposed on them by their families and the Catholic Church. Some postpone wedding and family life in order to secure independence and gain entrance to the job market. For others, having a baby is no longer necessary for a fulfilling life and Spanish birth rates are among the lowest in Europe. These changes affect female identity and establish new values in society and family, clearly influencing the psychological climate for adolescents.

Santos portrays strong unlikely heroines in complex novels of female development. The young women of *Laluna.com* and *Operación Virgo* are aware of the imposed limitations associated with their gender, but they struggle to find ways to overcome or circumvent those limitations, portray girls rising above their limitations, persevering in spite of obstacles and awakening to possibilities. As Judith Butler suggests in the opening passage, Santos' texts emphasize the changing nature not only of the womanhood of her characters, but of the idea and identity of womanhood more broadly. Her texts are emphasizing redefinitions of gender, family, self and what a life in progress looks like.

In Spain, girls are confronting models that are discordant with their construction of identity, due to the recent dramatic changes experienced in Spanish society associated with the end of Franquismo and the rejuvenation of the Spanish economy. Young women comprise forty-three percent of youth in the work force,* and are commonly active in feminist youth organizations ("Mujeres jóvenes de Valencia: Las Moiras," "La federación de mujeres jóvenes" in Madrid and the "Jornadas de mujeres jóvenes feministas" in

---

*See *El periódico feminista en red*, "Las jóvenes ganan un 27% menos que los chicos pese a estar más preparadas," <http://www.mujeresenred.net/print.php3?id_article=109>.

Barcelona). Moreover, in Spain today young women are greatly influenced by a global culture based on Internet technology.

Yet despite their visibility, and because of the transitory nature of youth and the acceptance of Spanish literature as universally masculine (Freixas 220), the representation of teenage girls has not been fully developed within the Spanish cultural arena. Anabel Sáiz Ripoll explains that the role models in youth novels are predominantly masculine: "el chico o la chica solitaria, el chico desencantado, el chico que rompe con los esquemas para hacerse oír, el chico sensible, el chico de espíritu aventurero" [The solitary girl or boy, the disenchanted boy, the boy who breaks the mold to make himself heard, the sensitive boy, the boy with an adventurous spirit] (Sáiz Ripoll 5).

Since many of the role models for youth are "chicos," it is significant that Santos chooses to focus on "chicas." But more important than the protagonists of these novels, is how the *readers* may benefit from the questioning of conventional forms of female identity presented in Santos' novels. Spanish teenage girls not only benefit from reading about brave and determined girl characters that can serve as role models for their own lives but, more importantly, that they are invited to think about what becoming a woman means to them personally. In these novels, girls perceive the shifting of conventional roles through characters who question and demand answers. Girls like the ones portrayed by Santos, are the object of this study, as they appear to elude the efforts of the adults around them who are trying to force them into conventional femininity. One could argue that books treating female development are especially valuable to young women readers, who similarly feel the confines of gender expectations closing in on them. Santos' books provide readers with options for eschewing traditional gender roles.

Though Santos' books are her primary instruments to reach youth, the author has caught on to the surge of Internet use by youth in Spain and Europe. Her website is multifaceted — including editorial information, translations, synopsis of her books, literary criticism, a link to up-and-coming Spanish authors, news about her latest social commitments (including workshops on writing for youth) and a section for teachers who may wish to administer classroom activities with her works. As youth across Europe spend less time watching TV and more time using the Internet,* Care Santos responds to this generation's web-based approach to communication by maintaining a blog and receiving emails and postings from her readers.

---

*"EIAA research reveals increasing and more sophisticated usage of the Internet among 15–24 year olds" at: <http://www.eiaa.net/news/eiaa-articles-details.asp?lang=1&id=66>.

The Internet also plays a major role within her narratives — especially in *Laluna.com* and *Operación Virgo*. The reality of youth in Spain today is strongly tied to computer mediated communication and mediated technologies, thus their fictions must shift accordingly. As Catherine Sheldrick Ross explains, "When for members of a particular cultural group the sense of reality changes, then the fictions that they tell themselves must change as well" (20). Santos, in tune with such social transformations, has chosen to portray these shifts in her works. Her narratives illustrate that, by communicating via Internet, youth call into question constructions of identity — including gender, race, sexuality and selfhood. For example, while online, limitations of real-world bodies may be overcome and users may bypass the cultural boundaries delineated by cultural constructs of beauty, ugliness and fashion. Online, participants may re-invent their own gender, race, class and age. Santos' novels represent how youth transcend boundaries, via computer-mediated communication and explore alternate identities.

Laluna.com and *Operación Virgo* explore the notion of *cómo ser una mujer* (or the female identity process) by portraying a young female protagonist who experiments with notions of selfhood in the early twenty-first century. They do this, not with a sense of loss, but with a confidence in their ability to determine their own destiny. The heroines of these novels struggle with abusive, absent or mystifying mothers (and sometimes fathers), with boyfriends and lovers, with school and with work, but they emerge with a sense of forging their own future. Ultimately, these texts can be taken as "blueprints" for the 21st century, as Spanish girls become new Spanish women.

Laluna.com is the name of the cybercafé that comprises the majority of the narrative space in the novel of the same name. The main characters Cira, Cris and Amador contend with gender identity issues. The narrator begins with Amador, Cira's cousin, who talks about the complexity of finding a girlfriend:

> Las tías piensan que sólo buscamos en ellas un culo duro y unas tetas bien puestas. Por eso se hacen las ofendidas[...]. Creen, por ejemplo, que sólo buscamos *eso* de ellas (ya me entendéis) y que antes y después de conseguirlo las dejamos de lado para entregarnos a nuestras únicas actividades en la vida: fútbol y cerveza.
>
> [Girls think that all we look for in them is a firm ass and well placed tits. That's why they act offended[...]. They think, for example, that we're only looking for *you know what* from them (you know what I mean) and that before or after getting it we'll put them aside to devote ourselves to our only activities in life: soccer and beer.] [33].

Amador voices the difficulties and pressures to get to know the "opposite sex," and the demands that young girls face to be physically pretty. He acknowledges that unlike most guys his age, he looks beyond physical beauty. Nevertheless, the norms governing girls' appearance and the violation of these norms, deserve special attention when reading Santos' novels — they crucially influence the life goals and routine practices to which girls (Cira in *Laluna.com* and Patri in *Operación Virgo*) are socialized. In order to reframe our perception of gender roles and thus dislodge such prejudice, Santos celebrates the power of dissidence, as her works portray the argument that we must supplant figurations that perpetuate negative gender stereotypes. Santos' works urge us to combat the social and self-ascribed status of those deemed "different."

Cira begins by telling the reader that the size of her nose is the source of inner conflict: "Tengo una relación más bien complicada con mi nariz. Si no me diera pánico, no es nada que un par de horas de quirófano y tres días con la cara como un bollo no pueda resolver" [I have a complicated relationship with my nose. If it didn't panic me, it would be nothing that a few hours in the operating room and three days with a swollen face couldn't resolve] (17). She goes on to tell us how she has never had a boyfriend and never successfully flirts with boys her age, due to her oversized nose. In characterizing Cira as a girl ridden with physical complexes, Santos is interpreting growing up — she proposes that adolescence is a particularly hard time, and that girls are faced with unrealistic physical expectations. Widening hips, developing breasts, curves and pimples, are inconsistent with media-generated images of ideal beauty.

The study of body image among youth in Spain is fairly recent. María Calado Otero, María Lameiras Fernández and Yolanda Rodríguez Castro from the Universidad de Vigo, note the following:

> En los escasos estudios con mujeres jóvenes se ha encontrado que la auto-objetivación se relaciona positiva y significativamente con alta vergüenza corporal y síntomas de trastornos alimentarios. Esto se podría deber a que el estándar de belleza que la objetivación envuelve es extraordinariamente difícil de conseguir, lo que conlleva un descontento entre el deseo de parecer y la realidad en definitiva, esto provoca un "descontento normativo" de la mayoría de jóvenes con sus cuerpos.
>
> [In the few studies done on young women it has been found that self-objectivity is positively and significantly related to shame of the body and eating disorders. This could be due to the fact that the beauty standard that envelopes the objectivity is extraordinarily difficult to achieve, which leads to a dissatisfaction between the way one desires to appear and the

definitive reality, which provokes a "normative dissatisfaction" in the majority of young women regarding their bodies] [360].*

This study connects diametrically with Santos' portrayal of girls in Spain. Her novels do not simply reflect the lived realities of adolescent girls, instead, they deliberately emphasize bodily experiences such as growth into womanhood and sexual desires, in an effort to subvert the cultural narrative that prescribes girls as passive victims, reframing the terms by which girls' bodies have been traditionally represented.†

Cira, due to her nose, has developed a strong character and is known as a "peleona" [feisty]: "Luego está la gente a quien le caes mal. En mi caso son muchos, porque no soy de ese tipo de personas que se preocupa por lo que los demás piensan de ellos. Y cuando alguien se mete con mi nariz les pego un bofetón y me voy tan tranquila" [Then there's the people who don't like you. In my case it's many, because I'm not the type of person who worries what others think of them. And when someone makes fun of my nose I slap them in the face and go on calmly] (20). Cira has a strong personality and is considered the leader of a group of adventurous girls who decide to go "fly-surfing" for Spring break. Cristina, Amador's girlfriend and the newest addition to the group of friends "las Lokas," is lost at sea during their vacation and found dead 72 hours after her disappearance. Amador is devastated upon the death of his new girlfriend, the first person he feels he has truly loved. The story is not about fly-surfing, but about teenage love, interpersonal communication and individual growth.

Laluna.com is mainly composed of emails between Amador and Cristina. Unbeknownst to him, his cousin Cira is the author of the emails he believes are from his girlfriend Cristina, prior to her death. Amador falls in love with Cristina via email. Having spent little time in person with Cristina, he does not realize that the emails cannot be from the same girl he is dating. The two girls have an agreement; Cira will be the words in the relationship and Cristina the body.

The ".com" of the title exemplifies the cybernetic focus of the story, which is emphasized throughout the novel. The main characters not only

---

*See "Influencia de la imagen corporal y la autoestima en la experiencia sexual de estudiantes universitarias sin trastornos alimentarios," *International Journal of Clinical and Health Psychology*, 4. 2 (2004) 357–370.

†Some important publications regarding girls' and gender roles are: *La guía para chicas* by María José Urruzola Zabalza (Ciudad Real: Junta de Castilla-La Mancha, first published in 1992) and Susana Checa's *Género, Sexualidad y Derechos Reproductivos en la Adolescencia* (Buenos Aires: Paidós, 2003).

communicate via email, but use the Internet as a primary source of information:

> Normalmente, cuando Cira sentía esa urgente necesidad de conectarse a Internet era para buscar páginas de su última chifladura o para encontrar datos nuevos de su chifladura más antigua. Lo normal, pues, era encontrarla consultando sitios web sobre todo tipo de diversiones arriesgadas o sobre cuestiones de interés fundamental para cualquier ser humano de dieciséis años.
> [Normally, when Cira felt the urgent need to connect to the Internet it was in order to look for pages on her latest craze or to find new facts about her oldest craze. It was normal, then, to find her looking up websites on all types of risky activities or about anything fundamentally interesting to any sixteen-year-old human being.] [59].

"Laluna" refers to the group of girlfriends, as they call themselves "las lunáticas," and create their own online discussion group — "las Lokas." "Las lunáticas" online become "las Lokas" denoting with a "k" the rebellious tone to the creation of their group in cyberspace. Their "body" as an online group is a site of contestation, a "battleground" where they struggle with cultural meanings of girlhood. Their identity as "Las lunáticas" offers them a community where as "crazies" they can avoid being coded in patriarchal discourse.

Since the Internet is a space where people can talk without having to disclose details or truths about their identity, or even use their real name, it is no surprise that Amador is easily misled. This negotiation of being present via chats and email and at the same time being absent (a result of the anonymity of the web), works particularly well for the young women in this novel — as they seek to combine a desire to organize and communicate with others, with a need to avoid surveillance. Cira's *pandilla* — "las Lokas," communicate through blogs and emails to one another. The Internet functions as an in-between space that allows them to negotiate between community and anonymity and create identities as they wish. Cira and Cris have mixed their identities, thus fooling Amador. Regarding the possibilities of the Internet as a safe space for young women, Lynne Hillier writes, "The internet is not a geographical space and it has until now been free of the surveillance that in the real world creates invisibility, hostility and frustration for this group" (126). Girls are able to write their bodies and identities without the restrictions of social norms. Cira describes how well the creation of a virtual Cristina comes about: "Cuando Cris leyó mi carta, la que yo le había escrito a su adorado Amador, y que había guardado en mi carpeta de borradores, se quedó pálida de envidia. Fue sincera y reconoció que a ella nunca se le ocurriría algo así. La firmó sin pensarlo dos veces y la envió" [When Cris read my letter, the one I wrote for her to her adored Amador, and had saved in my drafts folder, she became pale with jealousy. She was sincere and recognized that something like that would never occur to her. She signed it without think twice about it and sent it] (82). Cira and Cristina are able to mesh their identities, creating a new "version" of Cristina, the girl that Amador falls in love with.

Santos also proposes a reversal of social norms by including in her novel an age-old plot and revisiting Edmond Rostand's play *Cyrano de Bergerac*. The reference to this nineteenth century play is overt: Cira is Cyrano, Cristina is Christian and Roxanne is Amador. In Santos' lyric romantic comedy, love letters are not sealed and bound, but rather sent electronically as emails. In this fashion, characters negotiate the sketchy terrain of romantic attraction as they wrestle with expectations, reservations and pride. These distinct characters eloquently explore in their emails how we create identity on a screen and out of language. With moments of truth, hilarity and despair, *Laluna.com* makes the reader question conventional beauty by creating a "masculine" heroine. The reader also questions the degree to which physical attraction should dictate a relationship. The intertexual reference to *Cyrano* calls into question Spanish culture's central values and assumptions about girlhood by equating Cira to Cyrano. Santos' story links girlhood to power, showing that girlhood does not have to be an obstacle to self-agency. In *Retelling Stories, Framing Culture*, Stephens and McCallum suggest that "The major narrative domains which involve retold stories, have the function of maintaining conformity to socially determined and approved patterns of behavior, which they do by offering positive role models, proscribing undesirable behavior and affirming the culture's ideologies, systems and institutions" (3–4). I argue that Santos revises *Cyrano*, not to affirm Spanish patriarchal ideologies, but to subvert them, attributing protagonism and power to teenage girls.* She offers positive role models to girls in a narrative which has taken apart its pre-text and reassembled it as a version which is a new textual and ideological configuration.

Santos' novel takes a classic love story and adapts it to modern day standards. She alters nineteenth century love letters to twenty-first century emails and reverses the traditional roles of the "active" characters from a man

---

*These authors separate retelling from revising because "retellings do not and cannot, reproduce the discoursal mode of the source, they cannot *replicate* its significances and always impose their own cultural presuppositions in the process of retelling." The resulting version is a then not so much a retelling as a *re-version* (4).

(Cyrano) to a teenage girl (Cira). In *Laluna.com* girls partake in dangerous physical activities as men would and the love-object, instead of a female, is a passive boy who has been deceived. The ingenious character who in the nineteenth century work is a man-Cyrano, in Santos' contemporary version is a girl-Cira. The substitution of these protagonists exemplifies the importance that Santos confers to revisiting gender roles and focusing on girls' agency in her work. She creates a character whose mind and wit are exemplary, but who embodies an awkward teenager. Such a portrayal confirms Santos' aspiration to render teenage girls as empowered and intelligent individuals. Thus, *Laluna.com* negotiates the narrating and presenting of one's self, through technologies that allow teenagers to explore and create their identities, while undermining traditional gender roles.

The Internet allows these young women to actively manipulate the borders between public and private, to manage expression without resistance and appropriation, by writing their own script. The web is simultaneously there and not there, just as for Amador, Cira and Cris are both there and not there (one in words, the other in body). This capacity to be present and absent, public and private, is reflective of the position of young women today, as both too visible and not visible enough. Cyberspace is a reality that is constantly shifting. Girls find power in the shifting virtual truths that they create: identity, language and talk. Cyberspace can be read as a book that is forever being written, rewritten, revised and erased. In order to better appreciate the influence of technology on gender identities Jiménez Cortés affirms that:

> Para entender las relaciones entre tecnología y género, entre Internet e identidad cultural, entre dimensión social e individual hemos de delimitar la conceptualización de género y de tecnología. En este sentido, la tecnología es algo más que un conjunto de artefactos u objetos físicos ya que incluye una cultura, un conjunto de relaciones sociales legitimadas. Por ello, Internet se convierte en un terreno privilegiado para la articulación y el mantenimiento del poder.
>
> [In order to understand the relationships between technology and gender, between the Internet and cultural identity, between individual and social dimension we must define the conceptualization of gender and technology. In this sense, technology is more than a set of artifacts and physical objects since it includes a culture, a set of legitimate social relations. For this reason, the Internet becomes a privileged field for articulating and maintaining power.]*

---

*See http://cibersociedad.rediris.es/congreso.

These modes of communication maximize girls' ability to connect with one another across a range of contexts, discussing local affairs as well as more broadly felt concerns. In this respect, cyberspace is not completely cut off from the public sphere or from issues that shape contemporary youth politics. Instead, it is a space for participation, communication and activism. One of the "chicas del grupo" conveys this best: "Nuestro lema es <<Vivan las Lokas ke kedan pokas>>. Somos solidarias, defensoras de la naturaleza, cultas y feministas. Todo chicas, por supuesto (porque los tíos suelen estropearlo siempre todo)" [Our motto is <<Live on the Crazies for few remain>>. We are sympathetic, defenders of nature, cultured and feminists. All girls of course (because guys always tend to spoil things)] (99). This passage documents how ideas about girl power, success and self-invention, are borne from an online (and offline) community. These girls use their group space to resist traditional images of girlhood and re-imagine the place of girls in contemporary Spanish society.

Santos continues to portray the importance of sex and body image among girls in *Operación Virgo* (2003), the story of Lucía and Patricia, two best friends and aspiring ballerinas. "Operación Virgo" is a code name for their latest adventure: Patricia's quest to lose her virginity. "Virgo" has a dual meaning in this work; it refers to the fact that both girls are Virgo signs of the zodiac and Virgo*—as part of the Latin root word means "virgin." "Operación Virgo" is a plan that must be accomplished by September 15, Patricia's seventeenth birthday. Though the plan "Operación Virgo" centers on boys, it is important to note that it also subscribes to common notions of "girl power," in that it endorses and values female friendship over the pressure to get boyfriends. In addition, young readers have claimed to identify with *Operación Virgo*:

> Me leído Operación Virgo (en catalán: Ara o mai) no me gustaba leer asta k un dia me interesé por leer su libro y fue fascinante me lo acabe en menos de lo normal. Muchas gracias por darme esa pasión por la lectura. Es el libro k mas me a gustado de todos los que me leído. Ahora estoy pensando en leer y leer todo gracias a usted. Atentamente, su fan número uno. Besitos!!! María.
> [I have read Operación Virgo [in Catalán Ara o mai] and I didn't like to read until one day I became interested in reading your book and it was fascinating, I finished faster than normal. Thank you very much for giving me this passion for reading. It's the book I've liked most in all the ones

---

*According to the Oxford English Dictionary "virgin" is derived from Middle English and from Old French as *virgine* and from Latin *virgo*, "maiden." http://cache.lexico.com/dictionary/graphics/AHD4/GIF/omacr.gif

I've read. Now I'm thinking about reading and reading everything thanks to you. Faithfully, your number one fan. Kisses!!! María.]*

Messages such as this one and numerous others, reveal that Santos has a readership following and that girls connect with the characters in her novels.

The protagonists of *Operación Virgo* welcome their approaching womanhood. They reflect upon each other's lives, as well as those of their mothers and imagine a different future for themselves. In her diary, Lucía retorts to her mother the following:

> Voy a aclararte algunas cosas mamá. Primero: fumar, lo hago muy de vez en cuando, siempre que alguien me invita, porque es muy caro y yo no me lo puedo permitir con la porquería de paga que me das (y eso cuando me la das). Segundo: no bebo ni creo que beba nunca porque el alcohol me repugna y, además, engorda mucho. Tercero: los tíos no me repugnan, no engordan y no salen caros como el tabaco o como la marihuana, así que me siento muy bien, si quedo con varios de ellos en una semana.
>
> [I am going to clear up a few things for you mom. First: smoking, I do it every once in a while, only when someone offers, because it's very expensive and I can allow it for myself with the crappy allowance you give me (and that's when you give it to me). Second: I don't drink nor do I think I will ever drink because I find it repugnant y moreover, it's fattening. Third: I don't find guys repugnant, they're not fattening and they're not expensive like tobacco or marihuana, so I feel very good if I go out with a number of them in a week.] [129].

Here, Lucía expresses her agency and a separation from her mother. Her ability to assume the active position by using the first person (*hago, puedo, bebo, quedo, me siento*) [I do, I can, I drink, I go out, I feel] suggests a diversion not only from her mother's path on to her own, but also from the traditional masculine order that excludes girls, confining them to the realm of "nurturer."

For Christmas, Lucía gives Patricia a copy of *Kama Sutra* to aid in her sexual education. She dedicates the book to Patricia promising that they will achieve their goal to de-virginize her. "Erase una vez una niña virgen que tenía una amiga. Éranse dos amigas que siempre lograban sus propósitos. No olvides el quince de septiembre, cariño: lo conseguiremos" [There once was a virgin girl that had a friend. They were two friends that always achieved their goals. Don't forget the fifteenth of September, darling: we'll do it"] (19). The chapters following this initial claim describe the adventures that the girls undertake in order to find a candidate for Patricia. They put ads in the

---

*See <http://www.caresantos.com>.

newspaper, meet people online and even proposition an old friend. The novel handles the subject of teenage sexuality and puberty in a humorous fashion, while addressing serious topics such as pregnancy, contraception and sexually transmitted diseases. These girls are dealing with new, twenty-first century concerns in a hands-on manner. For example, girls of previous generations were not actively trying to "get laid," as revealed in a conversation between Patricia and one of her possible conquests:

> Tú eres el ideal para resolver esto. Guapo, con experiencia, y con tus veintitrés centímetros, jiji. No sé si cabrás, pero podemos intentarlo.
> — No seas bestia, Patricia, que no soy un semental.
> — Perdona. Era una broma. ¿Querrás ayudarme?
> — No sé, te veo muy lanzada.
> — Pues claro. ¿Tú no estabas lanzado la primera vez?
> — Sí pero era distinto, yo soy un tío.
> — Anda, y eso qué tendrá que ver. Si hoy en día somos nosotras las que llevamos la iniciativa...
>
> [You are ideal for resolving this. Handsome, experienced, and with your twenty-three centimeters, haha. I don't know if you'll fit, but we can try it.
> — Don't be a stupid Patricia, I'm not a reproductive stud.
> — Sorry. It was a joke. ¿Will you help me?
> — I don't know, you seem very forward
> — Well of course. ¿Weren't you forward the first time?
> — Yes, but it was different, I'm a guy.
> — So, and what that have to do with it. Today us girls take the initiative...] [78].

These girls have learned that equality means accessing realms and behaviors traditionally limited to men, they have chosen to appropriate traditional "boy" behavior, while maintaining their own individuality and femininity. Patricia and Lucía represent a new age in Spanish feminism — they are young, fashion-conscious, pop culture-savvy, single teens. Variously referred to as "girl power, "lipstick feminism," or "power feminism," these girls are well aware of patriarchal conceptions of femininity and use them to their own advantage. Insisting on women's right to be individuals, to make their own decisions about whether or not to wear make-up and miniskirts, to read pornography or participate in rough sex, Karen Lehrman sees this type of feminism as "not a set of commands, but a set of challenges." She views feminism as a guide to rational decision-making and self-affirming behavior, rather than a list of predetermined beliefs.

In the wake of Franco's death in 1975, girls realized, perhaps for the first time in Spanish history, that they could fight for the opportunity to rise to their potential — which they certainly did, as witnessed by the number of girls who went to college and on to have professional careers, penetrating the public sphere. With the advent of democracy, laws were made against sexual discrimination and adultery and the sale of contraceptives were decriminalized. Girls became influenced by the Spanish "movida," a sociocultural movement that took place during the 1980s, triggered by an explosion of liberties and the economic rise of Spain. This hedonistic cultural wave was confusing to girls — it implied that equality meant girls should integrate themselves into a "boys" world. In contrast to the Twenty-first century girl, the girls of Francoist Spain grew up deprived of access to "male" things and were forced to participate in "female" things. This left them to assume that in order to gain equality they had to master "boy things." Santos' characters do not have to master "boy things" (though they sometimes choose to), they embrace girlhood and find power in their femininity and female friendships. While it is true that being a ballerina and embracing the pink tutu is stereotypical of girlhood and this is not a radical gesture meant to overturn the way society is structured, it can be interpreted as a confident gesture. Santos portrays a new generation that embraces "girlieness" as well as power (making adult decisions, moving away from home, having a baby). This analysis is more akin to scholars who view third wave feminism as the visions and voices of feminists who positioned themselves "against," rather than necessarily "after," the second wave (Henry). Twenty-first century girls seek to refigure and enhance definitions of Spanish girlhood and womanhood from the 80s and 90s so as to make them more diverse and inclusive.

The teens in *Operación Virgo* are emphasizing the reality of Spanish girls today, who live in contrast to what some women of the previous generation anticipated their lives to be (a rejection of Barbie and all forms of pink packaged femininity.) Santos' work incites readers to think about what it means to be a teenage girl today and more importantly, what messages Spanish narratives are sending to girls about the significance of femininity. Spanish culture has been significantly transformed through the enormous growth in electronic technologies. The feminism these characters portray stems from changing social conditions. This generation's common foci are appropriation, deconstruction and de-centering — and Santos' depiction of power and identity are mirrored in macro-level processes like globalization, the changing composition of the Spanish family and work force and the complex nature and influence of mass culture on youth.

Sexual relationships and body image are of equal importance for the characters in *Operación Virgo*. Both Lucía and Patri watch their diets closely. As ballerinas, they must maintain petite figures and deprive themselves of food. Santos comments on the dangers of eating disorders when she describes Patricia as "esquelética" [very skinny] and when Lucía faints due to malnutrition and an unexpected pregnancy. The girls are required to visit a doctor on a regular basis in order to monitor their weight in a healthy fashion. "Nada de meterse los dedos en la garganta para vomitar ni de esconder comida, ¿de acuerdo?" [Nothing of sticking fingers down the throat to vomit nor hiding food, agreed?] (105). Patri has battled with anorexia before and her doctor knows her well. In the chapter "El doctor Gonfaus y los afrodisíacos naturales," [Doctor Gonfaus and natural aphrodisiacs] Santos portrays a number of important topics for teenage women: use of the birth control pill, weight gain and questions about aphrodisiacs and sexual pleasure.

Teenage pregnancy and abortion are discussed in detail when Lucía decides to renounce her dream of dancing in London to have a baby:

> Un hijo es la excusa perfecta para pasarse el día discutiendo: el agua del baño está demasiado caliente, no le has tapado bien, tardas demasiado en preparar el biberón, cómo es posible que aún no hayas aprendido a cerrar el cochecito.... Todo eso resultan trampas mortales para una pareja como nosotros, que se basaba en el sexo, las salidas nocturnas y la diversión sin freno.
> [A child is the perfect excuse to spend the day arguing: the bath water is too hot, you didn't cover him up properly, you take too long to prepare the bottle, how is it possible that you still haven't learned how to close the stroller.... All of these are fatal traps for a couple like us, that was based on sex, nightlife and non-stop fun.] [132].

Pregnancy is one of the most important social concerns regarding girls in Spain today. The recent ratification of the "morning after" pill is a prime example since many Spanish youth do not use protection. According to *Eroski Salud* in 2004: "Sólo el 12,7% de adolescentes de entre 15 y 17 años que reconoce tener relaciones sexuales utiliza anticonceptivos. Alrededor de 18.000 menores de 19 años se quedan embarazadas cada año en España" [Only 12.7 percent of adolescents between ages 15 and 17 who acknowledge having sexual relations use contraception. Around 18,000 minors under the age of 19 become pregnant every year in Spain] (Embarazos). The lack of education regarding reproductive health care among girls in Spain is depicted in *Operación Virgo* as Patri marvels at the "rent boy's" penis. She is unaware of how his anatomy works and is fascinated by the fact that his member continues to grow. She asks him questions: "¿Me va a doler? ¿Me lo voy a pasar bien? ¿Usaremos preservativo, ¿no?" [Is it going to hurt? Am I going to have fun? We'll use a condom, right?] (96). Care Santos is clearly conscious of the lack of awareness and responsibility among youth in Spain. She depicts the questions, repercussions and lifestyle that sex, pregnancy and motherhood entail. Lucía's choice between having her baby and giving up her career as a ballerina, or having an abortion and pursuing her career, is perhaps one of the key decisions that effects her understanding of "cómo ser una mujer" [how to be a woman].

Santos' teen girls are individualized, resilient, self-driven and self-made. Sherrie Inness argues in *Millennium Girls* that today's young women are "reinvisioning what girlhood actually means in numerous contexts [...] girls today are not passive consumers of mass culture around them but actively interact with popular culture in such a way as to re-imagine and reshape cultural norms of what constitutes acceptable girlhood" (196). They are girls who choose to follow nonlinear trajectories to fulfillment and success. Because of their flexibility and self-actualization, Patri and Lucía come off as confident, empowered, can-do girls that wear pink tutus. The girls may emerge stronger by refuting cultural standards of female beauty and accepting their own bodies, however imperfect, or by resolving conflicts with family and friends. Only after having undertaken a variety of experiments, do these girls finally claim their place with confidence and determination. Santos acknowledges that her readers are the recipients of mixed messages about being a "girl," and that these conflicts must be resolved before girls can take charge of their lives. Her protagonists portray young Spanish women who struggle with issues of gender in ways very different from their ancestors.

During the last twenty years, Spain has seen increases in divorce rates and in the number of unmarried couples, children born out of wedlock, and single mother families. Spain has also registered a rise in teenage pregnancies (Cómo). These changes in social norms have affected the composition of the Spanish household, creating alternative family models to the nuclear family. Because of such abrupt changes, girls face new notions of family and womanhood and have to negotiate their own female identity process or definition of "cómo ser una mujer" as norms and roles continue to evolve. In "Convivencia y relaciones desiguales" María Elena Simón Rodríguez affirms that it is currently very difficult for girls to identify with social models of women because the models offered are mere remakes of stereotypical and patriarchal beauty: Barbies, Lolitas and Misses (Simón).

The Spanish girls of today's world resist the behavioral codes of previous decades but do struggle when defining themselves. As Alberdi, Escario and Matas point out in *Las mujeres jóvenes en España*, the process of equalization in Spain has neither ended, nor been fostered with parallel intensity within the different confines of Spanish society (7). Each of Santos' heroines must determine if her own sense of "cómo ser una mujer" can be reconciled with the models that her culture offers. When it cannot, she is then faced with resolving the conflict, with constructing an identity that allows her an active place in the world. Modern day technology has changed the way girls in Spain create their own identities. Through technology they are able to appropriate the cultural scripts and make them their own. In *Laluna.com* and *Operación Virgo*, girls take culturally gendered scripts and subject them to significant revisions. Though this process of revision always involves both internal and external struggles, these struggles take a much different form and result in much different outcomes than those depicted in earlier youth literature in Spain.

Works Cited

Alberdi, Inés, Pilar Escario, and Natalia Matas, eds. *Las mujeres jóvenes en España*. Barcelona: Fundación La Caixa, 2000. Estudios sociales No. 4. <http://www.pdf.obrasocial.comunicacions.com/es/esp/es04_esp.pdf>.

Bakhtin, Mikhail. "Discourse in the Novel." Trans. Caryl Emerson and Michael Holquist. *The Dialogic Imagination*. Ed. Michael Holquist. Austin: University of Texas Press, 1981.

Barthes, Roland, and Lionel Duisit. "An Introduction to the Structural Analysis of Narrative." *New Literary History* 6.2 (1975): 237–272.

Calado Otero, María, María Lameiras Fernández, and Yolanda Rodríguez Castro. "Influencia de la imagen corporal y la autoestima en la experiencia sexual de estudiantes universitarias sin trastornos alimentarios." *International Journal of Clinical Psychology* 4.2 (2004): 357–370.

Checa, Susana. *Género, Sexualidad y Derechos Reproductivos en la Adolescencia*. Buenos Aires: Paidós, 2003.

"Embarazos en adolescentes: Sólo el 12,7% de adolescentes entre 15 y 17 años que reconoce tener relaciones sexuales utiliza anticonceptivos." *Consumer.es Eroski* <http://www.consumer.es/accesible/es/salud/prevencion_y_medicamentos/2004/10/25/110838.php>.

European Interactive Advertising Agency. "EIAA research reveals increasing and more sophisticated usage of the Internet among 15–24 year olds." <http://www.eiaa.net/news/eiaa-articles-details.asp?lang=1&id=66>.

Freixas, Laura. *Literatura y mujeres*. Barcelona: Destino, 2000.

Henry, Astrid. "Feminism's Family Problem: Feminist Generations and the Mother-Daughter Trope." *Catching a Wave: Reclaiming Feminism for the 21st century*. Eds. Dicker, Rory and Alison Piepmeier. Boston: Northeastern University Press, 2003.

Hillier, Lynne. "'I'm Wasting Away On Unrequited Love': Gendering Same Sex Attracted Young Women's Love, Sex and Desire." *Hecate* 27.1 (2000): 119–127.

Inness, Sherri. *Millennium Girls: Today's Girls Around the World*. Lanham: Rowman & Littlefield Publishers, 1998.

Jiménez Cortés, Rocío. "Internet y educación: La gestión de la identidad cultural de género." <http://cibersociedad.rediris.es/congreso>.

"Las jóvenes ganan un 27% menos que los chicos pese a estar más preparadas." *El periódico feminista en red.* <http://www.mujeresenred.net/print.php3?id_article=109>.

Lehrman, Karen. *The Lipstick Proviso.* New York: Doubleday, 1997.

McCallum, Robyn, and John Stephens, Eds. *Retelling Stories, Framing Culture: Traditional Story and Metanarratives in Children's Literature.* New York: Garland, 1998. 3–23.

Rostand, Edmond. *Cyrano de Bergerac.* Trans. Christopher Fry. London: Oxford University Press, 1975.

Ruiz Huici, Kiko. "Literatura juvenil y el lector jóven." *Cuadernos de Literatura Infantil y Juvenil* 17.174 (2004): 7–14.

Sáiz Ripoll, Anabel. "El adolescente en la literatura juvenil actual." *Othlo* 17.1 <http://www.othlo.com/hletras/escritos/10adolescente.htm>.

Santos, Care. *Laluna.com.* Barcelona: Edebé, 2003.

_____. *Operación Virgo.* Barcelona: Diagonal Junior, 2003.

_____. <http://www.caresantos.com>.

Sheldrick Ross, Catherine. "How to find out what people really want to know." *Reference Services Today: From Interview to Burnout.* Eds. Bill Katz and Ruth A. Fraley. New York: Haworth Press, 1986. 19–27.

Simón Rodríguez, María Elena. "Convivencia y relaciones desiguales." *Currículum y Género* <http://www.ciudadanas.org/ELENASIMON/DOCUMENTOS/CONVIVENCIA_Y_RELACIONES_DESIGUALES.htm>.

Stephens, John, and María José Urruzola Zabalza. *Guía para chicas.* Cuidad Real: Junta de Castilla-La Mancha, 1992.

The Elusive Self in Eugenia Rico's *La muerte blanca*

Kyra A. Kietrys

In 2002 Eugenia Rico published *La muerte blanca* against the fading backdrop of Spain's historical amnesia, in which those silenced during Franco's regime and then purposefully unremembered during the transition to democracy remained forgotten — especially women.* The turn of the millennium, in general, has heralded a climate in which the official culture of forgetting associated with the transition and consolidation of democracy gives way to a prominent intellectual effort to reclaim the past and thus offers an alternative discourse to the official history (Álvarez Fernández 221).† The publication of prize-winning novels such as Dulce Chacón's *La voz dormida* (2002) and Ángeles Caso's *Un largo silencio* (2000); historical studies such as Shirley Mangini's *Las modernas de Madrid: las grandes intelectuales españo-*

---

*An English translation of the title of this untranslated novel might be *White Death*. All translations, unless otherwise indicated, are my own. I would like to express my sincere gratitude to the careful reading of this essay by my colleagues Elizabeth Cummins-Muñoz, Montserrat Linares, and Mark Sample.

†This zeitgeist is evidenced by the formation in 2000 of the *Asociación para la Recuperación de la Memoria Histórica* (Association for the Recovery of Historic Memory) and the *Ley de la memoria histórica* (The Law of Historic Memory) passed by the Spanish Congress in 2007 in which "se reconocen y amplían derechos y se establecen medidas en favor de quienes padecieron persecución o violencia durante la guerra civil y la dictadura" [rights are recognized and increased and measures are established in favor of those who suffered persecution or violence during the civil war and the dictatorship] Ley 52/2007, ed. Leggio Contenidos y Aplicaciones Informáticas, S.L., Zaragoza, Spain, 1 July 2008 <http://noticias.juridicas.com/base_datos/Admin/l52-2007.html>. See also <http://www.memoriahistorica.org/>.

las de la vanguardia (2001); as well as the republication or publication of memoirs, works of fiction and monographs on intellectuals such as María Teresa León, Concha Méndez, Constancia de la Mora, María Zambrano, Margarita Nelken, and Victoria Kent all give voice to women who had been silenced for decades.* On a collective scale, there is an undeniable literary trend to remember and construct the female through memory.

Winner of the 2002 Azorín prize, *La muerte blanca* does not appear to recover Spain's collective past. Rather, it turns this preoccupation with memory loss and the construction of subjectivity through remembering inward, to an intimate context, focusing on a personal loss. *La muerte blanca* is, in Rico's own words, a novel about a search whose starting point is an absence."† Rico refers here to the absence of the narrator's brother, who died fourteen years before her narration begins. The unnamed female narrator mourns his absence and he — not she — is the subject of her writings. As the narrator puts it, she wishes to construct her brother out of words (19) — and the novel maps that attempt.‡ However, the temporally and thematically fragmented structure of the narrator's memories undermines this act of construction at every turn. We are left with an elegant dramatization of the failure of identity construction. It is not simply her brother's identity the narrator fails to conjure; ultimately, the narrator fails to effectively write an identity for herself. Despite this apolitical, perhaps even politically naïve narrator, *La muerte blanca* unveils through the intersection of writing and memory the lingering systems of Franco–era patriarchal power that suppress the female voice, thus explaining the narrator's elusive female agency.

Rico's novel is the story of a woman who, fourteen years after her teenage brother's accidental drowning on a school trip, recounts sporadic memories of her brother's life. Inserted into the narration of concrete childhood memories are others from her recent past, as well as musings more philosophical in nature, particularly those regarding the relationship between writing and memory — the mechanisms through which the narrator attempts to reconstruct her brother. The novel is bookended by assertions of identity: it opens with the sister acknowledging, "Si mi hermano no hubiera muerto, yo no

---

***Un largo silencio* was awarded Premio de Novela Fernando Lara 2000, and *La voz dormida* the Premio Libro del Año 2002. Chacón's novel was translated to French as *Voix endormies* by Laurence Villaume in 2004, to English as *The Sleeping Voice* by Nick Caistor in 2006, and to Chinese as *Chen shui de sheng yin* by Lei Xu in 2007.

†"*La muerte blanca* es una búsqueda, que parte de una ausencia." <http://www.elmundo.es/elmundolibro/2002/03/08/anticuario/1015603777.html>. All translations, unless otherwise noted, are my own.

‡"Quiero construir un hermano de palabras" [I want to construct a brother out of words] (19).

sería quien soy..." [If my brother hadn't died, I wouldn't be who I am...] (11) and ends with the sister directly addressing her brother, "...no sería quien soy si tú no hubieras muerto" [... I wouldn't be who I am if you hadn't died] (196). The narrator's identity is not simply dependent upon her brother's life; it is her brother's death that she sees as her own defining characteristic. What does it mean that this nameless narrator's identity is bound to that of her long-dead brother? And how does she interpret her own identity, that is, who exactly is she in her own eyes? The narrator seems sensitive to such questions, asking, "Cómo mostrar quién es alguien. ¿Quién era él? ¿Era su nombre, era su cuerpo, era su manera de pensar?" [How can we show who someone is. Who was he? Was he his name, his body, his way of thinking?] (19–20), but she offers no satisfactory answers to these questions. The entirety of her narrative, however, poses an unacknowledged answer: it is writing that makes us who we are.

The narrator first identifies herself as a writer, "ocupaba todo mi tiempo en escribir" [I occupied all my time with writing] (99), and also explores the relationship between writing and reality in terms of forgetting and remembering. When she sees her brother's name inscribed on his grave, she affirms that "aprendí que no todo lo que está escrito es más verdad por estar escrito" [I learned that not everything that is written is any more true because it is written] (179–80) in an attempt to prevent the symbolic and definitive death that forgetting him would represent. So then, because the narrator does draw attention to the status of her work as writing on several occasions, it is both the lack of explicit answers to her own initial questions regarding identity, as well as the subsequent lack of recognition of the implicit answers, which beg critical attention. In this regard, Carmen Martín Gaite's claim in *La búsqueda de interlocutor* becomes particularly relevant: the essential element of all literary creation is the ability to choose which memory makes up the text: "No es recordar, sino seleccionar los recuerdos de una determinada manera, lo que convierte al protagonista de cualquier situación, ... en narrador (o sea, sujeto y artífice) de ella" [It is not remembering, but rather selecting the memories in a particular way, that which converts the protagonist of a situation into a narrator (that is, subject and author) of it] (23–4). As Martín Gaite points out, the selection of memories takes on an importance beyond the memories themselves. So, in drawing attention to her story as a literary creation, the narrator reminds us that she is the architect of the scheme, intentionally including certain elements while excluding others. In this light, we can study the novel in terms of its own unanswered questions — which point to a pervasive presence of absence within the novel — as well as the types of memories ultimately selected. An examination of the narrator's memories of her sibling relationship as well as of those memories that evoke the power of patriarchal systems will reveal that female gender construction is linked first to an absence of her brother, and ultimately, to an absence of agency within larger systems of power.

In a book purportedly about her brother, the narrator includes sporadic memories that are but tenuously linked to her brother, thus signaling that they must be important for other reasons. These digressions from the narrator's declared purpose of the narrative — recreating her brother — remind me of Susan Stewart's observation about the interplay between narrative and digression. In *On Longing*, her study of the role narratives play in making sense of our world, Stewart notes that "digression in narrative [...] is a matter not just of additional information but of a restructuring of information [...]" (30). Building on this point, she continues:

> narrative digression articulates the narrative voice, its control over the material, and consequently its control over the reader's passage towards closure. Instead of offering the reader transcendence, the digression blocks the reader's view, toying with the hierarchy of narrative events. What counts and what doesn't count must be sorted [30].

It is through these digressions, which "block" any transcendent view of either the narrator or her brother, then, that the narrator, conscientiously or not, undoes her project. In a book that claims to be about a search for her deceased brother and to "construir un hermano de palabras" [construct a brother out of words] (19), the narrator's digressions complicate any narrative closure and muddy our true sense of who the brother was. Paradoxically, the digressions establish the narrator's authority as the originator of the narrative (depicting implies authorship, as Stewart notes) — leaving the reader to interpret seemingly unimportant memories.

But these memories *are* important. A number of them quite significantly revolve around matrilineal and sisterly relationships — as opposed to her sibling relationship. One key memory involving the narrator's great grandmother reveals an awareness of women's worth as measured by her exchange value. As the narrator recalls, her great grandmother had hidden under a table when she was eleven years because, "tenía miedo del hombre de los grandes bigotes negros que venía a buscarla" [she was afraid of the man with the big black mustache who came to look for her] (93). It turns out that this older man was to be her husband "en cuanto tuvo la primera regla" [as soon she had her first period] (94). The marriage for this man was little more than a financial transaction; he traded her for twelve sacks of flour (94). We later learn that this great-grandmother died during the birth of her eleventh child, a sibling of the narrator's grandmother. Feeling orphaned after her mother's death in childbirth, the narrator's grandmother chose to have only one child — the narrator's mother (94). From this anecdote we see a female — the grandmother — who rejects her mother's function as commodity and bearer of children, and makes her own decisions regarding reproduction. More importantly, the narrator points out to the reader that this grandmother — representing the succeeding generation — imposes a change in the role she is willing to play within the patriarchal family structure. It is important to note that the great grandmother was deceased before the narrator was even born. This detail is significant for two reasons: it reveals an existent oral tradition among female family members; and, it distances the great grandmother from the narrator's childhood — particularly a connection to her brother — and, in this way challenges the reader to justify the relationship of this memory with the claimed overarching purpose of the narrative.

In addition to the commodification of women, the narrator also uses this anecdote to criticize the ways in which women were confined to the private space of the home. She writes, "Era el bisabuelo el que iba a las ferias y los lugares públicos donde estaban los fotógrafos" [It was our great grandfather who went to the fairs and public places were the photographers were] and "De la bisabuela no había retratos, como si no hubiera existido" [There were no photographs of my great grandmother, as if she hadn't existed] (93). The narrator suggests that by keeping women in the home, their public presence was nullified and their very existence was ultimately left for questioning. By retelling this memory, the narrator foregrounds her great-grandmother, writing her back into existence, while at the same time relegating her brother to the background.

The narrator's stories of her mother's grandmother reveal the imbalanced role of women in family and public life — a historical fact that has shaped the narrator's own childhood, which I will consider shortly. But first I want to turn to two other digressions that amplify the narrator's implicit criticism of the institutions in Spain that have long silenced the voices of women, in this case, the institutions of medicine and law. At one point the narrator relates how her paternal grandfather was fatally struck by lightning while on his way to help his sister during a powerful thunderstorm. She says, "Así fue como murió mi abuelo por su hermana, cuando mi hermano y yo ni siquiera habíamos nacido" [That's how my grandfather died for his sister, when my brother and I hadn't even yet been born] (82). On the surface, this anecdote seems to portray a fraternal love that matches the narrator's own family tragedy two generations later. But, there is more to this harrowing story of her great aunt. We learn that this woman was terrified of lightning because it triggered her memories of electroshock therapy in Argentina, undergone when she was once overcome by depression at the end of a romantic relationship. While the effectiveness of electroconvulsive therapy may be debated in psychiatric circles, it is inextricable from a discussion regarding power dynamics (Hirshbein and Sarvananda 1). When we consider that "women are subjected to electroshock two to three times as often as men" and that "approximately 95% of all shock doctors are male" (Burstow 378), we can rightfully consider electroshock therapy as a form of violence against women. The narrator's motivation for including this particular memory becomes clear: another female member of her family fell victim to a socially sanctioned institution that claimed to act with her best interest in mind.

Another memory from the narrator's childhood illustrates the failures of the legal and justice systems to protect women. She recalls a story her father told her and her brother about an ill-fated woman they saw standing on the street, giving away candies (128). According to her father's story, the woman had just been released from jail for killing her older sister out of jealousy and blaming the murder on her younger sister. She was the middle of three sisters who had lived together, the eldest of whom was married to a man who was the lover of the youngest and with whom she, the middle sister, was impossibly in love. The father tells the children that the Civil Guard "colgó a la asesina en el granero como un jamón y casi la mató a palos, hasta que el amor se le escapó por las heridas. Y confesó" [hanged the murderer in a silo like a ham and nearly beat her to death until her love escaped from her wounds. And she confessed] (128). The attentive reader questions the veracity of this story, not because of the brutality depicted, but rather because of the way the narrator frames it. She says that her father told her brother and her the story to keep them from rolling around the ground in their Sunday clothes while the narrator's mother was in church at a funeral (127). The father's skilled art as an impromptu story-teller becomes evident. While the narrator might have naïvely believed her father's tale as a child, in recounting the memory to us the questionable authenticity of the link between the incidental woman on the street and the story itself loses importance. What matters is that the narrator chooses to recount the story to us in a novel that she claims is about her brother. In doing so, not only does she draw attention to a traditional system of authority dominated by the loathing of— or fear of— women's sexuality, but she also reveals a vestigial fear of the law enforcers and, by extension, the sexual repression they embody. Furthermore, by framing the story as a memory and in the words of her father, the narrator escapes being overtly critical and thus avoids responsibility, not only for the criticism, but also as author of her own narrative. As Stewart proposes, it is through this digression that the narrator paradoxically articulates her narrative voice by forcing the reader to decide its significance. Through these digressions the narrator offers a not-so-veiled criticism of three systems of power — family, medicine, and law — revealing a wrongful treatment of women by society through these systems. They serve to underscore a lack of female agency in history, while the memories focusing on her brother will elucidate the narrator's own, personal lack of agency. Below I demonstrate that her own psychosocial development has been imprinted by the collective weight of these social institutions. Her childhood memories that do deal with her brother and in which she makes repeated references to herself specifically as a female demonstrate a clear consciousness of her gender and sexual identity. Remembering her brother's identity becomes an attempt to understand her own gender and sexual identity, to become herself while recognizing her own voicelessness. For the reader, this understanding will come to light through the meshing of the brother's and sister's, male's and female's, two identities.

In the eyes of the narrator's father and grandfather — that is, the older male generations — the traditional roles are assigned to the children. The young girl is aware that others undervalue her because she is female: her grandfather says, "...ojalá hubieses muerto tú y no él, tú que sólo eres una niña..." [...I wish you had died instead of him, you who are only a girl...] (101). Meanwhile, her father views her in a utilitarian light objectifying her body, "...yo era el útero que podría darle otro hijo" [...I was the uterus that would give my father another child] (135). Literally, this disturbing statement raises the specter of incest, but what is really going on is that her father possesses not only her, but also what she produces. These paternal figures reinforce traditional gender codes: the female is inferior; and, not even a body, but a fragmented organ of a body whose purpose is to gestate offspring. Little has changed since the days of her great-grandmother who realized her worth as ten sacks of flour only after she was physically capable of bearing children. Two generations of men heap scorn upon the narrator, with her father and grandfather representing tradition and generational patriarchy. This denigrated estimation of her intrinsic worth affects and infects how she views herself: "Sólo era una mujer, y una hembra nunca había sido una verdadera descendencia" [I was only a woman, and a female had never been a true descendant] (189). When her brother dies, she gives herself permission to love herself, but it is only in so much as she is no longer fulfilling her family role of a female, but rather as that of a man, "Había decidido amarme desde que murió mi hermano. Me había convertido en hombre honorario y heredero" [I decided to love myself after my brother died. I had become the honorary man and heir] (135). In this way we see how it comes to be that her identity is bound to her brother's death — her sense of self, as appreciated by others within this patriarchal family system, does not develop until her brother is dead. Furthermore, her worth does not stem from who she was, but rather from her newfound likeness to her male sibling. The narrator is recognized by older males as valuable insomuch as she has now acquired her metaphorical penis.

La muerte blanca opens with the narrator recalling the morning her brother died. Like many of her memories about her brother, this memory is laden with sexual overtones. The narrator was sixteen years old that morning, in the bathtub, listening to her favorite song *"Juana de Arco"* [Joan of Arc] (12), a 1981 synthpop ballad by the English group Orchestral Maneuvers in the Dark (OMD). It is no coincidence that the narrator's favorite song is about a cultural and religious icon whose story, as the historian Francoise Meltzer puts it, reveals "the limits and illusion of any sovereign subjectivity, the insistence of desubjugation" (23). Just as Joan of Arc exemplifies a woman who challenges our notions of gender assumptions, so will the narrator of *La muerte blanca* portray herself in this light. Meltzer points out that Joan of Arc is "imagined either as a near-masculine individual [...] or as a highly feminine figure" (3). Sometimes she is depicted in "combination feminine/masculine attire" and more recently, "relatively androgynous" (3–4). What is clear in all of these representations of Joan of Arc is that she "is an indicator of a series of problematics: the question of feminine subjectivity and of subjectivity itself" (6). In this way she embodies the same principal dilemma of our narrator: both young women must battle the constraints set by the patriarchal world in which they live in order to exercise their agency. Moreover, our narrator appropriates the Joan of Arc story by unnecessarily translating the Saint's transparently intelligible proper name into her own native language: both the saint's French name, *Jeanne d'Arc* and the English song title, *Joan of Arc*, would have been comprehensible to the Spanish-speaking reader of the text. Yet, for the narrator, the song *Joan of Arc* becomes *Juana de Arco* sung by *Maniobras Orquestrales en la Oscuridad*, revealing an affective connection with the saint through her translation to her own mother tongue, thus ameliorating any trace of possible emotional alienation caused by a foreign language.

In the tub that day, the narrator is logically, but not incoincidentally, naked and, what is more, she is thinking about her first love. It is important to point out that this is not the moment she learns her brother is dead, but rather this is the morning of that day. And in the tub she believes she receives a phone call from him. The narrator abruptly picks up the phone (although she never says it rang, and it might be precipitous of us to conclude that it did) and the earpiece slips between her wet breasts while she hears her brother's voice in the distance saying, "es mi hermana..." [it's my sister] (12). The narrator's brother thus enters this erotically charged and highly feminized space. By beginning her entire narration with this piece, the narrator not only connects her sensuality to her brother, and subsequently, his death, but she also alerts the reader to the issue of female subjectivity that she will problematize in her text.

Elsewhere in the novel, the narrator remembers when she and her brother bathed together as children. She remembers that as a little girl she was unhappy, not because she was ugly, but because she was an ugly *girl*. Rather than wishing to be pretty, she wished to be a boy, because in her mind nobody cared if boys are ugly (76). This first instance of self-loathing and gender rejection at five years of age is a key moment of her psychosexual development as well as in the development of her relationship to her brother. He says to her at this time, while they are both in the bathtub, together, "Déjame que corte mi cosita y te la dé para que puedas ser un niño" [Let me cut my little thing off and give it to you so you can be a boy] (76), naively thinking identity can be changed with a single cut, and echoing his grandfather's attempts to protect his own sister. While Freudian overtones of penis envy and castration anxiety are evident in this scene, a more productive analysis focuses on the magical thinking of children, who ingenuously believe that identity is solely defined by body parts — ignorant of the incredible weight of social norms and rules that define us.

We then learn that the narrator and her brother bathed together not only as small children, but also through puberty and that "...él me enseñaba su cosita y su cuerpo juguetón de niño" [...he would show me his little thing and his playful boyish body] (75). The narrator thus invites us to interpret the sibling relationship from a sexual perspective. We begin to see that part of the narrator's sexual identity is bound to her brother. When she remembers "...que él me mirara era como si yo misma me mirara" [...him looking at me was as if I myself were looking at me] (75), Lacan's mirror stage comes to mind as a metaphor for the development of the narrator's identity. By equating "he" with "I," we see a subconscious meshing of identities, in which her subjectivity becomes dependent on his existence. During puberty, a moment defined by sexual development, the narrator did not distinguish between her female self and her brother's male gaze. In effect, her brother becomes an escape from her own sexual identity as she sublimates her identity into her brother's. The repressive context into which she has been born has caused her to define herself through him. Her only agency is accessed through the adoption of his gaze. His death during their puberty truncates his own sexual development, stalling him forever in the narrator's mind as pubescent, and more significantly, since her own identity is so intertwined with his, delays her discovery of her own mature sexual self. Consequently, we can conclude that her current search for her brother paradoxically becomes both a continued search for and escape from her own sexual self. In her brother's death — the permanent blinding of his gaze — the burden of subjectivity now becomes exclusively her own. In order to bear the due weight of this burden, she must first extricate her identity from his — which she does through writing.

The narrator later underscores issues of sexuality and power in her relationship with her brother by recalling the Egyptian myth, Isis and Osiris who were both siblings and lovers. The narrator describes her search for her brother's memory in terms of these gods, "Yo sigo buscando, como Isis buscó los pedazos de su hermano Osiris..." [I keep looking, like Isis looked for the pieces of her brother Osiris...] (95). According to one version of the myth, Osiris was killed by his jealous brother and his dismembered bodied was scattered around Egypt. Isis was able to find every part of her brother-husband's body except his penis. She magically turned herself into a hawk, hovered over where his penis would have been and used the flapping of her wings to create a new penis that would impregnate her to later give birth to Horus (Friedman 8). Incest, this time among siblings, is again alluded to in the novel through the narrator's reference to this myth. Unlike the previous allusion to incest which named the uterus, this account of incest draws our attention directly to the phallus. While incestuous relationships were legitimate among the Egyptian gods and pharaohs, we should recognize the forbidden latent incestuous desire that is apparent here and in which the female has the power. I interpret this desire in the context of the meshing of the narrator's identity with her brother's, arguing that in searching for the missing piece of her brother's fragmented body, she is in fact searching to construct a complete empowered identity for herself. The missing penis represents her recognition that in her society, women are not granted the same privileges as men. Yet, in this myth, it is the female who creates the power of subjectivity by creating (or restoring life to) a penis. Her brother's phallus is either missing (absent) or lifeless (useless), depending on the version of the myth, but in both cases, it is the sister who endows him with the phallus. That is, the phallus becomes a gift that only the woman can give. Finally, Isis eventually became the most important deity in Egypt and "her worship wholly eclipsed that of her male counterpart Osiris" (Budge, II 271). In sum, the female begins her trajectory existing only in relationship to the dead male, but eventually exercises agency over herself by granting it — the agency acquired through the phallus — to him. In this sense, we see a significant underlying parallel in the stories of Isis and the narrator.

The narrator complicates this seemingly quasi-erotic love for her brother by adding an element of proprietorship. As children, the sister assumed the role of not just protecting her brother, but also of preserving his phallus. For example, when she was six, the narrator had a neighbor whom she hated for no explicable reason, but "Sentía que ella quería quitarme a mi hermano" [I felt that she wanted to take my brother from me] (38). One evening she found this girl alone in a room with her brother with "los pantalones bajados y su cosita al aire, ronco de tanto llorar, y allí estaba Salomé experimentando con él como si fuera un ratón de laboratorio, jugando con la cosita que podía doler" [his pants pulled down, his little thing exposed, hoarse from so much crying, and there was Salomé experimenting with him as if he were a lab rat, playing with his little thing that could hurt] (39). We see here a reversal of stereotypical gender roles: the female is the abuser and the male is the abused. The narrator also reverses the story of her grandfather who aimed to save his sister, for here it is she — the sister — who comes here to the rescue of the brother.

Like Joan of Arc, the siblings repeatedly defy traditional gender roles. The narrator confesses, "Desde pequeños yo había sido la fuerte y él el bello" [Ever since we were little, I was the strong one, and he the beautiful one] and "A mí me gustaba jugar con pistolas y a él con muñecas" [I liked to play with guns and he liked to play with dolls] (166). Also, "Él era el niño más guapo del barrio, pero siempre me tocaba a mí defenderle" [He was the most good-looking kid in the neighborhood, but I always had to defend him] (167). We can interpret these repeated reversal of roles in the simplest of terms: the siblings' behavior simply does not conform to the gender-bound social norms of their preceding generations, but rather, represents a resistance to these traditions. A more complicated reading reveals that on a subconscious level, she has always believed herself to be the possessor of the phallus, but like Isis, she was not able to acquire control over this phallus until it was stripped from her brother in death, which thus afforded her the position to wield its power.

The narrator's feelings of ownership culminate with her attempt to preserve the memory of her brother after his death. As I have already suggested, the mechanism she relies on is the written word. But it is not at all clear she can succeed. As the novel progresses, her desire to write her brother back into existence develops in parallel to her acceptance of the limited power of the word and consequently, of herself as narrator: "Me doy cuenta de que de él solo quedan mis palabras, y éstas son menos que nada" [I am aware that, of him, only my words remain, and these are less than nothing] (20), and "Mi hermano quería dejar una huella. Yo soy su huella" [My brother wanted to leave a mark. I am his mark] (46). Like so many other aspects of their relationship, there is an inversion operating here: she claims to be his mark, but throughout the novel, he is her mark. It becomes unclear who exists for whom, and the narrator's identity becomes doubly elusive. Towards the end of the novel, she recognizes his once ineffable presence is fading, admitting, "Y yo soy todo lo que queda de él" [And I am all that remains of him] and this is, "Muy poca cosa" [Very little at all] (151). Her brother is fading and what little remains of him, in her, is very little at all. His lessened hold on their conjoined identity allows—though she does not realize it—her own individual self to emerge. Ultimately, the novel is not about recovering her brother (no matter what she says); it is about letting go of him so that she can begin to see herself separate from him.

As much as we do learn about her brother—his name, his age, his job—his identity has eluded her words, "...aquello que es él y no se puede contar con palabras" [...that which is he and can't be told in words] (183). We are reminded of what she said at the beginning, that "él no cabe en palabras" [he doesn't fit into words] (19). By the same logic, though, she does not fit into words either. That is, it is of no consequence that we do not know her name or hardly anything about her present life. The narrator has unwittingly answered a subtle "No" to those questions about identity which opened her narrative and began this analysis: "Cómo mostrar quién es alguien. ¿Quién era él? ¿Era su nombre, era su cuerpo, era su manera de pensar?" [How can we show who someone is. Who was he? Was he his name, his body, his way of thinking?] (19–20). Identity is not comprised of external tags and activities, but rather as a construction of the creative voice—the writing process as an exercise through which she acquires subjectivity. Caught up in the circularity of her narrative, the narrator fails in both successfully writing his identity, and recognizing that she is, in fact, writing her own identity.

On one level, the narrator writes to remember her brother and to accept the pain she has felt for fourteen years. It is an extended act of grieving and remembrance: "Éste es el libro que siempre quise escribir. Lo escribo para mí, pero, sobre todo, lo escribo para él" [This is the book I always wanted to write. I write it for me, but above all, I write it for him] (11). But beneath this all too predictable analysis, we see that the act of writing ultimately represents her power. It is the power to create her own identity. Through the narrator's relationship to writing, a pattern emerges which reveals her tenuous relationship to her own agency. When she writes that "quiero construir un hermano de palabras…" [I want to construct a brother out of words…] (19) she is recognizing identity as a construction, but also empowering herself as a writer in this construction. By the end of the novel, the narrator has essentially failed in recreating her brother for the reader, but what she has done is create her own authorial voice. Yet even as she exercises agency as a writer, she does not recognize it to herself or her reader. Rather, she claims to have made no progress, "Al final del camino tengo las misma preguntas y sigo sin tener las respuestas" [At the end of the road, I have the same questions and I still don't have the answers] (196). It is here at this intersection between power and the denial of acknowledgement of power that we can interpret her individual search in terms of the collective. By repeatedly displaying naivety, the narrator reveals a prevailing absence of awareness in her discourse. She is paradoxically aware of and sensitive to women's historically subordinate role in society and unaware of how, through her writing, she is rewriting this role. On a symbolic level, her brother's death becomes the metaphoric death of the power of the male gaze and the need to define the female self through the male. Therefore, his death is also the birth of the gendered subject — in this case, via the act of writing. In this way, the personal struggle with identity construction joins the larger, collective intellectual effort to recoup — in this case *subjectivize*— the lost voices of Spain's historical amnesia.

Works Cited

Álvarez Fernández, José Ignacio. *Memoria y trauma en los testimonios de la represión franquista.* Barcelona: Anthropos, 2007.
Budge, E. A. Wallis. *Osiris & the Egyptian Resurrection.* 1911. 2 vols. New York: Dover Publications, 1973.
Burstow, Bonnie. "Electroshock as a Form of Violence against Women." *Violence Against Women* 12.4 (2006): 372–92.
Europa Press. Eugenia Rico. "La muerte blanca explora los límites y la dualidad entre el bien y el mal." *El mundo.* 08 mar 2002. <http://www.elmundo.es/elmundolibro/2002/03/08/anticuario/1015603777.html>.

Friedman, David M. *A Mind of Its Own. A Cultural History of the Penis*. New York: Simon & Schuster, 2001.
Hirshbein, Laura, and Sharmalie Sarvananda. "History, Power, and Electricity: American Popular Magazine Accounts of Electroconvulsive Therapy, 1940–2005." *Journal of the History of Behavorial Sciences* 44.1 (2008): 1–18.
Martín Gaite, Carmen. "La búsqueda de interlocutor, Revista de Occidente, 1966." "*La búsqueda de interlocutor*. Barcelona: Editorial Anagrama, 2000.
Meltzer, Francoise. *For Fear of Fire: Joan of Arc and the Limits of Subjectivity*. Chicago: University Chicago Press, 2001.
Rico, Eugenia. *La muerte blanca*. Barcelona: Planeta, 2002.
Stewart, Susan. *On Longing*. Baltimore: Johns Hopkins University Press, 1984.

Fragmented Identities: The Narrative World of Espido Freire

Montserrat Linares

One of the most prolific and high-profile writers in contemporary Spanish literature, Espido Freire (Bilbao, 1974) is a commercial and literary success.* In addition to her eight narrative works, she has published a collection of poems and three nonfiction books.† Freire also enjoys a wide-ranging media presence. She maintains a website and regularly conducts and gives interviews in magazines, newspapers, and radio programs.‡

Espido Freire's work is generally included in two literary groups that are not mutually exclusive: women writers of the 1990s and the new generation of young novelists called "Generation X." While Freire shares with Generation X a historical moment, common life challenges, and the distinction of publishing in her early twenties, she stands apart from the Neoreal-

---

*I would like to thank Sandra Watts for her help in translating this essay, and Chris Klimchak and Kyra Kietrys for their invaluable input.

†Her novels are *Irlanda* (1998), *Donde siempre es octubre* (1999), *Melocotones helados* (Premio Planeta 1999), *Primer Amor* (2000), *La última baalla de Vincavenc el bandido* (2001), *Nos espera la noche* (2003), *Cuentos malvados* (2003), *Juegos míos* (2004) y *La diosa del pubis azul* (2005, in conjunction with Juan Manuel de Prada). Her book of poems is *Aland la blanca*, 2001. Her non-fictions books are: *Cuando comer es un infierno*, 2003; *Querida Jane, querida Charlotte*, 2004; and *Mileuristas*, 2006.

‡Freire's website is <http://clubcultura.com/clubliteratura/clubescritores/espidoweb/>. She also contributes to the online magazine Psychologies <http://www.psychologies.orange.es/index.html> and to newspapers such as *El País*, *La Razón* and *El Mundo*. In addition, Freire appears on radio programs such as Onda Cero's "Te doy mi palabra" and Cadena Ser's "La ventana."

ist vein of Gen X authors such as Jose Ángel Mañas or Ray Loriga. As Freire herself has said, "Yo con los nuevos narradores tengo poco en común, salvo la edad [...] Mi idea de la literatura es otra, va por otro lado, distinta a ese realismo tan urbano y todo lo que parece caracterizarles" [Apart from being of the same age, I don't have much in common with the "young writers" [...] I have a different conception of literature that takes another" direction, different from the urban flavor of realism and other characteristics shared by those writers] (Moreno).* As the present article argues, Espido Freire develops an alternative to the Neorealist novel of her Generation X contemporaries through her use of the imaginary, creating narrative universes of great lyrical and emotional intensity in which, among references to legends, myths and ghosts, female protagonists search for their identity.

Freire is also included in a broader group of female authors who belong to a wide range of generations and who are all still publishing in the last decade of the 20th century. Carmen de Urioste, in her article "Narrative of Spanish Women Writers of the Nineties," describes the characteristics that authors such as Espido Freire, Mercedes Abad, Lucía Etxebarría, Belén Gopegui, Dulce Chacón, and Luisa Castro, among others share: "preference for the first-person narrative; perspectivism through different points of view; the polyphonic novel; preference for a woman or group of women as protagonists; and finally, fragmentation as a narrative technique" (285).

In this article I will analyze two of Espido Freire's early novels, *Irlanda* (1998) and *Diabulus in musica* (2001). In these two novels, the use of fantasy and the aforementioned separation from traditional realism does not preclude a relationship to the reality of women's lives at the turn of the millennium. Fantasy does not convert the female subject into something "unreal" or entirely implausible but rather presents the "self" in a more refined manner, truer to its essence. For Espido Freire, the use of fantasy in her work arises from a conscious awareness, from a feminist revindication. Fantasy does not remove her characters from their identity as women, it just provides a new model for a serious female character. In fact, one of the reasons why Freire started writing is "la carencia de personajes femeninos dignos y

---

*In an interview published on the Internet, Freire also states her difference with her literary contemporaries: "ultimamente, entre los jóvenes narradores se ha derivado hacia un hiperrealismo urbano. Aun gustándome mucho esas novelas, esas tendencias, he preferido buscar un camino diferente" [lately, there has been a move towards urban hyperrealism among young narrators. Even though I like those novels very much, I have preferred to look for a different path] <http://www.mujeractual.com/entrevistas/freire/>.

creíbles" [One of the reasons why I began writing during my adolescence was the lack of believable and dignified female characters], and her novels draw from the tension created between "lo que las mujeres creen que deben ser y lo que en realidad son..." [what women think they should be and what they are in reality...] (Martínez).

Irlanda, Freire's first novel, introduces the reader to the strange events that take place one summer in the life of Natalia. This protagonist-narrator is a fifteen year old adolescent who, after her older sister Sagrario's death from a degenerative illness, goes to spend her summer vacation in the country with her cousins Irlanda and Roberto and some of their friends. Natalia leaves behind her younger sister, "la nena," a child obsessed with dead princesses and poisonous plants. We come to know Natalia well over the course of the weeks she spends in the country. She has a rich imagination and makes constant reference to a natural world populated by spirits, in which rivers, trees, and plants possess magic powers. At night she is visited by the ghosts of both a turtle and of her dead sister. At first such occurrences seem normal within the protagonist's world but, suddenly, we learn that the true reason for these apparitions is much more complicated: not only did Natalia kill the turtle, which was Sagrario's pet, but more shockingly, she suffocated her own sister with a pillow. Apart from these nighttime visits, Natalia does not appear to be very affected by these deaths nor does she show remorse for the killings. Over the course of the summer, her relationship with her cousin grows increasingly tense. Irlanda's vivacious and manipulative character clashes with Natalia's own shy and introspective nature. Natalia attempts to become part of her cousin's world of frivolity, popularity, and success. Irlanda's typical teenage cruelty, however, combined with Natalia's inability to fit into this world, leads to a tragic ending: as the two stand in a tower, Natalia pushes her cousin to her death. At the end of the novel, Natalia visits Irlanda's grave with the intention of continuing to torture her cousin even after death.

In the first place, it is important to note the influence of what has been termed "Female Gothic"* in *Irlanda*. The Brontë sisters and Jane Austen are among the authors Espido Freire admires most. In particular, Emily Brontë and *Wuthering Heights* are clear influences on Freire's work. Commenting on Brontë's writings, Ellen Moers notes that "[the] acceptance of the cruel as a normal, almost invigorating component of human life sets her novel apart" (99). Furthermore, both Brontë's and Freire's work are characterized

---

*"Female Gothic" as defined by Ellen Moers in *Literary Women*.

by the constant presence of cruelty in the childhood world. Moers' observation that "Emily Brontë's view of childhood comprised nature and freedom, but not innocence [...] the children in her novel are brutes, little monsters of cruelty and lust" (106–7) applies to Freire's work as well.

In this Bildungsroman, Natalia is an adolescent searching for her identity in a world of conventionality, which is represented by her cousin Irlanda. The opposition between the two teenagers can be transposed to a literary level as well. Irlanda is a character straight out of traditional fairy stories: beautiful and charming. Natalia stands apart from the myths and stories Western society tells its children. She is more original, and, after some struggle, creates her own definition of her place in society as a woman. In this sense, as Concha Alborg remarks, Freire's fiction belongs to a "tradición desmitificadora" [tradition of demystification of fairy tales] "que la lleva definitivamente al umbral del siglo XXI" [that situates her squarely on the threshold of the 21st century] (243). Other Spanish writers belonging to this tradition of desmytification are Carmen Martín Gaite, Ana María Matute and Esther Tusquets, who, as critic Elena Soliño points out "are actively engaged in unmasking the magic spells of fairy tales, often by distorting its pre-established forms" (267).

The connection between Irlanda's character and a particular tradition of female characters appears in the novel in the parallel between the teenager and one of her ancestors, Hibernia la Bella. This parallel might well be seen as a reincarnation, given that the lives of each character appear to follow the same path. In fact, the two even share a name: Hibernia is the Latin equivalent of Erin or Irlanda. Both characters represent the prototype of the beautiful "femme fatale" whom no one can resist. Irlanda's most notable trait is her beauty, which is accompanied by brightness, light and the color white. Irlanda's smile "con los últimos rayos de la tarde, era preciosa" [under the day's last light, was beautiful] (23), and she loves to wear white: "Irlanda y sus vestidos blancos. Siempre blancos. Siempre blancos. Y el brillo claro que le salía de la piel" [Irlanda and her white dresses. Always white. Always white. And the bright light that comes from her skin] (159). Her beauty is complemented by an ability to manipulate those around her with a smile and she herself is aware of this power, stating that everyone around her "Harán lo que yo diga. Siempre hacen lo que yo digo. Eso es lo bueno de la gente estúpida" [will do whatever I say. They always do what I say. That's the good thing about stupid people] (62). As we will see further on, Natalia is also aware of her cousin's power, to which she responds by refusing to wait passively for a fairy godmother or a prince to save her and to grant her the status she deserves. Irlanda is all that Natalia *should* want to be — but is not.

Natalia, in contrast to the light surrounding Irlanda, is obsessed with death and appears enveloped by shadows and darkness. As an ironic counterpoint to the somber reality she inhabits, Natalia's name derives from the Latin root "natus" meaning to be born or birth. She defies what is expected of her as both a young woman and a literary character. By contradicting her given name, Natalia manifests both her rejection of preconceived definitions and a separation from the legacy of the past. In this vein, her reality is populated by coffins, ghosts, and the dead: "de niña imaginaba que las ramas que se recortaban contra el cielo eran brazos de trasgos y muertos que trataban de atraparme" [as a child I imagined that the tree branches sketched out against the sky were the arms of goblins and dead people trying to trap me] (22). Her younger sister, "la nena," has also fallen victim to this obsession and fills all her drawings with cemeteries and dead princesses in their coffins. This fascination is due to growing up under the shadow of the illness of the eldest sister, Sagrario. Sagrario ends her days confined to bed without being able to walk, dreaming of being rescued by a prince who wakes her from her dream, her nightmare, like Sleeping Beauty. In Sagrario's case it is not a prince who saves her; rather, it is Natalia, who decides to end her sister's suffering.

Natalia, in stark contrast to her cousin Irlanda, is a rather antisocial young woman* who appears to be proud of this trait when she says: "yo nunca había tenido amigas. No las necesitaba" [I never had friends. I didn't need any] (38). In part, Natalia's attitude towards friendship and relationships with others her age derives from her refusal to grow up at the same pace as those around her. She does not want to enter the world of adulthood. Her trip to the country functions as a critical juncture at which she encounters the reality of the future as embodied in her cousins and friends, that is, the world which she must enter but refuses to join. Natalia does not want to grow up.

---

*Espido Freire says about the protagonist: "Natalia, que no destaca en nada, salvo por su meticulosidad, sus conocimientos sobre plantas y su carácter tímido y cariñoso, se enfrenta de pronto a una muchacha que representa lo que una adolescente debe ser: hermosa, inteligente, popular, afectuosa, rica y sensata. Ahí le muestran el camino a seguir, y ella, en un principio, intenta amoldarse. Sólo cuando decide no crecer, no ser otra cosa sino lo que hasta entonces ha sido comprende su poder y hace uso de él." [Natalia, defined only by her meticulousness, knowledge of plants and shy and affectionate nature, suddenly comes face-to-face with a girl who represents all that a young lady should be: beautiful, intelligent, popular, warm, rich and sensible. This is the model for Natalia to emulate and which at first she attempts to imitate. It is only when she decides not to grow up, to remain in the world of childhood, that Natalia understands her power and begins to make use of it.] (Martínez)

She prefers to remain apart from the world of adults, to allow them to play the part of those who are always right and never make mistakes, and to stay in the world of childhood where mistakes are always excused. She prefers to think that "...los mayores siempre tendrían razón, y que resultaba terriblemente lento y doloroso crecer" [...adults were always right, and that growing up was a terribly slow and painful process] (43). Despite her efforts to blend in, to be like the others, Natalia's actions constitute more of a protest than a desire to fit in. At this point Natalia stops eating, after noticing that her cousin is much thinner and that her own dresses are tight. On one hand this attempt at anorexia may be viewed as an attempt to grow up, to enter the world of adults, but in reality it serves as a protest given that an anorexic adolescent "realizes what she is becoming and what that means" (Pennycook 80). Anorexia is a symptom of adolescents who "find the terms under which they have to grow up impossible to comply with [and] ... seem to take on board fully the negative feelings about womanhood" (Pennycook 80). Natalia sees refusing to eat as a required step in the passage from childhood to womanhood, which requires to be "frágil, tan delgada como Irlanda" (165) [fragile, as thin as Irlanda] (165). In reality, this refusal ends up being a a way to cling to childhood. Natalia also displays a resistance to maturing, to becoming a woman, in her attitude towards the opposite sex. As Natalia herself states, she has no interest in boys (61). The world of men seems not to exist for Natalia, to the point that when she speaks about her family she barely mentions her father. Her mother and her sister are the only ones who appear to have a place in her emotional universe. After spending a few weeks in the country, Natalia becomes interested in her cousin's friend Gabriel, a young man with "demented eyes" who is haunted by the memory of his father's suicide. Because of his past closeness to death, Natalia views Gabriel as a soul mate, and she begins to daydream about him. Her fantasies, which lack any sexual overtones, contrast sharply with the highly sexualized reality that surrounds them. For example, on a day in which Natalia hopes to be alone with Gabriel, she imagines both that day's encounter and their future life together:

> Podría preparar una ensalada mágica con hojas de capuchina y aceite de rosas que crecieron en una pared al este y llevármelo a comer al prado, y allí continuar charlando de los otros mundos en los que naceríamos, de los que nada sabían las muchachas bonitas de cabellos claros[...]. Y viviríamos en la vieja casa del campo, caminando bajo las ramas oscuras del bosque para preguntar cada noche a los viejos espíritus del bosque por nuestra vida.
>
> [I could prepare a magic salad with capuchina leaves and oil made from

the roses that grow upon an Eastern-facing wall and bring it out to eat in the meadow, and there keep chatting about the other worlds in which we would be born, worlds unknown to pretty fair-haired girls[...]. And we would live in the old country house, walking under the dark boughs of the forest to ask the old wood spirits about our lives.] [117].

Yet reality once again shatters Natalia's fantasy world when, one night, she sees Gabriel leaving Irlanda's bedroom with scratches on his back. Irlanda, who has realized Natalia's interest in the young man, seduces him merely out of maliciousness: to prove that she can do it, to torture Natalia. Irlanda's cruel nature becomes apparent when she shares with Natalia the details of her physical relationship with Gabriel: "Me acariciaba la nuca mientras hablaba [...] Me tiene despierta durante toda la noche, hablando a mi oído, enredando sus manos en mi pelo. Y por el día me dice que siente mi olor en todas partes[...]" [He stroked the nape of my neck as he spoke[...]. He keeps me up all night, whispering in my ear, running his fingers through my hair. And during the day he tells me he smells my scent everywhere [...]] (170).

Such explicit details catch Natalia off guard. Sex has no place in her childish world of ghosts, dragons, spells and magic, so she decides to do away with Irlanda. Killing her cousin is a way of affirming her own will, of refusing to accept a world which she does not want to enter but which also denies her entry. Her hatred towards the world runs together with her hatred of her young blond cousin: "fue entonces cuando empezó mi odio hacia ella y hacia el destino que me negaba de un modo tan cruel mi participación en los rituales de vida" [it was then that I began to hate her and to hate the fate that so cruelly prevented me from taking part in life's rituals] (140). Natalia also asserts that "fuera de la historia de mujeres magníficas, Hibernias e Irlandas sin escrúpulos [...] la vida no me dejaba participar en sus ritos" [apart from the story of amazing women, unscrupulous Hibernias and Irlandas [...] life didn't allow me to participate in its rites] (167). The injustice of the situation becomes unbearable to Natalia, and for this reason she decides to put an end to it. The scene of Irlanda's death is preceded by an exchange between the two girls that allows the reader to identify more closely with Natalia and to create a sharp contrast to the impending death. The two girls are in the tower and Irlanda, leaning against the railing, says that everything is perfect: "Todo. El mundo. Esta casa en el ocaso. Los pájaros volando. La vida. Yo" [Everything. The world. This house at sunset. The birds flying. Life. Me] (179). This statement is the culmination of the tension that has been building throughout the novel, finally reaching the breaking point. Natalia, in a fit of rage, pushes Irlanda and feels the pleasure of death: "en la mente noté el crujido de las cadenas que ataban su vida al cuerpo; las sentí rechinar y romperse, con el mismo sonido con que mi hermana se apagó bajo la almohada y quedó luego en silencio [...] Nada estropeó la satisfacción de ver roto el hermoso cuerpo de Irlanda" [In my mind I could hear the groaning of the chains linking her life to her body; I felt them squeal and break, with the same sound with which my sister faded away under the pillow and then fell silent [...] Nothing could spoil the satisfaction of seeing Irlanda's beautiful body broken] (180–1). The tower in *Irlanda* is not the place where princesses wait to be saved by their prince; it is the place where, with impunity, Natalia exercises her agency to end Irlanda's tyranny. Everyone believes it was an accident.

This death adds to the complexity of the novel as clearly the reader will be repelled by Irlanda while feeling compassion and understanding for Natalia. Some critics have seen these characters as the embodiment of good and evil. But who is good and who is evil? *Irlanda*'s is not a manichaean world in which the two concepts are clearly distinguished from each other. Rather, good and evil blur together throughout Natalia's story. As Espido Freire notes, "El mal, que sería destruir a Irlanda, y el bien propio, el instinto de autoconservación, se confunden. Y la única versión, la de Natalia, no obliga, con su visión sesgada, a introducirnos en una mente en que la polaridad tradicional bien-mail se halla deformada." [Thus evil, in the form of destroying Irlanda, and Natalia's own good, in the form of self preservation, run together. And the only version–Natalia's, with its biased perspective — does not necessarily present us with a mentality in which the traditional opposition between good and evil has been deformed.] (Martínez)

In this sense, *Irlanda* may be read both as the story of a girl who employs unconventional means to rebel against the established order, and also as the tale of a character who refuses to define herself within the parameters defined by tradition. Concha Alborg observes that "De acuerdo con el arquetipo, Cenicienta, o aquí Natalia, debería convertirse en princesa, pero no nos extraña que no sea así. Se transforma en una bruja perfecta" [Following the archetype, Cinderella or here, Natalia, should turn into a princess, but we are not surprised that this does not happen. She turns into the perfect witch] (251). Natalia chooses to create her own self, just as Espido Freire decides to create a literary universe governed by its own rules. And she achieves this by creating a world in which darkness, shadows and death become irresistibly attractive to the reader.

Diabulus in musica (2002) also presents us with a protagonist and narrator in search of her identity, seeking to define herself in a world in which the real and the fantastic are inextricably combined. Her consciousness appears fragmented to the degree that identity and unity seem to be irreconcilable concepts. This fragmentation of consciousness is reflected in the novel's construction, especially in its handling of time. According to Espido Freire herself:

> La trama tiene como objetivo inquietar, no que se devore la novela sólo para averiguar el final. Busco un lector que se demore en la lectura, que le guste leer y no le importe volver unas páginas atrás para confirmar algo. El tiempo no es lineal en esta novela, sino que se da mediante capas, y he elegido un punto de vista desorientado y que desoriente al lector.
> [The plot's objective is to unsettle, to prevent the novel from being devoured in order to discover the ending. I am looking for a reader who takes time to read, who likes to read and who is willing to turn back a few pages to double-check a doubt. Time in this novel is not linear but rather is layered, and I have chosen a disoriented perspective that in turn disorients the reader.] [Vivas].

In the novel's opening pages we discover that the narrator, whose name we never learn, is a ghost who inhabits a school and who feels the need to tell her tale: "respecto a mí, estoy muerta. Todas las mañanas me levanto, me miro en el espejo y me dedico a recorrer la escuela [...] Mi vida se agotó hace tiempo y ahora debo conformarme con esta rutina y esta existencia. Un fantasma en un colegio" [about me, I'm dead [...] My life ran out some time ago and now I've no choice but to put up with this routine and this existence. A ghost in a school] (14–15). Just as *Irlanda*'s Natalia took us into her world of spirits and convinced us that her actions were completely justified, the narrator of *Diabulus* also makes us her accomplice in that we must, from the start, accept a premise that might seem entirely implausible. As Espido Freire points out, "las primeras personas son siempre engañosas, nos convierten a los lectores en aliados y en cómplices. No descubrimos que nos puede estar mintiendo, que nos puede estar dando una visión parcial de la realidad" [the first person is always deceitful, it turns us readers into allies and accomplices. We do not find out that it might be lying to us, that it might be giving us a biased view of reality] (Mora).

The story covers two different periods in the protagonist's life. It begins with the recent past, with her relationship with Christopher Random, an older actor whom she meets in London. For the protagonist this encounter with Chris was something magical as he had indirectly marked a different stage in her life, her adolescence in Bilbao. He brings her back to Mikel, the boy who she dated in high school, who bore an uncanny resemblance to the protagonist of the film "Ragnarok or the Twilight of the Gods" (Balder el

Blanco played by Christopher Random). Mikel grew obsessed with Balder's character and transformed his appearance to look more like the actor, eventually losing touch with reality. His life entered a downward spiral, and he commited suicide after the narrator ended their relationship. Wracked with guilt, she never recovered from the shock of Mikel's death. From that moment on, she has lived haunted by the thought that Mikel/Balder follows her like a ghost who, sooner or later, will track her down. Her relationship with Chris is filled with mystery and excitement in the beginning, but slowly deteriorates as she realizes that he is merely an actor, not only on screen but also in life. The protagonist grows consumed by worry, which leads her to commit suicide as well. At this point Balder/Mikel appears in order to lead her away to the world of ghosts where she will have "todo el tiempo del mundo" [all the time in the wold] (185).

These events form a circular structure, beginning and ending at the same moment in time, a fact emphasized by the repetition of the phrase "ése fue el último día" [that was the last day]. This circularity reflects the narrator's need to understand her current situation. Telling her story is her way to give meaning and order to her life. She wants to organize the elements of her reality to understand them. She wants to be able to explain her life from the vantage point of her death. The result is a narrative characterized by leaps in time between her teenage years and her relationship with Mikel/Balder in Bilbao, and her life as a young woman in London and her relationship with Chris/Balder. These timeframes overlap and at times two different events appear to be happening simultaneously. For example, when Chris is talking to the protagonist about the film "Ragnarok" he says about the movie that it happened "hace mucho tiempo" [a long time ago]. She replies, "no, te equivocas, está ocurriendo ahora" [no, you are wrong, it's happening now] (41). Thus, in the protagonist's mind, two different events distant in time overlap, collapsing into a single moment.

In spite of this fragmented temporality, the protagonist is obsessed with order. She herself speaks of her "afán por encajar las piezas, por abrillantar y ordenar las razones y las causas" [obsession with fitting pieces together, with polishing and arranging reasons and causes] (16). This need for order manifests itself in her life as a continual questioning of her own existence, in the desire to make sense of what happens to her. As a narrator, this desire for order is what urges her to write as she needs to find an explanation for her life and the best way to achieve this is by telling her story. The result is not entirely successful: she ends up killing herself and her narrative raises more questions than it answers. The world is too chaotic to attempt to set it in order, and the narrator herself realizes that by telling her story, her life, she "no muestra sino confusión, manoteos de ciego, acordes inconclusos, piezas rotas" [only produces confusion, blind fumbling, unfinished chords, broken pieces] (17). Thus, her identity is a fragmented one that can only produce a fragmented narrative.

In this context the novel's title takes on new meaning: the "diabulus in musica" is a combination of notes forbidden by traditional music theory because it produces dissonance. Furthermore, it was believed that such dissonance provided a gateway for the devil because something dissonant necessarily must be a reflection of evil. The narrator spends her life trying to find order in a world utterly lacking it, and she does not realize that the devil will inevitably slip in through one of the cracks in life: "El mundo, el orden, se había quebrado. Tal vez siempre había sido así, un eterno *Diabulus in musica*, y yo no había reparado en ello, ciega en divertimentos pequeños, en encontrar en las historias de amor antifaces contra la realidad" [The world and order itself had shattered. Perhaps it had always been that way, an eternal *Diabulus in musica*, and I had not noticed it, blinded by minor divertimentos in seeking in love stories a mask to hide from reality] (173). Disorder and the uncontrollable win at the end, just as the author herself points out while speaking of the novel: "El personaje principal, la narradora, está obsesionada con el orden y el desorden, está preocupadísima por encontrarse en el lugar adecuado, por que no haya ningún resquicio por donde se pueda colar un imprevisto. Y los imprevistos ocurren. Su diabulus se cuela en su vida y, por supuesto, la destroza" [The main character, the narrator, is obsessed with order and disorder. She is extremely worried about being in the right place, about leaving no cracks through which the unexpected might slip in. And the unexpected does happen. Her *diabulus* slips into her life and, of course, destroys it] (Mora).

One interesting aspect of the protagonist is her complete dependence on those around her. Whereas Natalia in *Irlanda* did not need others and proudly proclaimed her self-sufficiency, in *Diabulus in musica* we find a protagonist who "se define únicamente en función de los otros" [defines herself solely in terms of others] (Entrevista). Her personality thus seems blurred and fragmented, lacking in characteristic qualities or defects. The narrator is aware of this, and seeks her own center in the exterior world. For example, when she goes on her first date with Chris, the actor, she would like to disguise herself as a different person. She changes depending on those who are around there, since it's other people who have the power to create her identity. The same thing had happened in her youth, when Mikel lent a sense of meaning to her life. On one occasion she tells him, "Dejaría de ser quien soy, con los ojos cerrados, sin pensarlo, si alguien me indicara qué ser" [I would stop being who I am, with my eyes closed, without thinking, if someone told me who to be] (88). She even goes so far as to assert that she would not exist without him. Mikel's death implies her own death as well: "yo creía que si lograba que alguien me amara, si lograba convertirme en especial para alguien, estaría salvada [...] Cuando perdí a Balder, perdí el mundo. Perdí, por tanto, mi lugar, mi nombre" [I thought that if I got someone to love me, if I managed to become special to someone, I'd be saved [...] When I lost Balder, I lost my whole world. I lost, therefore, my place, my name] (118). Thus hers is a life without meaning until she meets Chris. He grants her a new chance to be, to exist. Over the course of their relationship she becomes increasingly dependent on him. She stops taking classes and spends her time locked up inside, doing nothing. Little by little she wastes away and disappears, foreshadowing her ghostliness. She neither eats nor sleeps. It is as though she were losing corporeality at the same time as her personality and her identity fade away. This progressive "disappearance" is no less than a symptom of the illness from which Chris, the one who possesses her, is also suffering. In reality, he is not as strong as his girlfriend believes him to be. Thus, when she discovers that he has been faking all along, that the sweet things he has told her are merely phrases lifted from one of his movie scripts, she disappears, saying to herself: "Yo, marioneta de otra marioneta, no existía" [I, the puppet of another puppet, didn't really exist] (173). Death, then, becomes inevitable. Although suicide puts an end to her physical existence, she hasn't fully existed during her life. In reality, the process of becoming a ghost had begun much before her death.

Her obsession with identity can be observed in this novel in the recurrent presence of mirrors, which serve as the place in which she seeks herself. She desires not only to recognize herself in them physically but also to find an existence that goes beyond her body. The only reflection she encounters is that of her loneliness: once, as Chris leaves, she says, "Lloré, sobre todo, porque una vez más me quedaba sola, yo sola con mi espejo, sin nadie que me dijera quién era, qué debía hacer, qué camino debía seguir" [I cried, above all, because once again I was left alone, just me and my mirror, with no one to tell me who I was, what I should do, what path I should take] (104). For the protagonist, the mirror becomes an object that duplicates her inexistence. The mirror also introduces the theme of the double, of identity as fragmentary and fragmented. This theme emerges in the characters of Mikel and Chris, through the mythical figure of Balder. The first to appear in the story is Christopher Random, although he is the last to enter the protagonist's life. His last name holds great significance: he is fortuitous, he could be anyone depending on chance and on the circumstances reality lays in his path. As the protagonist notes, Chris has accompanied her during most of her life. He is a chance to redeem herself, to end her guilt over Mikel's suicide. Nevertheless she is destined to fail. When the protagonist and Christopher Random meet, he seems mature, self confident, but he slowly disintegrates and his identity fades, the same way Mikel's faded. He becomes more and more involved in the life of his own characters and their personalities become his personality. Chris is an actor, both in the screen and in real life. He "se había convertido en demasiadas personas a lo largo de los años [...] había vestido tantas identidades que algunos le conocían por el disfraz, por el personaje" [had turned into too many people over the years [...] he had worn so many identities that some knew him only by his disguise, as a character] (21). He has no real essence, he just wears the masks of the characters he has played in his movies. The borders between reality and fiction become blurry. If Mikel decided to live on the other side of the screen (choosing to die and become his idol), Chris is the vehicle through which fictional characters become real, inhabiting the real world. The protagonist thought that Chris could give her life meaning, but he is merely a fantasy. He has no center, no core. What is most interesting is that she falls into a trap of her own making: she becomes interested in him not because he is Chris but because he is the actor who her first boyfriend looked like. As her existence depends on him, when she realizes that he does not exist she has no other choice but to die, to cross over to the world of the ghosts that inhabit her life.

The figure of Balder, who has also become an obsession for her, becomes the curse that prevents her from continuing to live. Balder leads both the narrator and Mikel to see the true nature of life: a series of mirages, masks, images. Nothing holds any meaning and for that reason the only possible choice in a world that hurls them into the abyss is death. As a ghost, Balder serves as a permanent reminder that nothing truly exists, that everything is a mere illusion and that many times that which we believe to be false is revealed to be much more true than what we have taken to be real. The underlying theme of the novel is the questioning of one's own existence. Life is no more than a succession of mirrors that reflect each other.

In this novel, death lacks the power to free the protagonist as we saw in *Irlanda*. Natalia affirms her existence, her agency, through ending others' lives. In *Diabulus*, the protagonist tries to find an anchor in the real world through her relationships with men, but ends up realizing that everything is no more than a game of mirrors, masks, and images. Life has no meaning, and death is all that is left in a world that points to nothingness.

Espido Freire has created in these two novels two narrative worlds where fantasy and imagination are essential, where the search for the self brings the female protagonist to two different ends: the adolescent who triumphs, finding herself and affirming her agency; and the young woman who disappears, defeated by a world that cannot control, where everything becomes images with no referent. Freire's narrative world is, without a doubt, intensely original and thought provoking.

Works Cited

Alborg, Concha. "Espido Freire: (re) Lectura y (sub) Versión de los cuentos de hadas." *La pluralidad narrativa escritores españoles contemporáneos (1984–2004)*. Angeles Encinar Félix y Kathleen M. Glenn (coord). Madrid: Biblioteca Nueva, 2005. 243–254
"Entrevista con Espido Freire." Anika entre libros. <http://www.clubcultura.com/ clubliteratura/clubescritores/espidoweb/b_anika.htm>.
Fraile, María José. "Entrevista a Espido Freire." <http://www.mujeractual.com/ entrevistas/freire/>.
Freire, Espido. *Irlanda*. Barcelona: Planeta, 1998.
_____. *Diabulus in musica*. Barcelona: Planeta, 2002.
Henseler, Christine. *Contemporary Spanish Women's Narrative and the Publishing Industry*. University of Illinois Press, 2003.
Ibáñez, Andrés. "Magia, magia." *Revista de libros*. 18 June 1998. <http://www.clubcultura.com/clubliteratura/clubescritores/espidoweb/rese_irlanda.htm#res3>.
Martínez, Yaiza. "La fabulación nos permite compensar el final de la infancia." Entrevista con Espido Freire. *TendenciaSXXI*, Septiembre 1998. <http://www.clubcultura.com/clubliteratura/clubescritores/espidoweb/entr_irlanda.htm>.
Moers, Ellen. *Literary Women*. New York: Doubleday, 1976.
Mora, María J. "Espido Freire y el hueco por donde se cuela el diablo." *Terra*. 2 October 2001.<http://www.terra.es/cultura/articulo/html/cul4008.htm>.
Moreno, Sebastián. "Début brillante de Espido Freire." *Revista Tiempo*. 13 April 1998. <http://www.clubcultura.com/clubliteratura/clubescritores/ espidoweb/rese_irlanda. htm>.
Pennycook, Wil. "Anorexia and adolescence." *Fed up and hungry: women, oppression and food*. Ed. Marilyn Lawrence. New York: P. Bedrick Books, 1987.
Soliño, María Elena. *Women and Children First: Spanish Women Writers and the Fairy Tale Tradition*. Potomac, MD: Scripta Humanistica, 2002.
Urioste, Carmen. "Narrative of Spanish Women Writers of the Nineties: An Overview." *Tulsa Studies in Women's Literature*, 20.2 (2001): 279–295.
Vivas, Ángel. "Espido Freire se acerca al realismo con la novela *Diabulus in musica*." *El Mundo*. 2 October 2001. <http://www.elmundo.es/2001/10/02/ cultura/1054793. html>.

About the Contributors

Mary Ann Dellinger is a professor of Spanish at the Virginia Military Institute. She has authored a number of beginning and intermediate Spanish language textbooks, including *Ventanas*, *Sendas literarias* and *Vistas*. Her other publications focus on incarcerated women and exile.

Kathryn Everly is an associate professor of Spanish at Syracuse University. She is author of *Catalan Women Writers and Artists: Revisionist Views from a Feminist Space*. She also was guest editor for the "Post-Franco Artistic Production and Beyond" issue of *Symposium*. Of her numerous articles and presentations, many focus and women and identity or women and violence.

Kyra A. Kietrys is an assistant professor of Spanish at Davidson College in North Carolina. In addition to her work on contemporary Spanish women writers, she also researches women of the Second Republic and is currently preparing a web-based archive of the sexual rights activist Hildegart.

Montserrat Linares is an associate professor of Spanish at Elizabethtown College in Pennsylvania. Her research interests include the novel of the Spanish Avant Garde, and contemporary women writers with a focus on Espido Freire, Lucía Etxebarria, and Laura Freixas.

Joanne Lucena is an assistant professor of Spanish at Arcadia University in Pennsylvania. Her areas of expertise are nineteenth and twentieth century Spanish literature. She regularly reviews contemporary Spanish novels for *Hispania* and films for *Crítica Hispánica*.

Ellen Mayock is a professor of Romance languages at Washington and Lee University, where she also serves as the associate dean of the College for Faculty and Program Support. She is the author of *The "Strange Girl" in*

Twentieth-Century Spanish Novels Written by Women and has published over twenty-five articles and reviews with a focus on women writers, particularly those from Spain.

Nina L. Molinaro is an associate professor of Spanish at the University of Colorado at Boulder, where she teaches contemporary peninsular literature and film, Hispanic women's literature and literary theory. She has served as the director of Women's Studies at the University of Akron and the interim director of the Women's Studies Program at CU-Boulder.

Vilma Navarro-Daniels is an assistant professor of Spanish at Washington State University. Her scholarly work is interdisciplinary and focuses on the relationship between political and social transformations and their literary and cinematic representations.

Esther Raventós-Pons is an associate professor and chair of the Department of Hispanic Studies at Glendon College of York University in Toronto. In addition to over a dozen articles that study the relationship between the visual and literary arts, she is the author of the book *Rupturas espaciales: Imagen y palabra en textos catalanes*. She is also the co-editor of *Literary Texts and the Arts: Interdisciplinary Perspectives*.

Sandra J. Schumm is an associate professor of Spanish at Baker University in Kansas. She is the author of *Reflection in Sequence: Novels by Spanish Women, 1944–1988*. Her journal publications concentrate on women writers from Catalonia as well as twentieth century poets.

Carmen T. Sotomayor is associate professor and chair of the Romance Language Department at University of North Carolina at Greensboro. Among her many awards are those from the NEH/MLA, Spain's Ministry of Culture, and the Program for Cultural Cooperation between Spain and the U.S. Her publications focus on contemporary Spanish writers, the Spanish Civil War, and women in the Second Republic. She is on the editorial boards of the *International Poetry Review* and *Letras Hispanas: Revista de literatura y cultura*.

Parissa Tadrissi is an assistant professor of Spanish at the College of Charleston. Her dissertation is titled "'Realismo sucio,' Women and Youth Culture in Present-Day Spain: Care Santos's Narratives of Identity Formation." Her scholarly work concentrates on gender and sexual identities in the fiction of women writers.

Index

Abad, Mercedes 136
abuse 4, 41, 49–51, 55, 94–101, 105, 108–9, 127, 134, 174, 201
adolescence 171–2, 74–5, 178
affair 40, 47, 49, 69–70, 124, 127–8
Aldecoa, Josefina 1, 4, 21–36
Algún amor que no mate (Chacón) 93–111
alienation 34, 109–10, 198
alterity 135, 137–41, 143–5, 147–51
anorexia 4, 41, 52–3, 55, 187, 210
Antolín, Enriqueta 136
Atrapados en la ratonera (Medio) 83

Bachelard, Gaston 24–5, 36
Bakhtin, Mikhail 171, 173
Balcells, Carmen 2
Barrios, Nuria 136
Barthes, Roland 16, 19, 172–3
Bataille, George 11
"battered woman syndrome" 94, 112
Beauvoir, Simone de 11, 140, 171
Beccaria, Lola 136
Berenguer, Sara 83
Bergson, Henri 11
Berguer, John 95
Betterton, Rosemary 106, 111
Bildungsroman 118, 150 208
Box Cospedal, Antonio 114
Brontë, Emily 207–8
bulimia 52–3
Bushnell, Candace 47
Bustelo, Gabriela 136
Butler, Judith 171, 175

Cabañas Alemán, Rafael 68
Caso, Ángeles 191
Castro, Luisa 5, 135–7, 141, 149–50
Catholic Church 80, 156–7, 168, 175
Cerro Umbría 86

Cervantes 12
Chacón, Dulce 1, 4, 37, 77–91, 93–111, 191–2, 206
China 125
Ciplijauskaité, Birutė 154
Civil War *see* Spanish Civil War
Cixous, Hélène 1, 77–8, 80–1, 90, 105, 111
Conjugal Crime (Davidson) 97
Conrad, Joseph 11
Córdoba 88
Cuba 148
La cuestión palpitante (Pardo Bazán) 60, 64
Cyrano de Bergerac 181–2

Davidson, Terry 97
democracy 133, 186, 191
depression 12, 41, 53, 78, 108–110, 163, 165, 196, 222
Desde el mirador (Sánchez) 1 3–131
detective novel 11, 18, 57, 61–2, 64, 72
Diabulus in Musica (Freire) 205–218
diaries 35, 77, 79–80, 83, 185, 166, 168, 184
dictablanda 116
dictatorship *see* Franco
The Divided Self: An Existential Study in Sanity and Madness (Laing) 103–4
domestic violence 4–5, 49–51, 94–8, 100–1, 196

eating disorders 128, 174, 178, 187
Eisenhower, Dwight 115
En la distancia (Aldecoa) 35
El enigma (Aldecoa) 32
Entre el sol y la tormenta (Berenguer) 83
Equatorial Guinea 23–5, 33–4
Escudero, Javier 58–61, 65, 74
ethics 134, 137–40

Etxebarria, Lucía 1–2, 5, 135–6, 153–170, 206
European Union 52
La Eva futura (Extebarria) 156–8
Eyre, Jane 11

female characters 4, 6, 35, 113–4, 117–9, 124–5, 128–9, 207–8
female friendship 45, 47–8, 183, 186
female self 1, 3–6, 62–3, 72, 77, 81, 201, 204
The Feminine Mystique 116
feminism 3, 58, 79–80, 116, 140, 185–6
La fiebre amarilla (Castro) 5, 133–151
film 9–18, 213–4
first-person 49, 62, 66, 73–5, 101–2, 118–9, 126, 143, 184, 206, 213
Flores-Ortiz, Yvette 109, 111
Fortes, Susana 136
Franco, Francisco 22, 31, 57, 66, 86, 116, 163, 168, 185; dictatorship 1–2, 5, 67, 88, 113, 115–7, 123, 154–6, 185–86, 191–2; Franquismo 115, 175
Freire, Espido 1, 2, 6, 136, 205–218
Freixas, Laura 2–3, 6, 176, 190
Freud, Sigmund 103
El frío (Sanz) 133–151
La fuerza del destino (Aldecoa) 21–36

"El gato con botas" (Martín Gaite) 15–16
gender 26–7, 48, 66, 78, 137–42, 150, 175–8, 179, 182, 188, 196–9; gender roles 48–9, 54, 113, 123, 153, 176–8, 197, 201; gender violence 110
Generation X 133–7, 205–6
girl power 174, 181, 183, 185
girlhood 171, 180–3, 186, 188
girls: teenage 5, 173–6, 181–2, 187; young 52, 82, 178
Gómez López-Quiñones, Antonio 78, 86, 89
González, Felipe 118
González, Julio 59, 61, 65, 74
Gopegui, Belén 1, 5, 135–7, 141, 144, 146, 149
Grandes, Almudena 136
Guardia Civil 51, 87
Guerra Civil see Spanish Civil War

Hamlet 11
hatred 101, 109
helplessness 42, 49, 95–6, 98
Henseler, Christine 2, 6, 219
Higiene sexual expuesta a los adultos ilustrados (Box) 114

La hija del caníbal (Montero) 57–75
Histoire de la littérature anglaise (Taine) 58
Historia de un abrigo (Puértolas) 39–55
Historia de una maestra (Aldecoa) 21–36
Historias del Kronen (Mañas) 134–5, 151
L'Hora violeta (Roig) 164
House Beautiful 128
Huertas, Begoña 136
Hutcheon, Linda 14, 19

Ibsen, Henrik 11
incest 128, 197, 200
infertility 119
Intemann, Marguerite 43
interlocutor 9, 17–8, 22, 31
"El interlocutor soñado" (Martín Gaite) 18
intimacy 17, 28, 30, 66, 106, 124, 139, 141, 144, 146–7, 149–50, 166
Irigaray, Luce 105
Irlanda (Freire) 205–218
Irse de casa (Martín Gaite) 3, 9–19
Italy 41, 44–5
Izquierdo, Paula 136

James, William 11
jealousy 94, 110, 181, 196
Joan of Arc 198, 201
journals 13, 35, 79, 145, 165, 153–4, 157–8, 165, 168, 205
Julia (Moix) 159
Jung, C.G. 5, 156, 159–60, 163–4, 170
Junta Suprema de Unión Nacional Española 86

Kama Sutra 184
Keats, John 11
Kort, Wesley A. 21–2, 27, 36
Kristeva, Julia 103

Labordeta, Ángela 136
Lacan, Jacques 93, 103–6, 112, 199
Laforet, Carmen 136, 155, 161
Laing, R.D. 103
Laluna.com (Santos) 171–190
Un largo silencio (Caso) 191
Larra, Mariano José de 28
The Laugh of the Medusa (Cixous) 1, 90, 111
letters 11, 13, 29, 44, 77, 79–84, 89, 94, 100, 106, 153, 166–8, 181
Levinas, Emmanuel 133, 135, 137–41, 143–4, 147–150
Loriga, Ray 135, 206
Luisa Fernanda 11

Macbeth 11
Machado, Antonio 34
Madrid 27, 29–32, 48, 52, 58, 60–1, 72, 78, 115, 117, 125, 146, 163, 175
"Los malos espejos" (Martín Gaite) 18
Mañas, José Ángel 133–5, 137, 206
Manchester 45
Mangini, Shirley 84, 91, 191
marriage 25, 27, 44, 48, 88, 94–9, 125, 130, 162–3, 194
Martín, Sabas 133
Martín Gaite, Carmen 4, 9–19, 117, 123 136, 155, 161, 193, 208
Maslow, Abraham 39, 41–6, 48–9, 53, 55
Massey, Doreen 21, 24, 26, 35–6, 179
maternity 25, 126, 128, 156, 167–8
Mayock, Ellen 116–7, 123, 131
Medio, Dolores 83
Memorias de Leticia Valle (Chacel) 71, 155
Merleau-Ponty, Maurice 95, 112
Metafiction 9–19
México 22, 27–30, 34–5
Un milagro en equilibrio (Etxebarria) 153–170
militia 78, 81, 84, 86–7
Un millón de luces (Sánchez) 113–131
mirage 5, 113–4, 119, 124–6, 217
mirror 62, 70–3, 103–6, 117, 130, 144, 199, 216–8
El mismo mar de todos los veranos (Tusquets) 159
Las modernas de Madrid: las grandes intelectuales españolas de la vanguardia (Mangini) 191–2
Moers, Ellen 207–9, 219
Moix, Ana María 159
Molina, Tirso de 12
Monod, Jacques 11
Montero, Rosa 1, 4, 57–75, 166
motherhood 25, 114, 122, 154, 162, 164, 167, 188
Moura, Beatriz de 2
movida 40, 68, 186
La muerte blanca (Rico) 191–204
Mujeres de negro (Aldecoa) 21–36
Mulvey, Laura 95
myth 97, 147, 153, 156, 200–1, 206, 208

Nada (Laforet) 71, 155, 161
narrative voices 22, 89, 101–3, 106, 194, 197
naturalism 57–8, 60, 64–5, 70, 74
New York 9, 44, 47, 51
La novela femenina contemporánea (Ciplijauskaité) 154–5

Los ojos del lobo (Santos) 172
Okupada (Santos) 172
On Longing (Stewart) 194
Operación Virgo (Santos) 171–190
Orantes, Ana 50
Orchestral Maneuvers in the Dark 198
otherness 104, 135, 137, 139, 144–5, 147, 149

Páginas amarillas (Sabas) 133, 136
Pardo Bazán, Emilia 59–60
Paris 46
Pasismo 118
photographs 87–8
photography 84, 88, 90
Place and Space in Modern Fiction see Kort, Wesley A.
Plan de Acción contra la Violencia Doméstica 50
Plaza del diamante 71, 78
Pope Pius XII 155–6, 163, 168
post-war 4, 30, 35, 66, 80, 115–6, 117
Pratt, Annis 71
pregnancy 25, 84, 154, 164–7, 185, 187–8
Premio Primavera 57
Primera memoria (Matute) 71, 155
prison, Ventas 78–9, 81, 83–4, 86–7, 89
Puebla 27
Puértolas, Soledad 1, 4, 39–55, 166

Queda la noche (Puértolas) 40

Ramona, adéu (Roig) 164
Recóndita armonía 71
Republic *see* Second Republic
Rico, Eugenia 1, 5, 191–204
Riera, Carme 165–7, 170
Riestra, Blanca 136
Rodoreda, Mercé 78
Roig, Montserrat 164–5
Romeu Alfaro, Fernanda 82, 91
A Room of One's Own (Woolf) 24, 93–4

Salabert, Juana 136
Sánchez, Clara 1, 5, 113–131
Sánchez, Cristina 79
Santos, Care 1, 171–190
Sanz, Marta 1, 5, 135–7, 141, 143–5, 151
Sarajevo 62
Scanlon, Geraldine 80, 86, 91, 155, 170
Sección Femenina 113, 115–17, 156, 160–2
Second Republic 22, 78, 80, 83–4, 86, 88, 113, 155, 193, 222
selfhood 10, 12, 15, 18, 95, 99, 108–9, 177

silence 51, 82, 90, 94, 96, 99, 101, 109, 154, 157, 161
silencing 5, 88, 168, 191–2, 195, 223
Soliño, María Elena 36
solitude 18, 25, 28, 31, 34, 43, 54, 73, 143–4
Sontag, Susan 87–8, 91
Spanish Civil War 2, 22, 25, 27–8, 31, 35, 65, 67–8, 77–90, 123, 155, 191
Speculum, de l'autre femme (Irigaray) 105
Stewart, Susan 194
"strange girl" (*chica rara*) 116–8, 123, 161
subjectivity 5, 12, 102, 105, 135, 137–44, 147, 172, 192, 198–202
suicide 101, 108–9, 120, 122, 129, 162, 210, 214, 216
S/Z (Barthes) 16

Taine, Hippolyte 58, 60, 64–5, 70, 75
technology 5, 173–4, 176, 182, 189
El temps de les cireres (Roig) 164
Temps d'una espera (Riera) 165–6
third person 47–8, 54, 58, 65–6, 73–4, 101–2, 119, 141 143
Tocarnos la cara (Gopegui) 133–151
Tolliver, Joyce 10, 16–7, 19
transition to democracy 1–4, 35, 114, 191
Trece rosas 81–2
Tusquets, Esther 2, 159, 166, 208

Últimas noticias del paraíso (Sánchez) 113–131
Urioste, Carmen de 1–2, 6, 133, 135–7, 152, 170, 206, 220
Usón, Clara 136

Vega, Lope de 11–12
Venice 47
Vienna 61
violence *see* domestic violence
Virgin Mary 5, 114, 149, 155–6, 158, 162–4, 168
virginity 156, 183
La voz dormida (Chacón) 77–91

Walker, Leonor E. 94–5, 98–9, 112
war *see* Spanish Civil War
Ways of Seeing (Berger) 95
Waugh, Patricia 10, 12–3, 19
Wolff, Janet 10, 112
Woolf, Virginia 24, 58, 93–4, 109
Wuthering Heights (Brontë) 207–8

Ya no sufro por amor (Extebarria) 161

Zapata Bosch, Pilar 136
zarzuela 11, 18
Zatlin, Phyllis 67, 75
Zola, Émile 58, 64
Zubiaurre, Maite 60, 75

www.ingramcontent.com/pod-product-compliance
Lightning Source LLC
Chambersburg PA
CBHW032052300426
44116CB00007B/696